EVIDENCE SCENE

Members of Missouri K-9 Search and Rescue met investigators on the gravel road that led to John Robinson's farm, outside La Cygne, Kansas. The K-9 teams went in first, about 9:00 A.M. The handlers had their dogs sniff around the trailer before crime scene investigators began processing the trailer's interior.

"It looked like it was going to be a disappointment," said Sergeant Rick Roth of Lenexa Police Department. "The inside was a wreck, and the only item of significance that I could see initially was a Big Boy box matching the ones that [one of the missing women] had brought from Michigan."

The K-9 teams worked east to a collapsed building and a nearby concrete foundation, then south to the pond near the back of the property. While detectives combed other areas, Overland Park's five-member underwater team began a hand search of the snake-infested pond, looking for bodies, weapons, clothes or anything else that might point to foul play. It was a hot, humid day. The chiggers were in legions.

During the lunch break, K-9 handler Petra Stephens approached Roth and asked if he could have someone move some barrels away from a small shed. One of her Border Collies had shown some interest.

Roth threw a few items out of the way and began rocking one of the yellow drums from side to side as he pulled it backwards. Hitting an area of grass and bushes, he laid the barrel on its side, rolled it to a clearing and stood it back up. That's when he saw it: a single bead of reddish liquid that rolled from the edge of the lid down the side of the barrel.

"Is that blood?" someone asked.

The first body had been found. It was far from the last. . . .

BOOK YOUR PLACE ON OUR WEBSITE AND MAKE THE READING CONNECTION!

We've created a customized website just for our very special readers, where you can get the inside scoop on everything that's going on with Zebra, Pinnacle and Kensington books.

When you come online, you'll have the exciting opportunity to:

- View covers of upcoming books

- Read sample chapters

- Learn about our future publishing schedule (listed by publication month *and author*)

- Find out when your favorite authors will be visiting a city near you

- Search for and order backlist books from our online catalog

- Check out author bios and background information

- Send e-mail to your favorite authors

- Meet the Kensington staff online

- Join us in weekly chats with authors, readers and other guests

- Get writing guidelines

- AND MUCH MORE!

**Visit our website at
http://www.kensingtonbooks.com**

SLAVE MASTER

SUE WILTZ
with Maurice Godwin, Ph.D.

PINNACLE BOOKS
Kensington Publishing Corp.
http://www.kensingtonbooks.com

Some names have been changed to protect the privacy of individuals connected to this story.

ACKNOWLEDGMENTS

Many people made this book possible.

First and foremost, my deepest gratitude goes to Sergeant Rick Roth, who spent countless hours recalling details from the Robinson police probe, generously offering his personal and professional insights with a wry sense of humor and an unfaltering commitment to accuracy.

I am likewise indebted to many others in the law enforcement community who so kindly gave of their time, talent and expertise: Johnson County district attorney Paul Morrison and Johnson County assistant district attorney Sara Welch, Overland Park sergeant Joe Reed, Overland Park detectives Greg Wilson, Bobbi Jo Hohnholt, Mike Jacobson and Scott Weiler, Lenexa sergeant Dave Brown, Lenexa detectives Jake Boyer, Brad Hill, Mike Lowther, Dawn Layman, Alan Beyer, Perry Meyer, Mike Bussell, Rick Dougan, and Dan Owsley, Liberty (Missouri) parole supervisor Stephen Haymes, Overland Park captain Keith O'Neal, Lenexa Police Chief Ellen Hanson, Lenexa captain John Meier and Cass County district attorney Chris Koster.

My sincerest appreciation goes to the Trouten family, Karen Moore, Vickie Neufeld, Suzanne and Debbie Lawrence, Sharon LaPrad, Carl Macan, Debbie Mahan, Peggy Breit, Jeff Roberts, Tony Rizzo, John Milburn, Lisa Carter, Gerald Hay, Terri Issa, Linda Carter, Shirley Fessler, Ron Keefover, Mike McLain, April Shepard and the many other wonderful people I met while reporting this book. I am obligated to still others who do not wish to be identified, particularly the defense source who provided me with access to certain police documents, lending this narrative some of its illuminating and previously unpublished details.

I also wish to recognize my agents, Jane Dystel and Miriam Goderich; my editor at Kensington, Michaela Hamilton, my friends and former colleagues at *People* magazine,

Elizabeth McNeil, Nina Biddle, Fannie Weinstein and Maria Eftimiades, for their guidance and editorial input; Maurice Godwin, for his astute observations about Robinson's criminal psyche; John Fleck, for his photo contributions; David, Donna, Caleb, Ellen and Geneva Miller for opening their home to me in Kansas City; and Susan Houriet at CourtTV.com for assigning me to cover the trial.

Thanks also to family and friends for their words of encouragement when I needed them most: Paul and Peggy Miller, Anne, Armando, Carolina, Lindy and Isa Hernandez, Susan Wilz and extended family, Lisa Conte, Jim Clash, Jessica Amato, Stephen Flanagan, Whitney Bennett, Itziar Bilbao, Trent Gegax, LynNell Hancock, Seamus McNally, David Gordon, Nick Charles, Anthony Duignan-Cabrera, Natasha Stoynoff, Julia Campbell, Patrick Rogers, Seema Nayyar, Michael Paulson, Alfons Luna, Mike Thomas, Stan Preston, Benji and Liesl Loudermilk, John and Cindy Liebenow, Mandy and Bill Stetzel.

And to Paul Wiltz, who unselfishly gave up months of companionship so that I might write this book: your love and support mean everything to me.

S.W.

I would like to thank my wife, Helen, who has graciously endured my long working hours during this project, and whose encouragement, help, and support have sustained me throughout.

My sincere appreciation goes to Sue Wiltz and all those at Dystel and Goderich Literary Management, without whom I would never have been involved in this book. I would also like to remember my father, Halford Godwin, who passed away in June 2002. To the numerous individuals whom I did not mention—you know who you are—I am grateful for your help.

M.G.

AUTHOR'S NOTE

The material in this book is drawn from personal interviews and recollections, police and court records, witness testimony and news reports, including *The Kansas City Star,* the *Olathe Daily News* and the Associated Press. Pseudonyms or first names were used for a few individuals on the periphery of this case, solely at the author's discretion. Lastly, no editorial promises were made or money offered in exchange for information.

Prologue

Detectives Jake Boyer and Greg Wilson had a surprise waiting for John E. Robinson Sr. back at the Lenexa, Kansas, police station shortly after his arrest on the morning of June 2, 2000. Escorting the shackled prisoner into a conference room, they instructed him to remain silent. "We are going to respect the fact that you have asked for your attorney," Wilson said. "But we want you to understand how much work we have done and how much we know about your activities."

On a table in the center of the conference room lay photographs of several women whom Robinson had recently met for sadomasochistic sex, including Vickie Neufeld and Jeanna Milliron. A second table held seven black binders, containing hundreds of pages from an exhaustive ten-week investigation. Taped to a bulletin board was a picture of Suzette Marie Trouten, her police case number scrawled beside it, grainy surveillance photos of Robinson and his wife, Nancy, and a hand-drawn map with directions to his rural Kansas farm.

Slowly and silently, the fifty-six-year-old prisoner—balding, pudgy and bespectacled—walked around the center table, pausing for several seconds to stare intently at each photo.

Returning to the police booking room, detectives removed his handcuffs and allowed him to phone his lawyer. Robinson explained to attorney Ron Wood that he'd been arrested on charges of aggravated sexual battery, blackmail and felony theft. Bond, he calmly added, had been set for $250,000.

"Yes, I'm *sure* that is all they've charged me with," he insisted when Wood apparently expressed surprise at the shockingly high amount.

Then Robinson dropped an even bigger bombshell. "They're talking about charging me with murder," he continued in a cocky tone, sounding as though he didn't have a care in the world, "and they have a bunch of pictures of women that you and I need to talk about."

Chapter 1

In February 2000, Suzette Marie Trouten was excited about the future. The twenty-seven-year-old nurse's aide recently had met a man on the Internet who offered her a job in Kansas caring for his diabetic, wheelchair-bound father. She told friends and family the job would last about a year and entail world travel, time off every three months and great benefits. But the best part, gushed the vivacious brunette, was that the $65,000 salary he promised would allow her to pay for the pricey training she needed to become a registered nurse.

Nursing was a dream that Suzette had nurtured since she was a young girl growing up in the small town of Newport, Michigan, the youngest of Harry and Carolyn Trouten's five children and every bit the baby of the boisterous, tight-knit family. She had always adored animals—riding at age two the family's pet bull—and it wouldn't be long before she became just as devoted to caring for the elderly and terminally ill.

Perhaps the trauma she endured in childhood made her particularly sensitive to the pain and suffering of others. When she was eleven, Suzette was raped by a member of a nearby boat club, her mother said. Roughly the same time, her parents separated and eventually divorced. Because of the assault and her parents' breakup, Suzette wound up spending nearly a year in the psychiatric unit at Monroe County Hospital.

Even after her release, Suzette kept trying to reunite her parents. One day, devastated by a teenage breakup of her own, she was talking to her mother when she pulled out a gun and shot herself in the stomach. The bullet caused no permanent damage but left unsightly scars on her abdomen and lower back. "I don't think she really meant it," said Carolyn, a slender middle-aged woman with curly blond hair. "I think it went off by accident. At the time, her dad and I were seeing each other again. And I think she thought if she staged something really good, that would keep us together."

Through the turmoil, Suzette remained close to her siblings and her parents. She and her brother Michael stayed with their mother; the older kids—Kim, Harry junior and Dawn— were already out on their own. Even after her father, Harry, a tall and handsome railroad engineer with a salt-and-pepper beard, moved to Florida, he and Suzette continued to visit back and forth several times a year. "There were a few rough years," acknowledged her mother. "But her dad and I were both there for her all the time. And I think she finally got over [her problems]."

By the time she graduated from Jefferson High School in 1991, Suzette had set her sights on nursing. That August, she started work in Monroe as a nurse's aide for LaPrad Home Care, a job she would hold for the better part of nine years. "There wasn't anything you couldn't ask her to do," said her former boss, Sharon LaPrad, who gave Suzette all the toughest patients, most of whom were elderly or terminally ill. "She was caring and compassionate—not only with the patients but with their families—and she knew her stuff. They just loved her."

LaPrad recalled the time Suzette took care of an elderly gentleman who eventually passed away. His wife, in her seventies, became so attached to Suzette in the months that she cared for him that she asked her to stay by her side at the funeral. She wanted Suzette's shoulder to cry on. Another time, Suzette had a young patient with MS, a woman in her forties who needed to be catheterized a few times a day. Even though she knew from her studies how to perform the tricky procedure, Suzette was apprehensive about doing it on her own for the first time. LaPrad had a nurse and the woman's husband show her how.

"When I called to check on her a little later that day, the woman's husband said she learned it like a pro," LaPrad recalled. "She was always willing and wanting to know more."

Suzette made about $10 an hour as a nurse's aide, which wasn't enough to save for nursing school *and* cover living expenses, including the $200 rent she paid for a room in the home of her friend John Stapleton. She began working two or three shifts a week as a cook at the local Big Boy restaurant, where her mother was the manager. By 1998, she had taken a lot of nursing prerequisite courses and saved enough for a nursing program at Monroe County Community College only to drop out after being hospitalized with an undiagnosed illness for several weeks. "She really wanted to get her degree," recalled her sister Dawn. "She wanted to be a nurse."

Suzette was disappointed at the setback, her mother said, but her daughter's spirits were once again buoyed when a wealthy businessman named John Robinson offered her the "dream job" in Kansas. She planned to work with him for a year, touring the world yet still saving money, then come home and finally finish her nursing degree. "She had been going part-time and working," Carolyn said. "This way, she thought she could save up some money and go straight through."

There was some confusion over how Suzette had met Robinson. She told LaPrad she had found the opportunity through the wife of a physician friend who ran a nationwide home-care business. She told her sister Kim Padilla that it had come through LaPrad. They wouldn't discover these discrepancies until later, however. What they knew in the fall of 1999 is that Suzette and Robinson had somehow connected through the Internet and were now exchanging e-mail and talking regularly on the phone.

Only Kim and close friends such as Lore Remington and Tami Taylor were aware that Suzette actually led a double life: she was secretly involved in what is known as BDSM—an umbrella term for sexual activities involving bondage and discipline, domination and submission, sadism and masochism.

But at the time, they had no idea Suzette was going to Kansas for anything more than a job or that Robinson had become her BDSM master and she his willing sex slave.

Suzette, by her own admission, had been attracted to "the BDSM lifestyle" when she was sixteen years old. She had served two masters, she said, including one she had lived with for several years until he crossed the line from dominance to alleged abuse, beating her so badly on one occasion that she couldn't walk for three days. She also "played"—BDSM parlance for having engaged in sex sessions—with a number of others, including a so-called "judge" in Toronto.

By the mid-1990s, Suzette had become involved in Gorean, a subculture of BDSM that mainly involves fantasy role-playing on the Internet, although adherents often apply its philosophy to their everyday lives. The subculture is based on a series of twenty-five science fiction novels, written by author John Norman between 1967 and 1988, about an imaginary planet known as Gor in which many of the women are slaves and subject to the whims of their male masters.

The primary thrust of Norman's philosophy, as one admirer eloquently stated, is "simply that the female human being has been biologically prepared, through millennia of evolution, to be attracted to a naturally strong and capable male. And that the ultimate expression of inherent dominance . . . would exist in a society wherein slavery existed and was institutionalized."

In reality, Gorean requires the slave to yield completely to the master and does not adhere to the "safe, sane and consensual" guidelines of BDSM, which is practiced, often secretly, by thousands of men and women around the world. Suzette's friend Lore, a housewife from Nova Scotia, would later explain the difference: "BDSM [practitioners employ] safe words," she would testify. "Most of them use colors—red meaning 'stop' and green meaning 'I'm fine.' In Gorean, there are no safe words. The master has total control."

Suzette had met Lore, also a submissive in the same lifestyle, in a Gorean chat room in 1996. They hit it off, conversing daily in ICQ instant-messaging sessions on the Internet and quickly becoming the closest of friends. Lore later introduced her to Tami, another Gorean submissive, who lived in Ontario, and the three were in regular contact, chitchatting about their everyday lives as well as their sexual experiences with dominant male partners. Suzette, a bisexual, became intimate with both women, separately, when each visited Michigan and they participated in three-way BDSM sessions with different masters.

In 1999, Suzette had placed an ad on ALT.com, a Fetish/ BDSM "personals" Web site that claims more than a million members. Calling herself "angelwithout," she indicated she was "looking for the right Master" and went on to describe herself in the following terms:

> I am a 27 year old female who has been in BDSM for the last 11 years. I was owned from 16 to a year ago. I am 5'6" long brown hair, dark brown eyes, olive skin tone. I have a good shape and is a total slave. I live in Lower Michigan close to Detroit. I enjoy bondage, spankings, whips, is some what of a pain slut. No scat, blood, animals, no children . . . this is hard limits that will not be testeddddddd!!!!!!

For Suzette, September 11, 1999, would prove to be a very unlucky day indeed. "Read your ad," wrote "John Rob," using the e-mail address midwestmaster@email.com. "Let's talk about the possibilities."

Within days—which was moving very fast even by the standards of BDSM—Suzette had agreed to become his slave, telling him all about herself ("I love to read, write, paint, horse back riding, walks, fishing. Enjoys the out doors greatly"), giving him passwords to her various e-mail accounts and laying the initial plans for her move to Kansas City. She signed many of her notes, "On bended knee, Suzette."

On September 17, 1999, Robinson sent Suzette an e-mail

in which he described his philosophy on domination. "slave: as the days go by, I will begin establishing more and more control over you," he wrote. He told her that he would not simply give her a collar (the BDSM equivalent of becoming betrothed), she would have to earn it. He also said he would probably mark her body—consisting of "bruises on her tits, ass or back"—and that this would be done to remind his "slave" of her place.

Robinson insisted that Suzette would be his "personal slut and whore" and that "your body, mind and soul will belong to me." He said she would be required to sign a slave contract that included a long list of rules of sexual behavior but allowed that they would first discuss them to be sure they were in agreement. He would also provide her with training, discipline and punishment. "Punishment can be mild, medium severe or extremely harsh depending," he wrote. "Punishment will always be completed in private."

In response to Suzette's confession that she had been intimate with other women, or "slaves," he told her he would be the one to choose her sexual orientation and to decide if and when she would be allowed to service or be serviced by other slaves. "This is totally up to your MASTER," he wrote. He also said that he did not believe in sharing his slave with other men, or "masters." He might allow them to see or even whip her but not to touch or "have sex in any way."

Robinson signed his e-mails to Suzette in such a manner that would later become very familiar to police: "Hugs, Kisses and Lashes, MASTER JR."

In October and again in November, Robinson flew Suzette out for quick visits, ostensibly to have her meet his father (in reality, his father had been dead since 1989) and sign contracts for an apartment and a car. Unbeknownst to anyone back home, she also posed for nude photos, signed his slave contract and, in her own hand, wrote out a twenty-five-page list of more than one hundred rules in which she pledged total submission to Robinson.

She returned to Michigan both times saying how impressed she was with what she had seen. She said Robinson was a wealthy man, who had picked her up in an airport limousine, taken her to his mansion and treated her like a queen. She described meeting Robinson's wife, a younger woman with blond hair. She also said she had met "Papa John," Robinson's elderly father, "a crotchety old man," as she put it, and the young woman who had been his previous caretaker and was now an attorney. "She had so many details, it couldn't have been made up," Carolyn insisted.

Papa John owned several international companies, Suzette explained, but Robinson had been running them for his father, who wasn't well and was eager to step down and travel the world. One of Suzette's first trips after she got to Kansas would be to accompany both of them to Europe, taking care of Papa John while Robinson handled business in Switzerland and Belgium.

Robinson suggested Suzette apply for a passport and begin researching nursing programs overseas because she would probably have time to take some classes. Her mother remembered Suzette spending an entire afternoon on the Internet, looking up nursing programs in Belgium, and filling out the paperwork in Michigan for a passport. She never submitted the application because she was told she would need to apply through her new home in Kansas.

Robinson certainly seemed friendly and normal enough whenever he called Carolyn's house and asked to speak to her daughter. "He called here a lot and she would talk to him and tell me what he said," recalled her mother, who knew him well enough to say hello to after Suzette had moved home shortly before leaving Michigan. "One time, she said he had been working all day at the shelter—that everyone in his company goes to feed the poor. He seemed like a very nice man."

Carolyn admitted it was "fishy" that Robinson had agreed to pay Suzette such a large salary, but then she decided it wasn't so unusual considering she would be working long hours. She also knew Suzette had a flair for the dramatic and thought perhaps her daughter was going to be paid substantially less but just wasn't saying so. "If Suzette found a quarter, she'd tell you it was five dollars," she said. "Everything had to be bigger than life."

Despite Suzette's reassurances, others definitely thought the job sounded too good to be true. LaPrad, who is very intuitive, said she had "a very bad feeling from the beginning" and tried on several occasions to dissuade Suzette from going. When Suzette stopped by the office to pick up her last paycheck, LaPrad tearfully recalled how she spun around just as she reached the door. "Don't worry," she told her boss, with a little giggle to her tone. "It's not forever. I'll be back."

Privately, however, Suzette was apparently torn between her desire to be with her master and the fear of leaving her old life behind. She had recently met a reserve police officer and disc jockey, John "Edge," also in the alternative lifestyle, who lived nearby, and they liked each other very much. "Where do I want to be is the question," she wrote in a journal she had begun at Robinson's behest on January 24, 2000. "Will I cross that line of complete surrender or will I just hold back enough to know that there is a part of me that will say no? Only time will tell."

Suzette asked her aunt, Marshella Chidester, the bookkeeper in the family, for the names, addresses and birth dates of everyone in the family, carefully jotting them down on a yellow legal pad. She also provided her mother with Robinson's cell phone, pager and business telephone numbers. With the help of her mom and sister, she packed her belongings, including books, clothing and knickknacks, into some twenty Big Boy boxes, easily loading them into a large Ryder truck Robinson had rented for her trip. She would also be bringing her beloved Pekingese dogs, Harry and Peka, for she didn't go anywhere without them.

On February 13, the night of her daughter's departure, Carolyn gathered the family for a farewell party. As Suzette looked at the loving faces around the room, she was a bundle of mixed emotions: excited and scared at the same time. She had never lived anywhere else. *It will be strange being in a place I don't know,* she thought to herself. *Everything here is so familiar.* She was just a big mama's girl, she realized, and it was going to be hard to be so far from home.

Chapter 2

Robinson greeted Suzette with flowers when she arrived in Kansas City on Valentine's Day, tired after the fourteen-hour drive. He had made arrangements for her to stay at the Guesthouse Suites, a comfortable hotel and apartment complex just off I-35 in Lenexa, one of the wealthier suburbs of the sprawling Midwestern city. Checking her into a quiet second-floor suite, room 216, he promised to return later.

After attending to her dogs and taking a nap, Suzette's first tasks were to set up the Compaq Presario desktop computer she'd brought from home and to call her mother to tell her she'd arrived safely. For the rest of the month, she would be in constant touch with her family and friends via e-mail, ICQ instant messaging and telephone—speaking to her mother almost every day.

Robinson visited on several occasions and engaged in sadomasochistic sex sessions with her on the queen-size bed, leaving her euphoric. However, she would grow lonely and bored after he left, feeling like a caged-up animal with only the television and her computer to keep her company. She had no way to get around and there were no stores or restaurants within walking distance to distract her. She was often homesick as she tried to get used to being away from her family and being completely on her own.

On February 16, Suzette ran into Janis Munn, the manager of the Guesthouse Suites, while walking her dogs. Munn politely told her that the dogs would have to go, as they had a strict policy against animals. Suzette told Robinson and he agreed to board them for her in a nearby kennel, Ridgeview Animal Hospital. "Strange being alone in my room," she wrote that day.

Over the next several days, she suffered through a cold, bouts of sleeplessness and the end of a heavy two-week menstrual period, which she referred to as her "vampire weeks" in conversations with Lore. She would be moody and anxious one day, happy and relaxed the next. "I came, I saw, I want to come home," she wrote on February 19 in an ICQ message to her sister Kim. "Am homesick."

Two days later, her spirits soared as Robinson told her they would be leaving on their first trip, a week from Monday. By this time, the plans had changed, however, and instead of Europe they would be driving to California to pick up a yacht Robinson had purchased recently and sailing from there to Hawaii. The new destination didn't seem to faze Suzette; she told friends she was eager to check out Thai restaurants in California. "I am excited about going," she wrote in her journal.

She wasn't really working just yet but settling in, she told her mom. Robinson was busy negotiating the sale of one of his companies and they would be leaving for California as soon as he was done. She did mention she was working on some sort of Web site, but Carolyn, who detested computers even then, never asked about the details.

Suzette was more candid with Lore, finally admitting that there was more to her move to Kansas City than the job. She acknowledged that not only was she going to take care of Robinson's elderly father but was also developing a Web site for him about a secret BDSM society called the International Council of Masters, and that he was one of its "elite" members. She also admitted very cryptically that she and the younger Robinson were engaging in sadomasochistic sex. "When she went to Kansas, it was for a job," Lore later said, "but she finally told me the truth. I said, 'You're involved with him, aren't you?' and she said yes. She didn't tell me [before] because she knew I'd be irate. You don't mix business with pleasure."

Suzette's anticipation grew as the trip drew near. She had a hard time sleeping the night of February 23 and woke up late the next morning. She wrote:

> I just kept thing [*sic*] about Master and what the next few months will bring. I am finally settling down and I can even say I am relaxed but still anious [*sic*] to see how thing will go. I am very happy to be here. A little home sick but that's to be expected I should think. I am the biggest Momma's girl. This is all so new to me. At times I feel like a different person. But I can honest say I am glad it happen. Mircles [*sic*] do come true if you wish hard enough!"

She ended the entry with a little smiley face.

When the trip was postponed again, Kim heard from her on ICQ chat on February 28. "hey I leave wensday [*sic*] [March 1] kimmy so you will periodically get an e-mail from me."

Suzette made her last journal entry the next day. "I am very relaxed and very happy," she wrote. "Everything is going well today. Master is on my mind a lot today. I feel like I am on top of the world."

Around midnight (CST) that Tuesday night, February 29, Suzette called her mom while she was at work. "What are you doing up at this hour?" asked Carolyn, who was getting ready to close the restaurant.

"I'm not tired," Suzette replied, telling her mom she wasn't as homesick as she thought she would be. She said she was calling to let her know that they'd be leaving the next morning or at the latest by Thursday, March 2. Carolyn asked Suzette to call before they set off and her daughter promised she would.

That same evening, Suzette spent several hours chatting back and forth with Lore, finally signing off just before 1:00 A.M. CST. At one point during their late-night session, she played a joke on Lore's master, sending him an ICQ message that Lore had gotten her nipples pierced without his permission—which infuriated him. Suzette also seemed to have decided by this point that she was going to keep her relationship with Robinson on a purely professional level. "Just don't fuck the boss," Lore had pleaded. "I won't baby. Will screw up a great thing if I do," Suzette answered. A little later, she wrote, apparently to placate her friend, "No I'm not doing him and him is boss you were talking about."

The next morning, March 1, Suzette logged on to her America Online account at 9:09 A.M. from the telephone line in her room at the Guesthouse Suites. While on the Internet that morning, she accessed her e-mail account at Hotmail.com in order to send and receive e-mail, signing off at 9:24 A.M. Before logging off, she also held an ICQ chat session with an Australian friend, who used the online nickname "ahsa." "We leave tomorrow," Suzette wrote. "Will be gone about 2 to 6 months . . . nothing like taking a vacation while working. Well sweets I have to run . . . am off to the farm this morning for a while . . . grins . . . love to both of you baby."

The "farm" was Robinson's 16.5-acre property, located about an hour south of Kansas City in rural Linn County, which he had bought in May 1994. Though it contained nothing more than a ramshackle trailer, an old barn and a fishing pond, it was his pride and joy.

On the morning of March 2, Lore received an e-mail from Suzette, writing now from her Hotmail e-mail account instead of from her usual ICQ chat. "By the time you get this I [*sic*] off," it said. "My computer crashed yesterday and it took hours to get it working. You would laugh, station wagon full, the dogs in the back and off we go on the adventure of a lifetime . . . sees ya . . . suz."

At first, Lore didn't doubt the authenticity of the e-mail and sent her friend a reply, telling her to "have a blast" on the trip. She also mentioned she had told her master "to take a fucking leap" when he insisted he would be the only one to decide when she could get her nipples pierced. She was through with him, she told Suzette.

She received another e-mail from her friend about an hour later. This one contained an unusual request: "caught you message just before I unplugged . . . if your [*sic*] interested in a MASTER who is really great, write him. He is a great MASTER. His e-mail addy is eruditemaster@email.com Wow, what news . . . I'm off, love you too, don't forget to write him!!!, hugs suz."

Lore was suspicious. First of all, Suzette would never recommend a master for her; that just wasn't like her. She thought it was strange that Suzette had addressed the note to her given name. She always called her "sis" or some other nickname. She also never signed her notes with "hugs," preferring "love you babe." And finally she was struck by the fact that Suzette had spelled master in all capital letters. She had never done that before, either.

Knowing that the person who was sending the e-mails was somehow linked to her friend, Lore decided to play along in order to glean any information she could. She wrote to "eruditemaster," saying they had a mutual friend who thought they might get along. She received a response the next morning. Describing himself as a master with twenty years' experience, he told her he understood she had just broken off with her "dom" and he was looking for a slave who was trainable. He asked her to describe her experience in the lifestyle and to send him a picture of herself. "I await all the possibilities in front of us," he wrote, signing the note "JT."

Lore wrote back, telling him a little bit about her previous relationship, the fact that she was married with two children, attaching some photos.

He promptly replied, saying that he approved of her photos and that "Suz" had already made him aware of her situation. "I am a very selective MASTER," he wrote. "I demand the best form [*sic*] my slave and will accept nothing less." He told her they would first get to know one another through email and phone calls before meeting in person. He wasn't sure how the travel would work but, if they could work out the details,

they would be on their way to a Dominant/submissive relationship. "I warn you up front I am a very demanding
MASTER," he wrote. "If I accept you, you will be my slave
and you will understand your place is at my feet on your
knees. There is no quarter given." JT said his first rule was
daily communication and he ordered Lore to e-mail him
every day before 9 A.M. CST.

Lore's suspicions grew as she noted that JT also spelled
master in all capital letters. She continued e-mailing him as
well as whoever was using her friend's Hotmail account. She
asked "Suzette" what she knew about JT, adding that her ex-
master was furious with her and she was now thinking of
"playing" with some other Doms.

Suzette was obviously miffed when she purportedly wrote
back on March 7. "Lore; you know sometimes I would like to
strangle the fuck out of you," she wrote. "I would not have
even mentioned this guy if I tought [sic] he would be bad for
you." She went on to say she thought Lore could use a little
"quality dominance" in her life and she shouldn't screw
things up with JT by telling him she needed to play with other
dominants. "I have been through the same bull shit you have,
bad scenes, bad Doms who only wanted to hurt me, bad shit
and you know how it bothers me," she wrote. "I hoipe [sic]
this is my knight in shining armour, sems [sic] to be, feels that
way, and I'm going to keep him as happy as any slut could
possibly keep him." She also told Lore to relax and stop always looking for the down side. "Look for the potential, the
hope, the real MASTER," she wrote. "I'm telling you, this
MASTER can have the pick of the litter, be flattered he is
thinking seriously about you!!!" Reminding Lore that she
didn't have her computer and was stopping where she could,
she said she would monitor her progress. Telling her to be
happy, Suzette signed off with "Love ya lots."

Over the next few days, Lore learned from JT that his full
name was "James R. Turner," or "Jim Turner," and he was a
vice president of human resources at a large company in the

Kansas City area. He told her he loved to take pictures of his naked slaves, telling her "to get used to it," ordering her to send him some naked pictures of herself. He also asked for her telephone number and soon began barraging her with phone calls.

In e-mail exchanges with "Suzette," she learned that JT was friends with JR, her employer, and that they had all "played" together in Kansas City before she and JR had left for California. "Suzette" described JT as being around fifty years old, 5'8" tall, weighing 185 pounds and educated, very powerful and extremely dominant. "I was introduced to him by my MASTER who by the way is the best fucking thing that ever happened to me in my whole life," she purportedly wrote, claiming that she was sitting in an Internet café in Arizona and making her way to California. She explained that JT was a teacher, who helped other masters to train their slaves properly. "Don't fuck this up" were her parting words. "This guy will make your toes curl."

When Lore accused "Suzette" of being less than fully honest about her relationship with JR, and that she'd been bought, she received a defensive reply within the hour. "Figured you would fuckin' freak," her "friend" wrote. "I have found a MASTER and I have not been bought. Don't assume things that are not correct." Calling him "exceptional," she explained that he had just finished selling off his company and they wanted to travel for a while. "Me and my dogs are OK with him, my fat butt and all," she wrote. "I have everything I need, so be happy for me, damn it! . . . When you meet him and we play, you'll drool."

About a week later, the person sending the e-mails apparently started becoming confused by the complex scenario he'd created for himself. He would have JT respond to e-mails that Lore had sent to Suzette and vice versa. For example, Lore told Suzette that she was thinking of having her nipples pierced and JT answered, claiming to have done hundreds of piercings and offering to do hers.

Remington also noticed a change in the tone of the e-mails coming from "Suzette." "The e-mails were getting aggravated and upset," she later said. "None of the questions I was asking were being answered. The hints and little things I was sending weren't being responded to, but I was getting phone calls from [JT] addressing them. The more questions I asked, the more the e-mails were getting angrier and had a don't-ask attitude. Then my questions were not being answered by the e-mail Suzette. I received one more around [March] twentieth and that was it."

By now Lore had confided in Tami, showing her the e-mails she'd received and telling her how worried she was for Suzette's safety. After discussing what to do, the two women came up with a plan. Lore e-mailed "Suzette," asking her if her new master had any single friends for Tami. "Does Tami think I am the clearing house for MASTERS?" joked "Suzette." She suggested that Lore send Tami's e-mail address to JT, who knew a lot of people in the lifestyle. JT, in turn, told Lore to have Tami contact a new master at another e-mail address, preipo@usa.net.

Tami sent a quick note to the address she'd been given, telling him she knew nothing about him other than the fact that he was seeking a new sub/slave. She told him she was divorced, with no children, and included a photo of herself. "Love those tits, oh you have really made my head swim," came the reply from a man calling himself "T" on March 16. "I am a tit person, I just love my slave to have nice large, firm tits just like yours." He outlined his needs, telling her that he was a total "MASTER" who wanted a long-term, 24/7 relationship. "What I require of my slave is 'everything,'" he wrote. "I want total obedience, total honesty and complete submission. I will use you, but I will also cherish you, care for you and love you. Now you ask me whatever questions you want and let's get on with beginning to develop a good solid, strong D/s relationship."

Within a few days, T, who also called himself "Tom," or "Thomas Anthony Thomas" was phoning Tami, leaving messages on her voice mail and urging her to come to Kansas City for a visit. While "T" wouldn't send her a picture of himself,

"JT" sent Lore two photos of himself—wearing denim and sitting on a tree stump in one and donning a cowboy hat and propping his foot up on the stump in the other. He refused to provide either of them with any kind of telephone number. After listening to the voice messages and comparing other similarities, however Lore and Tami were convinced that JR, JT and Tom were all one and the same person.

Meanwhile, in Michigan, Carolyn had started to grow concerned when she hadn't heard from her daughter by March 2. Suzette had promised to call and it wasn't like her not to check in with her mother on a daily basis—the longest they'd ever gone without speaking in their lives was about three days.

Confirming that she'd checked out of the Guesthouse Suites, Carolyn's next move was to dial Robinson's cell phone, only to receive a message that said it was turned off. A few days later, she received a letter from Suzette. *Thank goodness,* she thought as she anxiously tore it open. She recognized the handwriting as her daughter's, but something was terribly wrong: dated February 28, a few days before her departure, it had not been mailed from Kansas City until March 6, nearly a week after she was supposed to have left town.

Then she heard from her ex-husband, Harry, who had just received a similar handwritten note at his home in Florida.

Sick with worry, Carolyn again tried Robinson's cell phone but got no answer. About an hour later, however, Suzette's supposed employer called back, saying he'd been in the shower but he had seen her number on his caller ID and wanted to know who she was and what she wanted. When Carolyn identified herself and asked why Suzette wasn't with him, Robinson calmly told her she had decided not to take his job offer and that she instead had taken off with a man she met named Jim Turner and they were going to be sailing around the world.

Carolyn had never heard Suzette mention Jim Turner or that she was planning to travel with anyone other than Robinson. She instantly thought it was suspicious that Robinson didn't seem at all upset by the idea that her daughter had not taken the job. He had gone to great lengths—investing a lot of time and money on her trips out there—to be so nonchalant.

Shortly after Carolyn spoke to Robinson, several members of her family began to receive on March 21 e-mail from someone purporting to be Suzette:

> Well the wandering suz finally decided to drop everyone a note and say howdy. sorry no e-mail up until now . . . no excuses just lazy. Peka, Hari [sic] and I are fine, they travel really well. I'm in California and getting rested up for sailing . . . excited, what a opportunity. Promised Mom I would send her a doll from every country we go . . . John Edge has been trying to contact me and I told him to please leave me alone. He won't listen and sent me a threat about "finding me." don't worry about me, I'm a big girl . . . bigger than I should be, Love to all suz.

Marshella and her husband, Don, received another e-mail a few days later from "Suzette."

> By the time you get this we will be off. I have written mom and dad each a letter so mom can quit worrying. Will not be on line for some time, but will keep all posted on the trip every chance I get. I'm excited, Peka and Harri [sic] have taken to boat life like they were born for it. At first I thought they would start their wandering and fall off, but no problems. Well aloha . . . I love you guys. Suz.

Suzette was a terrible writer, but her family was certain she knew how to spell the names of her beloved dogs. They also thought she was crazy about John Edge and now she was telling them—uncharacteristically—she wanted him to leave her alone. The idea of Suzette on a boat didn't sit right with them, either. When Don and Marshella bought their 27' Sea Ray, Suzette told them she hated boats so much she wouldn't even go out for a day trip. "And now she's supposed to be sailing around the world?" Marshella said. "I don't think so!"

By this point, too, Lore had managed to get hold of Suzette's mom and sister Kim and told them what had been happening on her end. It was clear to them now that Suzette had simply vanished on March 1. Robinson was holding her somewhere against her will, they believed, or else she was dead.

Later asked by a defense attorney why her family waited three weeks to go to the police, Carolyn understandably bristled. She knew that police departments typically give missing persons reports very low priority. "Of course we knew there was something radically wrong," she answered, her voice cracking. "But she wasn't a child. She was twenty-seven years old. She is contacting us by letter and she is contacting us by e-mail. How much do you think the police would do?"

Carolyn was about to find out.

Chapter 3

Overland Park police officer Warren Neff was working the evening shift on Saturday, March 25, when he took the fateful call from Suzette's sister Dawn, then living in Florida. Dawn tearfully explained the situation: her baby sister had obtained a job with a Kansas City businessman, only to disappear after spending a few weeks in a local hotel. She told him what her family and Suzette's friends knew and gave him phone numbers for her hotel and purported employer, John Robinson.

The name meant nothing to Neff. But to his supervisors, Lieutenant Dan Minteer and Sergeant Marty Ingram, who had investigated Robinson in the 1980s, it held great significance. Late Sunday evening, Minteer sent an e-mail about Suzette to Sergeant Joe Reed, who was in charge of detectives investigating crimes against persons. "I'd give this one close look," Minteer wrote Reed, prophetically entitling his note, "Strange Missing Person Case." "We still have some missing women on the books who had contact with [Robinson]."

Reed wasted no time when he got in on Monday morning. The likable, mustachioed sergeant loved his job. He had hired on with Overland Park fresh out of Central Missouri State University, where he majored in criminal justice. He'd worked a lot of cases in his twenty-two years on the force—burglaries, thefts and, ultimately, crimes against persons. His experience and instincts told him the Robinson case was going to be big. "I think we all recognized that right up front," he said. "We could have a serial killer on our hands."

Reed called in Greg Wilson and Bobbi Jo Hohnholt, seasoned detectives who were familiar with the old cases. The prior September, Wilson, a Kansas native who'd been with the department for eight years, had attended a training class in Oklahoma for missing and exploited children. Before he went, Reed handed him the Stasi file, about a nineteen-year-old mother and baby who had simply vanished after an encounter with Robinson in 1985. "You might want to get up to speed on this case because it is one of the ones they use in the training class," he told him. Ironically, Wilson had the file out on his desk when his department received the call about Suzette.

While Hohnholt copied the old case files and contacted Dawn Trouten and other family members for more information, Wilson consulted a phonebook and found only one Guesthouse Suites located just over the line in Lenexa. Paying a visit to the hotel's manager, Janis Munn, he confirmed that Suzette Trouten had checked out on March 1. He also determined that her sixteen-day stay had been arranged and paid for by Robinson, who was affiliated with a company called Specialty Publications, located in Kansas City, Missouri.

Munn described Suzette as being friendly and in good spirits and remembered that she had two small dogs. When she informed Suzette that the dogs weren't allowed at the hotel, however, they disappeared. Munn thought she had subsequently boarded them but didn't know where. She also recalled that Robinson had been the one to check her out, at 3:04 P.M., and was fairly certain he had made arrangements for other women to stay at the hotel in the past, though she couldn't find the records because of recent changes in their computer system.

Upon learning from Wilson that the Guesthouse Suites weren't in their jurisdiction, Reed picked up the phone and called Sergeant Rick Roth, his counterpart at the Lenexa Police Department. "Boy, have I got a bag of worms for you!" he exclaimed, filling him in on the old cases of missing women and offering Overland Park's assistance. The two men were acquainted from having attended several of the same training seminars and having once worked the same murder investigation. Their departments—and their detectives—enjoyed a spirited rivalry as they policed adjacent upper-middle-class communities in the same county. The chief difference: Overland Park, with about 165,000 residents and 214 sworn police officers, was roughly three times the size of Lenexa.

Knowing that Overland Park was already familiar with Robinson's background, Roth decided to accept Reed's offer to commit Wilson and another of his detectives, Scott Weiler, to the investigation. (Hohnholt was finishing up another assignment.) While Weiler would return to his unit after three weeks to help with surveillance, Wilson would spend the next four months working out of the Lenexa detectives' conference room. Ultimately, Overland Park would play a major role as events unfolded.

Like Reed, Roth had spent his career in law enforcement. In 1974, he joined the Kansas City, Missouri, Police Department as a dispatcher, where he had met his good friend and future boss, Captain John Meier. Three years later, he had transferred to Lenexa, where he became a patrolman in 1979 and a sergeant in 1984, moving to investigations in 1997. A tall, dark and distinguished father of three grown sons and grandfather of two grandsons, Roth was about to become the immediate supervisor on the largest police probe in state history. Meanwhile, his twenty-five-year marriage to his high school sweetheart was starting to fall apart.

Roth immediately picked Dave Brown as the lead investigator. Experienced, organized and smart, the boyishly handsome detective was the perfect choice. But even as Roth talked to Brown, he realized the case might require even more than one crackerjack detective could handle. Returning to the training room, where a swearing in of new officers was about to begin, he pulled out Jake Boyer. A twenty-four-year police veteran, he was Roth's best "street" detective and brilliant at interrogating and sizing up people. "Do you have anything big going on right now?" Roth asked him.

Boyer knew better than to say yes. "In our division, even if you might be up to your ears, you always say no," he explained. Roth told him a young woman had moved to Kansas City from Michigan and had gone missing from the Guest-house Suites. He also suggested there might be more to the story and he wanted him to colead the case with Brown. " 'Okay, I'm up for this,' " Boyer said he thought to himself. "I'd worked several homicide cases . . . and most of them were brutal and senseless," he said. "But this investigation developed into the biggest case I was ever involved in. It almost consumed us all."

Brown and Boyer went to pick up the case from Overland Park. Captain Meier put a call into Johnson County district attorney Paul Morrison and spoke to the prosecutor's executive assistant, Terri Issa. "I was in my office working on another case when Terri poked her head in and said that one of the Lenexa detectives had just called about a missing woman," DA Morrison recalled. "She also said that this missing woman happened to be associated with a man who was associated with several other missing women. She said his name and I had never heard it before."

Morrison paused and chuckled during an interview for this book, perhaps he was amused at the thought of a time when John Robinson's name meant nothing to him. The investigation roared forward like the race cars, he said, "at the dropping of the flag at the Indianapolis 500!"

The prosecutor was no stranger to bizarre, high-profile murder cases. He had been district attorney less than a year when Richard Grissom Jr. was arrested in 1989 for the murders of three young women in a two-week period. A phenomenal athlete, Grissom was half black and half Korean, a chameleon who could change his appearance at will. He was also the closest thing to a serial killer that Kansas City had ever seen, taking his victims to ATMs and draining their bank accounts before killing them. Even though the bodies were never found, the young prosecutor managed to win a conviction against Grissom after a four-week trial in 1990 that focused on an abundance of circumstantial and physical evidence. The landmark case attracted widespread media attention and prompted an ex-FBI agent to write the book, *Suddenly Gone.*

Five years after Grissom, Morrison prosecuted the equally bizarre case of Debora Green, the wealthy physician who had tried to poison her husband slowly and ultimately set her house on fire, killing two of her three children. Facing the death penalty, which had been reinstated in Kansas in 1994, Green ultimately pleaded guilty in exchange for life in prison. Like Grissom, she became the subject of many news articles and TV shows, as well as the mesmerizing bestseller *Bitter Harvest,* by well-known true crime writer Ann Rule.

Tall and lean with his thick mustache, chiseled features and subtle drawl, Morrison never sought publicity yet always seemed at ease in the spotlight. Born in Dodge City, Kansas, he hailed from a blue-collar family full of railroad workers and farmers. Growing up in tiny communities such as Plainville and Hays, he attended high school in Kansas City, Kansas, where he loved and excelled at debate. He and his brother were also into their Mustangs and motorcycles. "It was kind of a weird deal," he later said. "I was half debater, half gearhead. My dad used to tell me, 'You've got to figure out what you want to do.' "

He almost became a bricklayer. Dropping out of college for a year, he worked as a hod carrier—someone who assists a bricklayer in transporting loads of bricks and mortar—for a big construction company. "I tried really hard to get a bricklayer apprenticeship, but I didn't get my union card and instead got laid off," he recalled. "I always tell people that if I would have gotten that card, I'd be building chimneys around here somewhere."

Instead, he became the first male in his family to graduate

from college, earning a degree at Washburn University in Topeka. And by the time he started law school, he knew he wanted to be a prosecutor. To improve his chances in what had become a very competitive field, he interned at two different prosecutors' offices in rural counties, where he handled hundreds of misdemeanor cases and several jury trials. "For a lawyer, I don't think there's any better job in the world," he said. "It's always interesting and you go home most days feeling really good about what you've done."

He was hired out of law school in 1980 by then-prosecutor Dennis Moore as one of his ten Johnson County assistant district attorneys. "When I was growing up, I had only been to Johnson County a handful of times because that's where all those rich people lived," he said. "I didn't feel comfortable coming down here. It's interesting now seeing that from the other side. So when I moved here after I got out of law school, it was like moving to a whole new city."

By then, he had started dating Joyce Eisenmenger, a Topeka television reporter who would become his wife in 1981 and later the mother of their three children. With her encouragement, he decided to run for district attorney in 1988 when Moore decided he would not seek a fourth term. Basically apolitical, Morrison ran as a moderate Republican and won both the primary and general elections despite a tough campaign in which his boss supported his Democratic opponent. "I quickly realized, (a) I didn't know what I was doing and (b) if I didn't win, I would be out of a job," said Morrison, who has since been reelected three times. "Fear kicked in. I hit over five thousand doors personally while working full-time."

During the Grissom and Green cases, Morrison's wife was working as an assignment editor or producer for one of the Kansas City television stations. They quickly learned how to separate their marriage from their high-powered careers: he didn't talk about his cases and she didn't ask. "We got it to where it worked out fairly well," said Morrison, adding that his wife had since left the news business and launched her own PR firm. "With Debora Green, it was a little tense. She'd be under pressure to get something and a lot of people didn't understand. When [Green] was arrested, channel 41 got the scoop. Turned out a cop had leaked the story. Well, my wife would not speak to me."

Before John Robinson, Morrison figured he'd probably already prosecuted his most sensational cases. "When Richard Grissom was done in 1990, I remember telling people, 'Gosh, it's too bad it came so early in my career. Everything's downhill from here—in terms of the really interesting and bizarre stuff,'" Morrison said. "Then five years later, along comes Debora Green. I think what it all means is that I am never ceased to be amazed by some of the things that people do."

To help with the Robinson case, Morrison called on ADA Sara Welch, one of his most experienced and skilled assistant district attorneys, who had just returned to work after major back surgery. Because she had been out for six weeks, all of her cases had been assigned to other attorneys and her calendar was clear for a big project. Morrison gave her the scoop and asked if she could go to Lenexa the following day to attend a police meeting on the subject. "This could be a huge deal or it might be a routine missing person case," Welch remembered him saying. "But women who associate with John Robinson seem to disappear."

Welch had grown up in the tiny town of Halstead, Kansas (the setting for the 1955 Academy Award–nominated movie *Picnic*) before spending nearly eight years as a cop in the Kansas City and Denver suburbs. She had worked the street and done a stint in undercover narcotics when, without much consideration or forethought, she applied and was accepted to the law school at the University of Colorado in Boulder. "I distinctly remember driving to my first law school final in December of 1985 and thinking, 'What in the hell am I doing? I don't even want to *be* a lawyer,'" recalled Welch, who soon changed her mind.

Upon graduating near the top of her class, she worked for a year at the Jefferson County District Attorney's Office in Golden, Colorado, before returning to Kansas in late 1999 to be closer to her family. Morrison, who had known her from their undergraduate days at Washburn University in Topeka, immediately hired her. "It has worked out great," she said. "I was a mediocre cop. Couldn't shoot worth a darn. In fact, I was probably a public-safety hazard. Also, I lacked the burning curiosity that leads a good cop to ferret out criminal behavior from seemingly innocent conduct. Last but not least, I always overanalyzed everything. This is a great attribute for a lawyer but a bad one for a police officer, who needs to make quick decisions with not a lot of information."

Unlike Morrison, Welch had never been involved in the kinds of cases that garnered much media attention. She had spent most of her tenure in the DA's office as the section chief of the drug unit, prosecuting her share of marijuana busts and three homicides, one of which went to trial. But the cases nearest to her heart dealt with animal abuse. She won a six-month jail sentence for a man who had stuffed his beagle into a plastic garbage bag and left him under the crawl space of his rental home to die. Fortunately, the landlord came over to start the furnace and found the starving beagle, which was rushed to an emergency vet and miraculously survived. Welch also won a full year in jail for a man who beat and tortured his fourteen-year-old daughter's pug to death. "The little girl had to watch most of it," Welch remembered. "The little dog Pugsley had to be put down. These might not seem like high-profile cases in the traditional sense, but they are cases that were important to me."

Roth, Brown and Boyer met early on Tuesday, March 28, to brainstorm about where and how to proceed. The sergeant assigned Brown as the main contact for the Trouten family and the one who would investigate Suzette's association with Robinson. Boyer would have the pleasure of handling Lore Remington and Tami Taylor, the Canadian women. Brad Hill, a former marine who was on light-duty status because of a recent knee surgery, would immediately hit the phones to try and locate Suzette's dogs and any storage lockers where her belongings might be found.

The investigators agreed they should seal room 216 at the Guesthouse Suites and call in the Johnson County Crime Lab to process the scene. At Brown's suggestion, they wisely decided to put Robinson under surveillance and begin going through his trash. The responsibility of "trashing" went to Detective Dan Owsley, one of the department's two narcotics detectives who had experience collecting and retrieving evidence from suspects' garbage. Lenexa's Directed Patrol Unit, under Sergeant John Browning, was recruited to begin surveillance. Divided into two shifts, with detectives supplementing the officers, they would track Robinson's every move.

Roth was sitting at the conference table in investigations with his detectives that Tuesday morning when Sara walked in. "I still remember she was wearing a long black dress and she was walking with a cane!" Roth said. "Turns out she was wearing some sort of brace because of her recent back surgery and was in some pain. She was in such shape that she couldn't sit down during the meeting but instead leaned against the wall."

Up to that point, Roth had never worked with Welch, but he had heard she was highly regarded and also tough and tenacious—particularly in cases involving animal abuse. "She would drop anything to go after someone who was abusing [an animal]," Roth said. Welch only knew about the sergeant from what she had heard from his troops. "I had heard he was a real 'hard-ass,' never smiled, real aloof, all business, no joking around," she remembered. "I was intimidated by him and was very deferential to him when we first met."

Morrison, who joined the group a few minutes later, had

always enjoyed an unusually good working relationship with the police who served in the various departments of his county. He commanded their respect and, at the same time, he was extremely well liked. On the big cases, he routinely sent an ADA or went himself to the regular police briefings. "We usually attend every meeting so we have intimate knowledge of a case as it unfolds," Morrison said. "We are not policemen and we are not the policemen's bosses. But it's a team deal, where we confer on tactical as well as legal issues."

The district attorney warned the group that the Robinson investigation could take as long as a year and they needed to be prepared for the long haul. But that didn't mean the case would take a low priority. In fact, just the opposite was true. "Everybody was very much aware of the fact that, with Robinson, we were dealing with somebody who was very dangerous," Morrison said. "There was an absolute urgency from the outset to work this case hard."

Chapter 4

From what the detectives knew going into the investigation, the balding fifty-six-year-old "businessman" didn't live in a mansion, as he had apparently claimed to Suzette Trouten. Instead, he resided in an immaculate but very modest gray-and-white trailer on Monterey Lane in a 486-unit mobile-home community called Santa Barbara Estates, located in the less affluent suburb of Olathe, just south of Lenexa and west of Overland Park.

Surveillance began on March 29, 2000. Browning and three of his officers watched as Robinson puttered around his trailer park all morning but never left. The afternoon shift was a different story. Detective Alan Beyer was just joining Officer Dustin Frackowiak around 2:00 P.M. when Robinson, driving his white Dodge Ram pickup, exited Santa Barbara Estates. They tailed him as he got on I-35 heading south, excitedly radioing the news back to headquarters. It wasn't long before he exited I-35 onto 169 Highway that their radios were all but worthless. They had reached an area so rural that soon their cell phones gave out, too.

Some of the detectives who had jumped in their cars to follow Beyer and Frackowiak could hear bits and pieces of radio traffic. Once in a while, they could make phone contact. Roth and Boyer were just plain lost. One officer stopped in the tiny hamlet of Paola, Kansas, and used a pay phone to call the Lenexa dispatcher, who in turn was able to reach the detectives and tell them where to turn. "We just kept driving," Roth remembered. "Once in a while, we'd hear someone on the radio and they would tell us what road they were on. It was no help. We weren't on that road, couldn't find that road and didn't have a map. We were in the country: no service stations, no QuikTrips, no landmarks."

Finally Roth and Boyer heard an address, east of Maddox, crackling over the radio. Flagging down a dairy delivery truck, they were directed to the even tinier community of La Cygne, Kansas, where they gassed up and caught up with the other detectives. Robinson, they discovered, had pulled down a dirt driveway off a gravel road a few miles outside of town. As he parked his truck and entered a ramshackle trailer, the detectives, who numbered about eight, kept their distance. Several of them sat in their unmarked cars a few miles away—and quietly celebrated one of the first big breaks in the investigation. "I lit up a stogie, as did [Officer Rick] Dougan and Frackowiak," Roth recalled. At 4:33 P.M., Robinson emerged from the trailer, climbed into his truck and left for home.

Back at the station that evening, Boyer spoke for the first time to Suzette's friend Lore Remington, in Nova Scotia. To his surprise, she informed him that JT had called her around 2:30 that afternoon (CST) and remarked that, judging by the background noise, she thought he was phoning from his car. *If only she knew,* Boyer thought. Lore also told Boyer that JT was becoming insistent upon her flying to Kansas. When she brought up that she couldn't afford it, he told her not to worry. He had money.

Lore told Boyer she was willing to cooperate with the investigation by continuing to maintain contact with JT. She added that she had been pretending as though she were interested in having JT become her master; as a result, many of their conversations had been sexual in nature. He was demanding she perform several daily BDSM assignments, such as putting clothespins on her nipples and inserting "ice cocks"—condoms filled with ice—in her vagina. She had lied and told him she was adhering to his instructions, one of which included e-mailing him every morning. Boyer, who was unfamiliar and shocked by the mechanics of BDSM, asked her to forward any correspondence she received. She agreed.

The next morning, March 30, Roth sent Detective Dawn Layman on a mission that defense lawyers would object to later. She returned to Robinson's property, which she would learn from records was a 16.5-acre parcel in Linn County. Parking in the driveway, she began taking photos of the trailer, a nearby shed and two rather beat-up–looking pickup trucks: a yellow Toyota and a red 1986 Ford. The windows on the trailer were covered with sheets of newspaper or black plastic; Layman got the impression it was vacant. There was also an odd assortment of junk in a heap next to the shed. One photo she took that morning revealed a lawn mower, an outboard motor and several barrels, including two yellow eighty-five-gallon metal drums. Of course, Layman had no clue at the time that she'd just captured a crime scene on film. "It was a little spooky," recalled the petite, athletic woman with short brown hair, who had been promoted to detective about three months before. "I wanted to get in and out of there as quickly as possible."

Records from the Linn County Assessor's Office listed Robinson as the owner of the parcel and affiliated with another company called Hydro-Gro, Inc., in Kansas City, Missouri. When Layman checked, she found that the address actually belonged to Accent Insurance, located in a small strip mall just south of I-470. Similarly, when Detective Perry Meyer ran a check on the address for Specialty Publications, which Robinson had used when he paid for Suzette's room at the Guesthouse Suites, he found three businesses: Home Equity and Personal Loans, Mail Plus and 1-Hour Photo. On the surface at least, it appeared that Robinson's businesses were phony.

On March 31, Brown received a call from Carolyn Trouten, whom he'd interviewed for the first time a few days earlier. She had just received a typed letter purportedly from Suzette that had been postmarked from San Jose, California, on March 27. Carolyn explained that this letter, like the e-mails her family already had received, sounded nothing like her daughter. She was a terrible writer yet she was constructing complete sentences here. At the same time, she always referred to her sister as Kimmy—not Kim—and never misspelled the names of her dogs. Carolyn told Brown she believed the handwritten signature of "Love Suzette" was the only part of the letter that was authentic.

"Well, I'm off on the adventure of a lifetime," Suzette purportedly wrote. "Peka, Harri [*sic*], Jim and I will be leaving shortly but I wanted to drop you a note before we left." The letter went on to explain that she and Jim had met on her first visit to Kansas City the previous fall and had been talking for almost six months. "He is caring, loving and accepts me just the way I am." She also added that she wouldn't be able to contact anyone until she got to Hawaii, begging her mother not to worry. "Mom, I got an email from Kim saying that you were freaking out that I haven't called. I told you what I was doing, calm down! . . . I am a big girl. I am happy, healthy and safe. I need some space, I need to find out who I am and I need to be able to enjoy myself and see the world."

On April 1, Brown spoke to Suzette's sister in Florida who told him she and her father had also just received some letters supposedly from Suzette containing a San Jose postmark and dated March 27. Dawn Trouten carefully opened the one addressed to her and found a birthday card. It didn't make any sense; Suzette hadn't written her a card in years. Receiving their packet the next day, Brown carefully opened Harry Trouten's letter and saw that it was very similar to the one Carolyn had described. Typewritten and signed "Love Suzette," it, too, was postmarked from San Jose and dated March 27. Brown was stumped: who could be mailing the fake letters from California?

Meanwhile, Detective Derrick Pierce was assigned to follow up with the staff of the Guesthouse Suites. Speaking to Tim Herrman, the assistant manager, he learned that the hotel videotape should have caught whoever checked out of room

216. Herrman went into the back room and returned with the tape from March 1. The time shown on the tape, he said, was approximately one hour and eleven minutes fast.

Pierce also spoke to housekeeping staffers, who told him Suzette had discarded a number of bloody sheets and towels during her stay. One of them, Isabel Paulin, who would later marry and take her husband's name, Clark, said it was as though she'd been on her period for more than two weeks, yet it didn't appear that Suzette was in any distress. On the afternoon of March 1, Paulin had also observed a man matching Robinson's description backing his pickup truck into a parking space outside Suzette's room and loading it with belongings from the room where she stayed.

Back at the station that afternoon, Pierce popped the hotel videotape into a VCR and several detectives watched with excitement as the balding, pudgy man they knew as Robinson entered the front lobby and dropped the keys on the front desk. The time on the tape was 4:19 P.M. or—accounting for the fact that it was fast—3:08 P.M. It was consistent with the time, 3:04 P.M., that the Guesthouse Suites had swiped Robinson's credit card to pay for the room. Suzette was nowhere in sight, they noted.

While Pierce was at the Guesthouse Suites, Brad Hill had been calling kennels, animal shelters and storage lockers all over town. He hit pay dirt with the ninth locker on his list: Needmor Storage, located on North Kansas City Road in Olathe. Speaking with manager Linda Harvey, he learned that Robinson had rented a 10' x 15' locker, B-18, on June 5, 1998. Hill was able to obtain the activity log for the gates of the storage units. Robinson had entered the gate on March 1 at 2:24 P.M. and left six minutes later.

Hill got another break when Tina Clark, the animal control officer (ACO) for the Olathe Police Department, remembered colleague Rodney McClain picking up two Pekingese at Santa Barbara Estates. Calling the trailer park's front office, he was transferred to a woman named Nancy, who said her husband had seen the dogs running loose near their home and managed to trap them one morning inside their back fence. Nancy said the dogs wore no tags but were very friendly. She had no idea who owned them. Hill had no idea he was talking to Robinson's wife—and he wouldn't make the connection for at least a few days. "We were going over his conversation, the ACO reports and information we had gathered on John and Nancy," Roth remembered. "We all thought, 'Oh shit!'"

Checking the Olathe animal control records, Hill also discovered that the dogs had been picked up at Santa Barbara Estates at 2:35 P.M. on March 1 and were adopted by different owners within a few days. First he called on Dan and Vicki Wagner of Olathe, who introduced him to a small Pekingese dog with a black face they had named Tara. Showing them a poor quality fax of the missing dogs, the Wagners agreed that Tara resembled the smaller dog and that the larger dog looked like the one that had been with Tara when they adopted her.

Hill called the pooch by what he suspected was her real name: "Peka!" The spunky little dog jumped up from her bed and instantly came to him, wagging her tail. He snapped several photos of the Pekingese, who knew how to sit up on her back legs and had a scar on her abdomen, presumably from where she'd been spayed.

Laura Notley, who worked at an animal clinic, was taking care of the larger dog, a male whom she called Andy. Visiting Notley next, Hill snapped more photos as the friendly dog also sat up on his hind legs and wagged his tail.

By April 3, Hill had received photos of Suzette's dogs from her aunt and godmother, Marshella Chidester. Comparing them to the photos he'd taken of Tara and Andy, he confirmed that they shared identical colors and markings. He had found Suzette's dogs.

The significance of Hill's discovery was hardly lost on the detectives. Suzette never went anywhere without her dogs— she even took them to the grocery store and brought them to Christmas dinner, often carrying them in a large bag she wore over her shoulder. "Carolyn told me that those dogs meant everything to her daughter—they were her babies," said Brown, who had begun talking to Suzette's mother on a regular basis. "If Harry and Peka were found without Suzette nearby, something was very seriously wrong."

Preparing to meet with the family in Michigan, Brown decided to wait and deliver the bad news in person.

Meanwhile, Owsley was up to his ears in trash. Beginning on March 31, the narcotics detective would stop by the trailer court around 4:00 A.M. on Tuesdays and Fridays. After replacing Robinson's garbage with identical bags, he would return to the Lenexa police station and meticulously sort through the refuse, keeping only what he thought was of evidentiary value.

Owsley got a surprise in his very first pickup when he opened one of the bags and discovered a separate plastic bag full of shredded paper. Working at long tables in two-hour shifts, detectives went through each strand and started piles according to colors, types and lengths of paper. As the piles grew, detectives began matching the individual shreds. By April 4, Layman was able to photocopy eighteen documents they had reassembled. They provided a wealth of information: phone bills, credit cards, checking accounts, e-mail addresses and—most valuable of all—a bill for another storage facility, Stor-Mor For Less, on 58 Highway over the state line in Raymore, Missouri.

Roth assigned Pierce to follow up on the Raymore locker. From manager Loretta Mattingly, he learned that in 1993 Nancy Robinson had rented locker 23. Then Mattingly casually dropped a bombshell: Nancy's husband had rented a second locker, E-2, in the name of Beverly J. Bonner back in January 1994. At the time, Robinson said Bonner was his sister and he was storing her belongings while she lived in Australia. Funny, though, Mattingly couldn't remember ever meeting Bonner. She also noted that Robinson instructed her never to send the bill for this locker to his home. Instead, he came by the storage facility every month, paying in person. "Beverly Bonner's locker was very exciting," Roth said. "Why would he keep it secret from Nancy? The possibilities were endless."

Within days, investigators had installed cameras on three different storage lockers—B-18 in Olathe and 23 and E-2 over the Missouri state line in Raymore. This created a logistical nightmare because a detective, usually Dan Williams, had to drive to Olathe and then to Raymore every morning to change the VHS tapes and batteries.

By April 4, Owsley had also begun to clear up the mystery of the California letters to the Troutens. He discovered an Express Mail receipt in Robinson's trash for a 3.7-ounce package sent to a Jean Glines in Milpitas, California. Detectives ran the address to a business called Post and Parcel; it was within a few miles of where the letters had been mailed. Inundated with more pressing leads, the detectives would have to wait until later to follow up with Glines.

That same morning, surveillance officers followed Robinson for the first time to an address on Grant Avenue in Overland Park. Parking his Dodge Ram in the driveway of the duplex, however, Robinson looked directly at one of the officers before he entered the house. Fearful that the investigation had been compromised, Roth decided they should halt surveillance for a few days. In the meantime, they now had a new mystery to ponder: just who was Robinson visiting at the duplex?

Investigators were constantly worried that Robinson might be trolling for new victims. Conducting his third trashing on April 11, Owsley recovered receipts from Horizon Travel Service with the name of Jeanna Milliron and Extended Stay America in Overland Park. Wilson and Weiler headed to the hotel, only to discover that Robinson had paid the bill for a woman named "Ginna Jones," who had checked in room 200 on April 6 and stayed five days. Robinson had also paid for a one-way ticket for Jeanna Milliron (aka Jones) to return to

Texas. During the lapse in surveillance, they had missed her visit.

Through credit card bills, detectives also learned that on April 5 Robinson had charged another hotel room in Clinton, Missouri. Initially they had no idea what he had been doing there—until, that is, they applied for and received a court order on April 14 that allowed them to begin monitoring Robinson's cell phone activity. Though they couldn't listen in on the conversations, they could now at least determine whom he was calling and when. It didn't take them long to identify a woman in nearby Springfield—Linda G.—as Robinson's mystery date.

Both incidents sparked heated debates on how the detectives could possibly protect the women coming into town of their own free will to meet Robinson. "It was true that they were grown women and making these rendezvous on their own," Roth said. "But the thought of him hurting or killing someone chilled us to the core." It also made them appreciate the importance of surveillance, which they had restarted on April 10. "We had been lucky," he added. "Two women had been with Robinson in motels. They were alive but not because we knew about it."

While Brown flew to Michigan on April 13 to meet with the Trouten family, his unit at home put the mystery of the missing dogs completely to rest. Robinson's MasterCard bills, which came in the mail through subpoena the same day, revealed not only a transaction for Guesthouse Suites but also one for Ridgeview Animal Hospital. Boyer and Meyer collected paperwork from the animal clinic showing that Robinson had claimed to be Suzette's employer as he checked in the dogs on February 16. He, not Suzette, checked them out on March 1 at 2:13 P.M.

On April 14, 2000, surveillance officers again followed Robinson to the Grant Avenue address in Overland Park. After a forty-five-minute visit, he exited the duplex about 2:00 P.M. A plump, middle-aged woman with shoulder-length reddish brown hair followed him out to his white Dodge Ram. Robinson climbed into his truck and leaned out the window to kiss the woman on the lips. He kissed her again before driving off.

Detective Dawn Layman was assigned the task of identifying the woman on Grant Avenue. Through subpoenaed phone records, she got a name: Barbara Sandre. When Layman showed Sandre's Kansas driver's license photo to Browning and Officer Mike Bussell, they agreed that she was the one they had spotted in the embrace with Robinson. "For a long time, we wouldn't know much about Barbara," Roth said, "but she would one day be very important to us."

So would the email accounts Robinson was using on his home computer. Through trashings, detectives Hill and Brown had discovered that their suspect was accessing his email through the Internet provider, Grapevine.net. They knew from talking to Suzette's family that she used an AOL account to make her Internet connection and then accessed her email through a Hotmail account. They were aware that Lore Remington was communicating with someone calling himself James R. Turner and using the "eruditemaster" address at a company called Email.com. As technology experts, Brown and Hill also knew that navigation of email through the Internet requires the use of Internet Protocol (IP) addresses to coordinate both the destination and the source of the communications.

The detectives made an important discovery when they received the subpoenaed records from Grapevine, Hotmail and Email in mid-April 2000. "The IP address that is handed to a user when they log onto their Internet account is similar to a license plate on a car," Hill said, explaining that it enabled them to determine the source of the emails purportedly from "Suzette" to her family and friends. "Trouten was last heard from on March 1. The next day (March 2), there was a change in the IP addresses captured when her Hotmail account was entered. Grapevine logs showed that the IPs used were specifically issued to the account of John Robinson while he was online."

Likewise, the subpoenaed records from Email.com confirmed that Remington was right in suspecting that Robinson was posing as JT or James R. Turner using the "eruditemaster" address. After comparing the logins at Grapevine to those for Email.com, Hill said, "it was determined that the same IP address was in use by the account of John Robinson."

Detectives now had proof that their suspect was using the Internet to pose as ficticious individuals as well as one person who was real: Suzette. "For me," Brown said, "That was, 'Okay, we gotcha, ya bastard.'"

By this point, Roth had decided to run the Robinson investigation like a "Metro Squad" case, a concept that began under Chief Clarence Kelly and the Kansas City, Missouri, police department in the 1960s. The idea was to bring together detectives from several agencies to crack a big case—usually involving a homicide. Brown, who suggested the idea, thought it made sense since Overland Park was already involved and there could well be other jurisdictions before they were done.

Typically, in a Metro Squad case, a sergeant would write a lead on an index card and give it to a detective to investigate. When the detective was done, he or she would turn in the lead card and an accompanying report. Within a couple of days, Brown helped Roth load special computer software onto his laptop and from then on the lead cards were automated. "This may not seem like a big deal," Roth said, "but when the leads reached into the hundreds, it was a lifesaver."

The first days and weeks also led to many differences of opinion among investigators and prosecutors—as most complex cases do. There was a continuous string of closed-door meetings. One of the first issues they had to face was what kind of case they had. Some thought Suzette had been sold into "white slavery" or was being held somewhere against her will. Others were convinced she was already dead. The way they leaned would determine how to pursue the case:

"We decided she was dead," Roth said, "and that's how we directed the investigation."

Another hotly debated issue was whether to confront Robinson about Suzette's disappearance. From the old case files, as well as from talking to retired detectives, they decided he would only clam up and ask for a lawyer. Besides, they didn't have any hard evidence—yet. They would have to continue building the case against their suspect very cautiously without his having a clue he was being investigated.

Chapter 5

There was nothing obvious in John Edward Robinson Sr.'s childhood that suggested to detectives he would one day become a serial killer. Born two days after Christmas in 1943, his parents had introduced him to the world in the customary Catholic manner, baptizing him at Mary Queen of Heaven, their parish church in the bleak Chicago suburb of Cicero. Church records show that family friends William Conway and Johanna Harwell stepped in as proxies when godparents Edward and Agnes Robinson couldn't attend the April ceremony.

Henry Robinson Sr. worked as a machinist for Western Electric Company's Hawthorne Works, whose large stacks often belched thick black smoke into the air of the staunchly working-class community. His wife, Alberta, was a homemaker who had her hands full raising five children. Henry junior led the brood, followed by Joann, John, Mary Ellen and Donald. They lived in a three-story modest home on West Thirty-second Street—in a neighborhood of corner bars, tree-lined streets and the famous Sportsman's Park Race Track, which drew crowds of gamblers and drinkers from all over Chicago.

John Robinson would later describe his family in contradictory terms. Talking to prison psychiatrists in 1987, he referred to them as "traditional American," saying he respected them for their accomplishments and had felt great support throughout his lifetime to achieve great things. "He could think of nothing negative to include which would characterize his family as imperfect in any way," wrote psychiatrist Dr. Thomas Newberry in his clinical evaluation.

Just two years later, however, Robinson told another team of psychiatrists a different story. He said he felt his mother severely disciplined him when he failed math at St. Dionysius Grade School, a Catholic institution a few blocks from his home. "She made him sit at the kitchen table every day for a whole summer, practicing the math he had failed at," wrote prison psychiatrist Dr. George Penn. Later in life, Dr. Penn continued, "[Robinson] also reportedly could not discuss with his mother anything about relationships, questions regarding sex, or family problems. He felt that she could not deal with these issues."

Robinson, moreover, told Dr. Penn that his father was a binge drinker who failed to provide much parental guidance. "During their high school years, they drifted apart, because of the teenage rebellion," wrote Dr. Penn. "Their relationship improved after high school, but never to the level where the inmate could discuss intimate relationships."

Detectives would later debate whether Robinson had been honest in either of those reports.

However, father and son did appear to share a love of Scouting. Robinson was encouraged to join Boy Scout Troop 259, sponsored by Mary Queen of Heaven Parish and led by his father, who was a Scoutmaster and committee chairman for district training. By the fall of 1957, the thirteen-year-old senior patrol leader had completed the twenty merit badges—including nature, swimming, lifesaving, canoeing and rowing—required for the rank of Eagle Scout.

On the Sunday afternoon of November 3, Cicero police cleared the streets and directed traffic as a parade of cars carrying top Scouting officials, including Leland D. Cornell, made their way down Cermak Road and Austin Boulevard to the large auditorium at J. Sterling Morton East High School. A 12' figure of a Boy Scout was posted at the entrance as a welcome to the Eagle High Court of Honor of the Chicago Boy Scout Council.

James Krcmarik, of Cicero Explorer Post 2259, led the audience in the Pledge of Allegiance and a prayer of invocation. Then Cornell, Scout executive for the Chicago Boy Scout Council, told the 155 Chicago-area Scouts about to receive their Eagle and Silver awards that they were the city's "elite" future leaders. "The kind of a city that Chicago will be is in your hands," he said. "It can be beautiful or ugly, clean or filthy, honest or corrupt."

John Robinson's parents sat in the audience, proudly watching as their son, along with sixteen other Scouts, filed to the podium to receive their Eagle badges. "We were like the youngest Eagle Scouts ever made," recalled Krcmarik, who received his badge with John that day. "He wasn't a big guy. He was a little guy. He was kind of quiet and nondescript."

Somehow, however, the "quiet and nondescript" boy managed to finagle his way into representing American Scouts in a royal variety show put on for the queen of England. Eleven days after receiving his Eagle badge, as several newspapers reported, John Robinson flew to London to begin rehearsals for a dazzling three-hour production that included Judy Garland and legendary British actress Gracie Fields.

According to an article in the *Cicero Life* newspaper, John Robinson—then a freshman at Quigley Preparatory Seminary—was chosen for a singing scene from the Boy Scouts' own *Gang Show* because of his scholastic ability, scouting experience and poise. "Besides having a bright and friendly smile, John sings in the choir at Holy Name Cathedral and Quigley Seminary," the article stated.

His trip even made the front page of the *London Daily Sketch* and the *Chicago Tribune,* which proclaimed him as one of its own: CHICAGO BOY SCOUT LEADS TROOP TO SING FOR QUEEN. In the article, journalist Arthur Veysey described a cocky John Robinson trading quips with Judy Garland before the show. "We Americans gotta stick together," Robinson said when they met in her dressing room. "You're right," said Judy, planting a big kiss on his forehead. "I wasn't scared," he confided to Veysey afterward, "but I was surprised all right."

John Robinson also managed to seduce Gracie Fields. "You're a mighty handsome youngster," she told him during rehearsals. He cheekily said she was all right, too. Fields asked if he planned to come to Italy, where she had a home on the Isle of Capri. He replied that he was going to study for the priesthood after Quigley and would certainly come to Rome. "Good," said Fields, extending an open invitation for him to visit her anytime. A hug, Veysey reported, sealed the deal.

When the big night arrived, John donned a bright scarlet uniform and led 120 Boy Scouts onto the stage of the London Palladium. Described as the youngest American ever to appear at the home of London vaudeville, he then bowed to the queen and, with the others, sang a *Gang Show* tribute that went: "Freedom belongs to you. You are the emblem of our flag, red, white and blue." The queen reportedly smiled as she looked down upon Robinson from her royal box.

The story of John's London visit ironically shared the *Tribune*'s front page with that of Ed Gein, the mild-mannered bachelor from Plainfield, Wisconsin, who would later become the inspiration for *Psycho, The Texas Chain Saw Massacre* and *The Silence of the Lambs*. Gein had just been arrested after the body of a hardware-store owner was found hanging by the heels from a hook in his woodshed, with all vital organs removed. Investigators would ultimately find the remains of ten women on his farm—parts of which had been used to make a lampshade, an armchair and even a suit made entirely of human skin.

Upon his return from England, John described his adventures in another article in the *Cicero Life*. Included in his two-week trip, he said, were visits to the Tower of London, Westminster Abbey and 10 Downing Street, the house of England's prime ministers. John told the newspaper that it took him a few days to get the hang of pounds and shillings and to understand the way the English talked. He also said he enjoyed meeting the queen and seeing London, but it was nice to be home. In a scene of apparent domestic tranquillity, a smiling Robinson was pictured posing with his heavyset mother, Alberta, as she looked through a souvenir album while his blond-haired younger sister, Mary Ellen, adjusted his Scottish tam.

Things, however, were not going so smoothly for John at Quigley, the imposing Gothic-looking institution in downtown Chicago founded in 1905 to educate the city's future priests. As a freshman, John was required to take Latin, English, algebra I, general science, physical education (consisting of tumbling, wrestling, swimming and track), music (studying the "fundamentals of Gregorian chant and intelligent appreciation of modern music") and, of course, religion. "The seminarian learns from the spiritual directors how to love Christ and his Church, and how to order his life as a seminarian," states the 1958 Quigley yearbook, *Le Petit Seminaire.* "Nevertheless, before such action and love must come a solid knowledge of the Faith, a knowledge supplied by the religion course at Quigley. This course includes the study of Catholic dogma, or morals, and of the different forms of religious worship, with special emphasis on the Mass."

John, who had a just above average IQ of 102, was flunking out of the academically demanding school. According to school records, his attendance was good—except for the two weeks he was in London—but he had failed both semesters of Latin and algebra I and received a grade of Poor in English and religion, Satisfactory in general science and Good only in physical education and music. Most telling, however, was his grade for deportment, which was Excellent in the first quarter but had slipped twenty-two points by the end of the year to Poor. He finished the year at the bottom of his class, ranking 379 out of 390 students.

"You did not have to be a 'genius' to succeed at the school," said one former classmate, who did not wish to be identified. "But you first did have to pass an entrance exam to win admission to the school and you had to really work to succeed in a no-nonsense academically rigorous environment."

If Quigley wouldn't have him, there were other high schools in the Chicago area that would. Robinson bounced around, attending St. Philip's before ultimately landing at the Cicero public institution, J. Sterling Morton East High School, where he had been awarded his Eagle badge. Known by his classmates as "Little R," he seemed to fit in, serving on the swim team, the activity committee and even as the cochairman of the social committee, which sponsored the homecoming, Christmas, Valentine's and spring dances each year.

"What I will, I can," was Morton's motto and, as Robinson's yearbook noted, it had brought honors to many students who had "walked various pathways through the years to become great and successful citizens." Ironically, it concluded, "And yet who knows how many more hundreds of Mortonites will become well known personalities through the Morton way."

Graduating from high school on June 14, 1961, John Robinson enrolled the following fall at the two-year Morton Junior College. Then still administered by officials from his high school, the community college didn't have its own home and was forced to lease classrooms in the high school, community churches and even storefronts. John took courses through the spring of 1963, never declaring a major and dropping out without earning a degree.

John Robinson would later tell prospective employers that he had taken X-ray technician courses at Morton. "I don't know how he could've taken those courses," said a school spokesman, "because we've never had them." He told others he had trained at West Suburban Hospital in Oak Park, Illinois, which typically offered its lab for other colleges preparing students in medical technologies. But officials at West Suburban could find no record that Robinson had been certified there, either, or that he had ever registered with the Illinois licensing board.

It was at the end of his studies at Morton that John Robinson met Barbara Sandre, then a fifteen-year-old Canadian girl who had become involved in a Toronto production of the Boy Scouts' *Gang Show.* On the last night of the show, May 12, there was a cast party and Robinson, who had come from Chicago with several other Scouts to see the production, had been invited. Though they saw each other just that one night, the two began a correspondence and a romance that would span not only continents but also decades.

Back in Chicago, however, John Robinson apparently fell in love with a pretty blond wisp of a girl named Nancy Jo Lynch. After a whirlwind three-month courtship, they married in March 1964 and, within the year, moved to Kansas City and began raising a family. Their first child, John junior, was born in January 1965, followed by daughter Kimberly in April 1967 and twins Chris and Christine in May 1971. By then, the young father of four had already experienced several run-ins with the law.

Chapter 6

In Kansas City, Robinson wasted little time getting into trouble. By January 1965, when his first son was born, he had landed a job as a pediatric X-ray technician at Children's Mercy Hospital, located downtown. Producing certification of X-ray technician training and letters of recommendation, he told radiologist Dr. Charles Shophner he had been accepted into medical school and was looking for a night job to finance his day classes.

"He had a very sweet, innocent baby face," recalled Jo Bermel, who was assigned to teach him the hospital's system before he took over the evening shift. "He really looked like the boy next door—handsome and fair and very friendly. You'd think he was a great guy. But I remember working with him on special procedures and I just thought, 'Wow, pediatric radiology must be so different for him' because he didn't get it. He didn't catch on real quick. We had to teach him how to do it."

Shophner sent Robinson back to Bermel a second time when he still struggled with the younger pediatric patients, especially infants. "I remember [Dr. Shophner] saying, 'This young man's been accepted into medical school, so we have to give him a chance,'" Bermel said. "Pediatric radiology required a little more immobilization than adult radiology. Positioning is important and the machinery is intimidating. [Babies] don't understand when you say, 'Take a deep breath.'"

Shophner gave Robinson several chances, in fact, but eventually grew wise to the fact that his new X-ray technician was completely unqualified and dismissed him. That was the end of his short stint at Children's Mercy. But it was hardly the last time that Bermel would hear about her confident, cheerful coworker.

In April 1966, Robinson managed to talk his way into an even better job, actually running the lab at Fountain Plaza X-Ray Laboratory, owned by Dr. Wallace Graham, who had an upstairs medical office. Graham, who died in 1996, had impeccable credentials, as an Eagle Scout, local Golden Gloves boxing champ, World War II hero and the personal friend and physician to former president Harry Truman.

He could also be accommodating to a fault. In 1946, Truman wrote a note to Dr. Graham's father in which he praised "that son of yours" but also warned: "The young doctor will work himself to death if he lets all the chiselers take advantage of him."

Robinson, chief among chiselers, apparently saw his opportunity. Dr. Graham's son, then a fifteen-year-old lab technician working summers for his father, remembers his new boss as a "can-do guy."

"He had all these papers saying he was board certified by the American Board of Radiology and he had all these references," recalled Dr. Bruce Graham, now a successful colon and rectal surgeon. "He looked good on paper and he really put on a good show. He was very confident, very articulate and pleasant. He was also an Eagle Scout, which impressed my father very much."

The younger Dr. Graham added that his father was the kind of man who, once he felt comfortable, would let someone take the ball and run with it. "That was my dad's way of doing business," he said. "He was not a micromanager, and he had an extremely busy practice."

By Christmas, 1966, though, Dr. Wallace Graham was losing so much money that he couldn't afford to award holiday bonuses. While fellow employees worried about the grim finances, court records later stated, Robinson bragged of buying lakefront property, horses, a Saint Bernard and a new car for his wife. There was talk that he was running around with women in the laboratory and had even seduced a patient after telling her a story about his wife being terminally ill. Meanwhile, Nancy was in fine health, pregnant with their daughter Kimberly.

In a rather strange twist, Robinson also didn't hesitate to tell the boss's son how he liked to frequent a particular transvestite club in downtown Kansas City. "At the time, it was really, really bizarre to go to a place where men dress up as women and parade around," Dr. Bruce Graham said. "I said, 'Why would you want to do that?' And he just said, 'It's a lot of fun.' He said he used to take his wife there. To me, that was just creepy."

Robinson was apparently having so much fun he was either shirking his duties or was simply in over his head. When Graham's partner, Dr. Philip Reister, criticized his skills, saying he worked too quickly to perform accurate tests, Robinson brought in a newborn poodle as a gift to Reister's family, which reportedly kept the dog for thirteen years. "He was very smooth," Dr. Reister later told *The Kansas City Star*.

It would take another six months before an employee would discover the reason why the office was so financially strapped: Robinson had been using Dr. Graham's signature stamp to process and pocket numerous checks. He also had asked literally hundreds of X-ray patients to pay him directly in cash instead of directing them to the bill counter.

When Dr. Graham confronted Robinson in the summer of 1967, the young scam artist reportedly admitted, "Well, I transferred funds."

"What do you mean—from my pocket to yours?" Dr. Graham later claimed to have responded. "We had quite a conversation. He said that he would make it back to me the best way possible. . . . I said, 'Didn't you know you were going to get caught someday?' And he said, yes, he did."

Police charged Robinson with theft, escorting him from the medical building in handcuffs. Two years later, a Jackson County jury convicted him of embezzling $33,000, though Dr. Bruce Graham estimated he stole six times that amount. "We thought it was around two hundred thousand or more, but we could only prove thirty-three thousand dollars," he said. In the end, Robinson got off with a slap on the wrists, receiving just three years' probation. And though he was ordered to pay full restitution, Dr. Graham said, "We never got a cent."

Shortly after Robinson's firing, Bermel—of all people— answered a classified ad seeking his replacement at Fountain Plaza X-Ray Laboratory. She took the job and was impressed by all of the certificates and diplomas still hanging on the walls of her new office. "I was in awe," she said. "I thought, 'Wow, this guy was really educated. I don't know if I'm going to be able to [fill his shoes.]' "

Cleaning out the X-ray darkroom, however, Bermel came across a box and was stunned as she looked inside to see hundreds of blank certificates wrapped in cellophane. After showing them to Dr. Graham, she said, "He was in shock. He asked, 'Where did you get these from?' " When she told him, Dr. Graham shook his head and said, "I always thought he was awfully young to have all of those degrees."

Not long afterward, Bermel received an eye-opening long-distance call. "They asked for [Robinson]," she said. "I asked who was calling and it was some doctors in Chicago who said he had stolen from them, too, and he had been paying restitution, but they hadn't received any money for some time." Later on, she heard a similar story from another doctor, a podiatrist in Kansas City. "This young man really turned out to be a terrible, terrible crook!" she exclaimed.

By the fall of 1969, Robinson had obtained a new job as systems analyst at the Kansas City office of Mobil Oil Corporation (Ironically, a woman named Beverly Lake—later known as Beverly Bonner—was also working there.) Probation Officer Douglas Pimm remarked in a progress report that Robinson was earning $760 a month at his new job and "they are not aware of his probation status."

This did not seem to worry Pimm, who noted that Robinson "does not appear to be an individual who is basically inclined toward criminal activities and is motivated toward achieving middle-class values, therefore we anticipate his being a good probation risk." In September 1970, the man described as being "a good probation risk" was accused of stealing sixty-two hundred postage stamps—valued at just $372—and fired yet again. According to Clay County, Missouri, court records, the charge was reduced to a misdemeanor when he paid restitution.

The following month, Robinson and his growing family moved back to Chicago, where he landed a job with a company called Illinois R.B. Jones. He embezzled $5,586.36 over the next six months before being caught and fired. According to the same court records, the Illinois attorney general ultimately agreed to dismiss the case when Robinson confessed to the fraud and borrowed money from his father to make full restitution again.

In the midst of his troubles with Illinois R.B. Jones, Nancy gave birth to twins, Chris and Christy, at Chicago's Loyola University Hospital. Robinson formed an especially tight bond with his youngest daughter, calling her his "bonus" child, since they weren't expecting twins. "When he came back from Chicago, they were just babies," recalled Evalee McKnight, a neighbor and surrogate aunt to Robinson's kids, who lived near their home on Orchard Road, in Grandview, Missouri. "He was still carrying them in his arms and he brought them over to my house to show them to me. He was so proud of them."

McKnight, a retired schoolteacher, soon began to give Robinson a great deal of money—$30,000 in total. "He was buying stock for me," she said, still emotional decades later when the subject was raised. "It was in increments. He would come and say there was some stock he wanted to buy for me and I would give him maybe several thousand dollars or so. Of course, I didn't know at the time that the investments didn't mean anything." It would be several years before McKnight learned the truth.

Shortly after his return to Kansas City, Robinson was arrested and, this time, thrown in jail for two weeks when he failed to notify the parole board of the change in his residence and employment. Robinson's probation officer demanded that he make a complete turnaround in his daily behavior or the parole board would have to revoke his probation and consider him a menace to society—due to his constant lying, cheating and stealing. "Prior to 9-8-71 Robinson had never served any jail time," wrote Probation Officer Gordon Morris. "Thus it was felt that a period of time in Jail, combined with extensive counseling, would be a sufficient force to not only catch his attention but to provide a strong motivation for a complete reversal in his behavior."

Robinson apparently fooled the probation officer—much like he would many others down the road. "[He] has been making some definite progress in the reorientation to his thinking," Morris continued, "and thus we feel that Robinson is now ready to function once again in society."

Even so, however, he recommended that Robinson remain under strict supervision—securing a type of employment that could be checked by a probation officer for any "abnormal deviations," having his wife handle all of the family financial transactions and bookkeeping and attending regular group therapy sessions. A judge agreed to extend his probation by two years, though it's not clear if Robinson adhered to any of his probation officer's recommendations.

By this time, Robinson had decided to go into business for himself, with a company called the Professional Services Association, Inc., (PSA), which was supposed to provide financial consulting to doctors in the Kansas City area. Two groups of doctors at the University of Kansas Medical Center hired Robinson to manage their financial affairs but quickly dismissed him because of accounting irregularities.

Undaunted, Robinson continued to send letters to potential investors, portraying PSA as a thriving firm. He even had his young secretary, Charlotte Bowersock, draft a couple of fake letters in what would result in one of his most unsuccessful scams.

One of the letters, dated January 9, 1974, was purportedly written from the Board of Regents at the University of Missouri to Robinson, informing him that he had been voted the full rights and privileges of professor. The letter bore the name and signature of the dean of the School of Dentistry, Hamilton B.G. Robinson. In reality, the university did not have a Board of Regents and the dean's name and signature were fakes.

But it was another letter that ultimately did him in. Dated November 19, 1973, it falsely suggested that Marion Laboratories, founded by Ewing M. Kauffman, who was then the owner of the Kansas City Royals baseball team, was negotiating to acquire PSA and to purchase $364,000 worth of training manuals. Robinson, in typical careless fashion, misspelled both Kauffman's last name and that of one of his executives, John Hartlein. The forgery read:

> Dear Mr. Robinson:
>
> At Mr. Kaufman's request, I have received the material you submitted on November 15, 1973. It is the decision of the Executive Committee that we continue discussions toward making Professional Services Association, Inc, a wholly owned subsidiary of Marion Laboratories, Inc.
>
> We will begin discussions for your training manuals at $364,000. Of course, you will be a necessary part of our overall plan, if we can reach an agreement in the near future.
>
> If you have any questions, please do not hesitate to contact me.
>
> Yours very truly,
> s/John Hartlin
> John E. Hartlein
> Group Executive

In January 1974, Robinson placed an ad in *The Kansas City Star* under the Career Opportunities section: "Corporation with a proven program in the service industry looking for individual who will assist in developing the program nation-wide," the ad read. "If you are a go getter, willing to invest in your own future and want to make your own opportunities for financial security. Call Monday."

Whenever Robinson received a reply, he would send out a PSA prospectus that contained the two forged letters. Anyone with inside information that the publicly owned pharmaceutical giant was planning a takeover of PSA could make a killing. Though the letters were a hoax, Robinson could still make money by convincing unsuspecting investors to buy shares of his worthless company stock.

One of those investors was the late Prairie Village businessman Mac F. Cahal. When Cahal called Robinson, he received not only the prospectus but also a balance sheet that vastly inflated the value of PSA's training and reference manuals, which were the company's only assets. Unluckily for the con man, however, Cahal also happened to be good friends with Ewing Kauffman and called him after sending off a $2,500 down payment for ten thousand shares of PSA at $1 apiece. Kauffman "hit the ceiling," Cahal later told *The Kansas City Star*. He immediately stopped payment on his check and called the U.S. Securities and Exchange Commission, which opened an investigation into Robinson's stock solicitation scam.

In December 1975, a federal grand jury indicted Robinson on four counts of securities and mail fraud. Five months later, he pleaded no contest to reduced charges and Judge John W. Oliver fined him $2,500, placing him on another three years' probation. "He was engaging in schemes that, in my view, pretty much ensured he would get caught," said Bruce Houdek, Robinson's lawyer on that particular case. "He was a small-time, penny-ante con guy who spent more time getting out of trouble than getting into it—and he got into trouble pretty easily."

Chapter 7

Robinson quickly rebounded from his stock solicitation scam and moved his family across the state line to what was then just a rural township called Stanley, Kansas, located in the southern reaches of affluent Johnson County. The budding Pleasant Valley Farms neighborhood, where they settled in the summer of 1977, was a big step up for the Robinson family, and they were very happy in their comfortable nine-room home, a modern building of wood, brick and stone on four levels, with two big fireplaces. The four-acre property also boasted a horse stable and corral; the Oregon and Santa Fe Trails, once traveled by thousands of nineteenth-century pioneers heading west, ran along the back of their property.

Robinson started a new company called Hydro-Gro and began looking for investors to buy his water-based kits for growing indoor tomatoes, cucumbers and other vegetables. He even produced a glossy booklet, *If It Grows, It Grows Better Hydroponically,* which featured a photograph of his blond-haired twins, Chris and Christy, grinning in their "Grow Your Own" T-shirts. "We hope that as you read this book you will form an acquaintance with John Robinson as a sensitive and stimulating human being," stated his self-penned brochure. "John Robinson's lifetime goal in hydroponics is as far reaching as his imagination." It also portrayed him as "one of the nation's pioneers in indoor home hydroponics" and a "sought after lecturer, consultant and author."

Some people initially viewed him that way. Neighbor Nancy Rickard first met Robinson when her father, Brooks, recently retired and with his wife dying of cancer, agreed to invest in Hydro-Gro. At the time, Nancy was in her early twenties and an aspiring artist and Robinson allowed her to illustrate his how-to gardening booklet. "He was very nice to me, very encouraging," she later told *The Kansas City Star*. Ultimately her father and other family members invested more than $5,000. An aunt reportedly sunk $20,000. They would never recoup a dime.

In his new community, Robinson held himself out as a leader, taking an active role in Scouting, The Presbyterian Church of Stanley and other civic engagements. In December 1977, he even received a commendation from the mayor for his work with the handicapped and was named Man of the Year at a luncheon sponsored by a local "sheltered workshop association" and attended by the former state Senator Mary Gant. GROUP FOR DISABLED HONORS AREA MAN was the headline in the December 8 edition of *The Kansas City Times*. Two weeks later, however, *The Kansas City Star*—then the afternoon paper—revealed that the event was just another of Robinson's schemes. With the headline, MAN-OF-THE-YEAR PLOY BACKFIRES ON HONOREE," the story provided details of how Robinson had engineered the entire affair—down to his Man of the Year plaque—through an elaborate sequence of fake letters of recommendation sent to city hall.

The following year, in 1978, Margaret Adams saw Robinson at a downtown trade show, where he was demonstrating his hydroponic kits and giving away beautiful-looking tomatoes. Moving with her family to Pleasant Valley, the avid gardener soon discovered that Robinson was her new neighbor and asked him to demonstrate his hydroponics systems. "He couldn't have been nicer," Margaret said, until she told him the kit was out of her price range. With a withering glance, he snapped that she was "small potatoes" and had wasted his time. "He was rather sharp and could put you down with just a look or a comment," she said. "I found out later that that was his way of controlling people."

As neighbors soon discovered, Robinson was a man who

liked to be in control—at one point even electing himself as president of the homeowners association. He was often heard yelling at his wife and children and ordering them about. When a dog chased John junior, causing him to fall off his bike, Robinson nearly came to blows with its owner. "He was a loud man," remembered Margaret Adams's daughter, Hilary, who was the same year in school as John junior. "He kind of frightened me. We'd have a yearly cleanup where we went around the lake picking up stray branches, and I remember him walking ahead of us very briskly and yelling at his kids. That was my first impression of him as an abrupt person."

Scott Davis, whose parents grew close to John and Nancy after they moved into the neighborhood in 1978, described him as someone who could also turn on the charm. "If you had met John at a cocktail get-together or a business conference, he would be the life of the party," he said. "He was conversant, witty and always had good stories. He would keep you laughing. Nancy was very introverted, even in a group setting. She would sit back and watch John take center stage."

Nancy, to be sure, was an enigma. Some of her former neighbors believed Robinson psychologically—if not physically—tormented the painfully thin, quiet woman with white blond hair, who always seemed to have a cigarette dangling from her lips. "I think she was afraid of him," Margaret Adams said. "She cowered. You could look at the woman and know she was abused." Davis carefully explained his theory: "Personally, I think Nancy does not feel a whole person. And her involvement with John for good or ill is what made her feel complete."

While the majority of residents in the small neighborhood didn't care for Robinson and didn't really know Nancy, they liked his children, especially the twins. "They were adorable," recalled Hilary. "They were as blond as blond could be. They didn't look anything like Robinson. They looked more like Nancy, who, I believe, was a natural blond. They were well mannered, friendly and always came over. They used to watch our pets while we went on vacation."

The mischievous twins would steal the go-cart belonging to their neighbor Dorothy Davis and drive it up and down the street for hours, causing Hilary and her parents to break into laughter as they watched their antics. Christy also loved to help Margaret Adams pick the strawberries in her garden. "She was a tiny little thing and she would tiptoe around the strawberry bed," she recalled. "She was a sweet little girl, very small, and I'd say, 'It's only fair that you get half.'"

John junior was very nice, Hilary said, and quite different from his father in that he didn't seem to rub anyone the wrong way. "He was into the theater, always in some play or musical, and very left-brained, more artistic," she remembered, adding that he always wore his Scouting uniform to school, which she thought was quite geeky. Kim, on the other hand, was more reserved. "When I think of Kim, I think of a straight A student," Hilary said. "She was extremely smart, very studious and quiet."

In 1980, Robinson, who had put Hydro-Gro on the back burner, took a job as the personnel manager at a Liberty, Missouri, subsidiary of Borden, Inc., known as Guy's Foods. James Caldwell, the operations manager until the company went belly up in 2001, remembered the period as chaotic. Borden had recently bought the snack food company and, somehow, no one bothered to run a background check. "He was the personnel manager and they're typically outgoing, friendly and very helpful people and that's the way he was," said Caldwell. "He also embezzled a lot of money."

At the time, Borden had just decided to sell its fleet of Ford Econoline vans and was offering them to its salesmen and other employees at very good prices. Caldwell, whose uncle had founded the snack food company, got the first clue that something was wrong when he started getting calls from employees who wanted to know if he had received their checks for the vans they had purchased from Robinson. He tracked their checks—and several others—to a dummy bank account disguised to look like a legitimate corporate account. "John Robinson had set it up in his name and he was the only one able to withdraw from it," Caldwell said. "Because he was the personnel manager, the local bank allowed it to happen."

Besides stealing dozens of checks, Caldwell said, executives also discovered that Robinson had added a number of phantom employees to the company roster and had been quietly pocketing their paychecks. "I'd never been around dishonest people," Caldwell said. "I couldn't believe he would think nobody would notice. He was a dirty rascal, you know."

According to court and police records, Robinson spent some of the money on an Olathe apartment, where he conducted sexual liaisons with two women who worked for Borden, including a secretary he had hired named Becky. She later admitted to police that he had bought her a gold necklace, given her money to pave her driveway and taken her to Tan-Tar-A, a Missouri resort.

It was at this time that police in Liberty also discovered Robinson was sending $650 checks from his unauthorized Borden account to former neighbor Evalee McKnight. Upon questioning her, they learned that he was supposed to be investing $30,000 and had begun sending the unauthorized checks after she began inquiring about stock dividends. "I was not suspicious until the police called and wanted to talk to me," said McKnight, who never recouped the $30,000. "They wanted me to sue him, but I didn't want to because of the children. That's a mistake I made. I should have gone ahead."

Robinson ultimately faced felony stealing charges as well as a civil lawsuit for his illicit activities at Borden. Missouri, however, again let him off easily. After being ordered to pay more than $41,000 in restitution in the civil case, he pleaded guilty to just one count of stealing a $6,000 check and was sentenced in December 1981 to a mere sixty days days of "shock time" at the Clay County Jail, though he would remain on probation for five years.

Not long after, Caldwell said, he was driving along I-435 on his way to work and suddenly passed Robinson: "He had stolen this huge amount of money and here he was out loose.

He smiled and waved at me—as if to say, 'I got out of it.' It sent chills down my spine."

Back in Pleasant Valley Farms, Nancy Robinson had confided in Scott Davis's mother, Dorothy, that she knew about Becky and had started divorce proceedings. (She later reconsidered after the couple received marital counseling.) "My mom and [Nancy] became good friends and through that I heard a lot," said Scott Davis, now a computer consultant. "I knew he was having an affair [with Becky] because I was asked by Nancy to follow his car to see where he went. But I couldn't keep up with him and I lost him."

Neighbors later learned that Robinson had also tried to grope a woman who lived in the subdivision. When the woman immediately reported the incident to her husband, her spouse became furious and headed to confront Robinson. Robinson saw him coming, though, and jumped in his car and took off. The woman's husband—a giant of a man—followed him for miles. "I think he would have torn John's head off," said one of the neighbors. "But John was good at getting away."

On May 8, 1982, Robinson arrived at the Clay County Court to start his sixty-day sentence. Davis said the Robinson family tried their best to keep a lid on the embarrassing situation. "I don't think everybody knew, but a lot of people did," Davis recalled. "I was told, 'Hush, hush.'" Robinson and his wife actually told their kids he was going away on a "business trip"—though by the look on their faces as they boarded the school bus, Hilary Adams figured they knew the truth. "It was kind of scandalous in a neighborhood where most of the fathers were executives working for Bendix [Corporation] or Marion Labs," she said.

Upon his release in July, the convict was as cocky as ever. "He hadn't learned any lessons," Scott Davis said. "There was no shame or remorse. In fact, he came back bragging about the contacts he'd made there." Davis said Robinson had also bragged to him about inventing the phantom employees at Guy's Foods and even demonstrated his expertise at forgery, showing him how to use a Xerox copy machine, whiteout and a fake signature to produce a convincing document. "Here's where I'm good," he allegedly told Davis, who would shake his head in disbelief.

That same summer, Robinson started a new consulting company called Equi-Plus, which was supposed to help struggling businesses get back on their feet. He hired a couple of partners and his wife as the full-time secretary, moving into comfortable offices on Barkley Street in Overland Park. Erecting a big sign outside the building, he also produced a colorful brochure in an effort to attract clients.

Two of the first were Scott Davis and his father, Bob, who had started a company, Online Computers, and were having financial difficulties. Robinson offered to have Equi-Plus find venture capital to help them return to the black. In exchange, Davis and his father agreed to pay the company $1,000 a month and provide them with free computers. "He was just learning about them then," he said. "There was no Internet then, just word processing, but he welcomed technology." Within a few weeks, Robinson told them he had set up a $240,000 bank loan to bail out their struggling computer retail operation.

Scott Davis grew suspicious when he had to drive to one of the seedier parts of Kansas City to meet with Robinson's attorney. "This was a con job and I know it now," he said. "[Robinson and I] drove downtown in separate cars and ended up in this spot with no windows. It [now] reminds me of the kind of place where Tony Soprano would hang out."

The secretary had them wait in the lobby of the nondescript building while she went to find the attorney. Noticing a door ajar, Davis peeked through and saw what looked like a tavern that hadn't been cleaned up from the night before. There were cigarettes in ashtrays and popcorn on the floors. Over the bar was a picture of Mussolini and an Italian flag. Upon the secretary's return, she quickly closed the door. Finally the attorney appeared and the three men left for the bank. On the way over, Davis agreed to pay Robinson and the lawyer $30,000 each in commission if the bank approved the loan.

The meeting with the bank president made Scott Davis even more suspicious that something shady was going on. They handed the president a business proposition. He asked a few questions and then told them to leave while the attorney stayed behind to finalize the loan. "It was so perfunctory, it wasn't even funny," Davis remembered. "There was no discussion of the details, no due diligence, none of the things you would expect in a normal business transaction." Davis waited a week, then two. Finally calling the bank, he learned that it had closed down and the Feds were investigating.

By 1983, Davis and his father were forced to file chapter 7, which only served to infuriate Robinson, who hadn't received any real money for his services. According to Davis, Robinson's response was to forge some documents that said Bob Davis had agreed to pay him $125,000 no matter what happened to the company. Scott Davis, who said he was all too familiar with Robinson's cut-and-paste talents, demanded that he produce the original. "He never did," Davis said.

Then Robinson wanted to handle the liquidation and went so far as to organize the creditors, putting himself at the top of the list. "He wanted to get paid first," Davis said. "He went to my bankruptcy attorney and said, 'Wouldn't it be nice if I went to the head of the line?'"

When that didn't work, Robinson left an angry letter to Dorothy Davis on her doorstep, stating that he was organizing the creditors to fight and warning her that she would lose her home if he didn't get his money. "John could talk to you for an hour and know what buttons to push," Scott Davis said. "And that was a button with my mother."

Ultimately, though, the Davis family refused to pay him a cent. And Robinson, looking for other fish to fry, moved on. Expanding upon Equi-Plus, he formed a new company, Equi-II, which engaged in a variety of so-called management consultant and philanthropic ventures. This time, however, Robinson would not only use his companies to defraud and steal. He would use them for something more sinister.

Chapter 8

Before she disappeared forever, Paula Godfrey was looking for work. The pretty nineteen-year-old brunette had recently graduated from Olathe North High School, where she made the honor roll, contributed to a literary magazine and was active in a school pep club known as the Senior Rowdies. A talented figure skater, she had her career hopes temporarily dashed when a case of the flu kept her from performing well enough to win a spot in a professional ice show. She planned to try again; in the meantime, she answered an employment ad in *The Kansas City Star*.

Paula subsequently told her parents that a man named John Robinson had promised to help her get a start in the business world, offering her an office job with his company Equi-II, and making arrangements for her to fly to San Antonio for a weeklong clerical skills training course. On August 23, 1984, while her mother was home, Robinson picked up Paula and drove her to the airport. She was carrying a suitcase and about $40. The family heard from her just once, five days later, when she called home and let them know that she was staying in room 306 at the Airport Ramada Inn. When she failed to return as scheduled on August 30, they called the Overland Park Police Department.

According to police records, Paula's mother, Diane, reported on September 1 that her daughter had "been living away from home for the past seven or eight months" and was "feeling very independent." She acknowledged that it was conceivable that Paula had returned home and left again for the holiday weekend without telling the family. Her father, Bill, who had been away on a business trip when Paula left, drove to the Equi-II office in the Windmill Square Shopping Center in Overland Park to question Robinson about his daughter's whereabouts. Robinson, he said, was in his office with a middle-aged receptionist and told him he hadn't heard from her since he sent her for training. He didn't know where she was.

Within a few days, the Godfreys received a handwritten letter, purportedly from their daughter, who apologized for not calling and explained she had some things she needed to work out for herself. She told them she was fine and that she would call as soon as she could get her "head on straight."

"Maybe then we can all sit down and talk and be a family again," she wrote, telling her parents to say hello to her sister and brother.

Though the handwriting looked authentic, the Godfreys had a gut feeling after receiving the note that something was very wrong. "We thought it was very out-of-character for her," Bill Godfrey later told *The Kansas City Star*. "We weren't mad at her, and she wasn't mad at us. She was a mature young lady looking to get involved in business."

Bill Godfrey told police he returned to the Equi-II office. With the same middle-aged receptionist as a witness, Godfrey said, he pointed a .32-caliber handgun at Robinson and angrily threatened to kill him if he did not receive a telephone call from his daughter Paula within three days. Robinson reportedly became very nervous and said he would get word to Paula to call home—which sounded strange coming from a man who previously professed not to know where she was.

No phone call ever came. However, the Godfreys would receive two more letters from Paula that didn't seem to make much sense. In the letters, both handwritten in September, she referred to the great time she was having with a girlfriend named "Jackie"; her parents didn't have a clue who Jackie was. Godfrey's wife talked her husband out of going back to see Robinson, convincing him to sell the gun and leave the investigating to police. Godfrey soon grew frustrated, however, when the detective assigned to his daughter's case did not return his calls. As a last resort, he hired a private investigator, who ultimately failed to locate Paula or any trace of her.

In their defense, the Overland Park Police Department didn't have much to go on. They, too, had received a letter purportedly signed by Paula stating that she was living in western Kansas, was "O.K." but did not want to see her family. When a person goes missing, as several detectives repeatedly said, they often don't want to be found. With no concrete evidence of wrongdoing, the investigators soon suspended their investigation. It was a decision they would come to regret.

John Robinson was warming to his new role as a "philanthropist" when he presented himself in December 1984 to social workers at Truman Medical Center in Independence, Missouri, a hospital well known for its care of the indigent, and Birthright, an organization that counseled and aided unwed pregnant women. Robinson told both groups that he and several other Johnson County businessmen had established "Kansas City Outreach," an organization that provided housing and job training for single mothers with newborn babies.

In late December, several law enforcement sources say, Truman social worker Karen Gaddis put Robinson in touch with a nineteen-year-old woman named Lisa Stasi. Beautiful yet troubled, she and boyfriend Carl Stasi had gotten married in her hometown of Huntsville, Alabama, in August 1984, when she was eight months pregnant. "We were going to stay and start our lives there," Carl later testified. "But I didn't have no insurance and the baby was due and so we came back [to Kansas City]."

Their daughter, Tiffany Lynn, was born a few weeks later at Truman. She was an adorable baby, with bright red hair and blue eyes, and her parents doted on her. Broke and without a home, though, the Stasis' marriage quickly went downhill. There were quarrels and some of them, allegedly, turned violent. "It was shaky," Carl stated. "I was irresponsible and I wasn't working at the time. It was going down from there." He and Lisa separated in mid-December and Carl returned to service in the navy, just outside of Chicago, a few days after Christmas.

Lisa and Tiffany checked into Hope House, a shelter for battered women, but kept in touch with Carl's family and other relatives. Kathy Klinginsmith, his sister, agreed to watch her four-month-old niece after Lisa dropped by on January 8, 1985. Before she went out for the evening, Lisa told Kathy about a Johnson County businessman, "John Osborne," who was purportedly involved with helping young mothers. Osborne, Lisa said, wanted to help her get her GED and find a job. He was also putting her up in the Rodeway Inn in Overland Park, which raised Kathy's eyebrows. "I told her she ought to be cautious because, for one, she didn't know him all that well," she later testified. "She didn't know what his intentions were."

After spending the evening at a neighborhood bar and her in-laws' house, Lisa returned to Kathy's house the next day and called the front desk of the Rodeway Inn. Osborne was looking for her. She left a message for him to call her at the Klinginsmiths'. When the phone rang a few minutes later, Kathy gave Osborne directions to her house. While they waited, Lisa mentioned that Osborne had bought train tickets to go to Chicago that week about a job. A stocky man with brown hair, glasses and a deep voice arrived just twenty-five minutes later—driving across the city through a bad snowstorm to fetch Lisa and her baby. Osborne didn't waste any time on pleasantries, insisting they leave immediately. "He didn't say a word to me," Kathy Klinginsmith later said. "Nothing. He was just evil."

Lisa carried Tiffany to Osborne's car, which was parked down the street and out of view, leaving her own yellow Toyota Corolla and most of her belongings behind. Kathy's five-year-old son seemed petrified of Osborne, which only served to frighten her more. "I wanted to run after her and get her, but I was too scared," Kathy Klinginsmith said. "I was afraid of him. I knew deep down that was the last time I would see Lisa."

Betty Stasi, Lisa's mother-in-law, received a call later that night. "I took it for granted she was at her motel," she later testified. "She was crying real hard, hysterical. She was telling me that 'they' said I was going to take her baby from her, that she was an unfit mom." She didn't explain who "they" were, said Betty, who assured her she'd never said anything of the sort. In the same conversation, Lisa also told her "they" wanted her to sign four blank sheets of paper. "I said, 'Don't sign nothing, Lisa,'" Betty recalled. Her daughter-in-law calmed down. "Then she said, 'Here they come,' and she hung up."

Kathy Klinginsmith phoned the Rodeway Inn the next morning—January 10—only to discover that Lisa and Tiffany Lynn had checked out of room 131. Their bill had been settled not by John Osborne but by a man named John Robinson, who used his American Express card with the business name of Equi-II. "That really scared me," said Kathy, who drove the next day from northeast Kansas City to the Overland Park police station to file missing persons reports. "Now we were dealing with a guy who was using a false name."

Much like Bill Godfrey a few months earlier, Kathy's husband, David, paid a visit to Robinson's Equi-II offices in the Windmill Square Shopping Center. According to police records, he reported speaking to a very tall man with light brown hair, who was in his late twenties to early thirties. He said the man told him he was an associate of Robinson, who was out of town. He grew angry when he heard David's name, grabbed his arm and pushed him out the door.

Both David and his brother-in-law John Stasi told police they had received calls that week from a man claiming to be a priest named "Father Martin" of the City Union Mission. The priest stated that Lisa and her baby were fine; they had stayed at the mission the previous night and then left with a guy named Bill. When the men called the mission, they learned there was no Father Martin.

Chapter 9

Stephen Haymes had picked up Robinson's trail just before Lisa and Tiffany went missing. It all started with a disturbing call the soft-spoken mustachioed probation supervisor received on December 18, 1984, from Ann Smith at Birthright. Smith told Haymes that Robinson had approached her organization, saying he was on the board of directors of an Olathe bank and affiliated with The Presbyterian Church of Stanley, Kansas, which was developing a program to help young women who had just delivered babies. The church, he had explained, wished to place young mothers in a duplex in Olathe and pay their expenses while they got back on their feet. Robinson wanted to know if anyone at Birthright might fit the profile.

Smith told Haymes she became suspicious and decided to check out Robinson's story when he became insistent upon finding a young mother by December 24. Calling the church, she learned that Robinson was a member of the congregation but he was not representing them in any way and they had no program to help young women. Likewise, the bank said Robinson did not sit on its board of directors. In fact, as Smith relayed to Haymes, the bank had never heard of him. Upon learning that he was on probation out of Clay County, Missouri—on the old Guy's Foods conviction—Smith had called the Missouri Board of Probation and Parole and been connected to Haymes, the district supervisor.

Haymes also had never heard of Robinson, for his office in Liberty, Missouri, had transferred Robinson's supervision by means of an interstate compact agreement to a probation officer thirty-five miles away in Olathe, Kansas. But listening to Smith, he was instantly suspicious. Then he pulled Robinson's file and discovered his long history as a con artist. "I was even more suspicious," he said. After checking in with Robinson's Olathe probation officer, who had experienced no difficulties, he wrote the parolee a letter, ironically dated January 10—the same day that Lisa and Tiffany went missing—and asked him to report to the Missouri probation office the following week.

When Robinson failed to appear for the appointment, Haymes sent a second, registered letter for a January 24 meeting. Robinson called him on January 21, saying he'd just gotten back from a Denver business trip and received his letters. "He was self-assured, articulate and appropriately apologetic for having missed the meeting," Haymes said. "He was also real curious as to why I was having him come in. I said, 'We'll talk about it when you get here.'"

Before the meeting, Haymes phoned a contact he had in the Kansas City field office of the FBI to ask if they were currently investigating Robinson or were aware of any "baby-selling rings" operating in the area. The supervisor checked and said that the answer was no to both of his questions—though he acknowledged to Haymes that "they were aware of John Robinson."

The stocky, middle-aged felon arrived at Haymes's office in a suit and tie and calmly explained that he had not told Smith he was affiliated with The Presbyterian Church of Stanley. She had asked what church he went to and he had simply answered, he said. In the course of the conversation, he also mentioned that he had met with Truman Medical Center social workers Karen Gaddis and Sharon Jackson Turner and they had referred two young black women to the apartment he had rented for the program on Troost Avenue in south Kansas City.

When Haymes asked him what he was getting out of the program, Robinson told him he was simply getting the satisfaction of being a help to the community and people less fortunate than himself. "I didn't buy the story," Haymes said. "Probably because I'm cynical." He paused to laugh. "But a certain amount of cynicism is healthy in this profession. I didn't believe that a person who had a history of embezzling money was going to be giving to charities. He was also too good of a talker. Little things didn't match up. He would twist the truth—not enough to make it blatantly obvious he was lying but just enough that you'd have to go out and reinvestigate that what he was telling you wasn't true."

Haymes subsequently spoke with Gaddis and learned that while the two black women were doing well, a young white woman and her baby had gone missing after staying in an Overland Park hotel. Detectives, he said she told him, were investigating. "Gaddis cautioned this officer that there was some question about the program as the white girl that they had helped to arrange placement with had disappeared approximately three weeks earlier," wrote Haymes, whose careful notes about Robinson would later be filed in Clay County Circuit Court.

When Haymes called the Overland Park police, Detective Larry Dixon told him that they had been unable so far to find any evidence of wrongdoing in the Stasi investigation. The detective also mentioned that a second young woman who had worked for Robinson—Paula Godfrey—had been reported missing a few months earlier, but they had received a letter from her stating that she did not want to see her family. Haymes and Dixon agreed to keep in touch on any new developments in the Robinson case.

When Haymes sat down for another talk with Karen Gaddis and Sharon Jackson Turner on January 30, he learned even more disturbing details. In approaching the social workers before Christmas, John Robinson had stressed the importance of a 50-50 racial mix as this had been stipulated by potential contributors such as Xerox and IBM. Since they had already found two black women for the Troost Avenue apartment, Robinson strongly urged them to find a white woman. That's when the Truman social workers told Haymes they checked with other agencies and found Lisa and Tiffany.

Haymes subsequently spoke to Stasi's relatives and learned about the four blank sheets of paper that Lisa had been asked to sign. He also found out that two suspicious typed letters signed by Lisa had arrived for her mother-in-law, Betty Stasi, and Cathy Stackpole, the executive director of Hope House. In them, she said she was leaving Kansas City and spoke of needing to get away and "start a new life" for her and Tiffany. The letters didn't sound like Lisa, he was told, and the young mother didn't know how to type.

Haymes paid a visit to Robinson, on February 8, specifically to ask him about Lisa and her baby. Robinson told him that a guy named "Bill" had been waiting at the hotel when they returned from her sister-in-law's on January 9. The next morning, he added, Lisa and Tiffany came with "Bill" to his office and told him they were going off to Colorado. Robinson also commented that he couldn't understand why everyone was giving him such a hard time about their disappearance when he was only trying to help people. "He was taking the martyr role," Haymes remembered. "He told me, 'I'm just trying to do something nice.'"

By now, Haymes's suspicions had turned into deep concern. He called his contact in the FBI once again. "You need to take a look at this," he said, pointing out that there were now two missing women and a baby with links to Robinson. The alleged disappearance involved the crossing of not only municipal but also state lines. Unlike the Overland Park Police Department, he noted, the FBI didn't face jurisdictional obstacles. "At the time, we're scratching our heads, going, 'What in the world is he up to?'" he said. "Most con men are considered nonviolent. They go out of their way not to hurt people. We know he's doing something terribly wrong, but we're having a terrible time trying to figure out what it is."

Over the next several months, two FBI agents—Thomas Lavin, a veteran, and his young partner, Jeffrey Dancer—

along with Overland Park detective Cindy Scott and the now relentless Haymes were looking into Robinson's activities. While the Stasi leads seemed to be drying up, Haymes recalled that the parolee was creating big trouble for himself on an astonishing number of other fronts.

Larry McClain, then a Johnson County assistant prosecutor and now a disctrict court judge, told Haymes his office was building a case that Robinson's Equi-II had cooked up several phony receipts to defraud a company called Back Care Systems out of about $5,000. McClain also said he had received a complaint from a woman in Kansas City named Mildred Amadi. She said her former landlord, Irv Blattner, had introduced her to Robinson, who claimed he was an attorney and could help her obtain a divorce. Giving him the title to her car as payment, she waited and waited for the divorce papers. "He said . . . I didn't need a copy of the divorce papers," she stated, fuming, when she still hadn't gotten them months later. "He keeps telling me I'm divorced—go out, get married."

Amadi's story convinced Haymes that there was no con too small for Robinson. "He loves the con game," he said. "He loves the challenge of it. And it doesn't always matter what he wins. Here he took a 1970s American Motors Pacer, which was probably the worst car in history, as payment for his services as an 'attorney,' and that car didn't even run."

Meanwhile, the Secret Service was investigating both Robinson and Blattner, who, as it turned out, was his pal and fellow ex-convict, for forging the signature and cashing a paltry $741 government check. Blattner, however, quickly agreed to help authorities nail Robinson in exchange for lenient treatment.

Haymes felt he had enough evidence at this point to prove Robinson was in clear violation of his parole. Ordered to appear for another visit, on March 21, Haymes informed him that he was under arrest and would be transported to the Clay County Jail. "I had just put handcuffs on him," he remembered, "and he'd gotten very, very nervous and panicky about having gotten arrested. He didn't like the thought of going to jail. Boom, all of a sudden he regains his composure and says, 'Oh, by the way, Lisa's been found. That girl you asked me about, she's here in town and she's just fine.'"

Robinson, who was soon released after posting bond, had cooked up another story: a young woman in town, he said, had called his office looking for Stasi because she needed to pay her for some recent baby-sitting. Robinson told Haymes how the woman mentioned that Stasi and her daughter were with a guy the young woman had known for some time. He also said he had instructed the woman to call his attorney, Ron Wood, who in turn had relayed the information to the Overland Park Police Department. Detective Cindy Scott had verified the information, Robinson insisted, and was satisfied that Stasi was okay.

In fact, just the opposite was true. Scott paid an initial visit to Cora Kristine Pebley, who told her that "Bill Summers," a man she knew from playing pool at the Country Club Inn in Lee's Summit, had asked her to baby-sit for Tiffany for a few hours on January 25. Kristi—as she was then called—said that she had also met Lisa, who told her they were going to be going to Arkansas.

According to police records, Scott asked Kristi to view a photo of a woman and tell her if it was Lisa. Kristi replied that it was, but her hair was a little lighter. Scott then asked her how tall Lisa was. Kristi told her she was about 5'5". She was wrong on both counts: the woman in the photo was not Lisa and the missing woman was nearly 6'. For the moment, Scott didn't let on that she knew Kristi was lying.

Returning a few weeks later, Detective Cindy Scott and Agent Tom Lavin confronted Kristi, who admitted she had agreed to help Robinson by telling a false story because she owed him money. She went on to say that she had met Robinson through a friend, Misty Barber, who used to date a male dancer named Mark Boothroyd. Using the nickname M&M, Boothroyd had taken nude photos of both women and given them to Robinson. They added that Boothroyd's wife, Sandy, described by the women as "twenty-seven years old, blond and fat," also worked for Robinson.

Based on these and other interviews, investigators came to believe that Robinson was attempting to organize a ring of prostitutes and that Equi-II was more of an escort service than a consulting company. Boothroyd and Blattner, they realized, were both involved in recruiting women for Robinson, who would typically take them to a hotel, photograph them in various stages of undress and often require sex before hiring them. Prostitution, however, was just the tip of the iceberg.

Chapter 10

One of the women Boothroyd introduced to Robinson as a candidate for prostitution was Theresa L. Williams, a pretty twenty-one-year-old from Boise, Idaho. According to a statement she gave to FBI agents later, Williams had gone out barhopping in September 1984 and met Boothroyd at Jeremiah Tuttles, a nightspot in the Ramada Inn off I-435 in Lenexa. They danced and exchanged telephone numbers.

Within a couple of days, Boothroyd called and asked her out, inquiring of Williams on their first date if she was interested in working for Robinson's escort service. He insisted it was safe because all of the clients' information was on a computer. He also asked if she enjoyed rough sex. When she asked why, he told her that one of Robinson's customers was an older gentleman who was into that sort of thing. Upon learning from Boothroyd that she could make $1,000, she said she would give it a try.

Williams returned to the Ramada Inn a few days later, she told agents, where she met Robinson and they checked into a room. "He took pictures of me fully clothed and in various stages of undress," she stated. "He also took some pictures of me in various bondage poses, some when I was tied up and some when I was handcuffed. John also asked me at this meeting if I knew of anyone who just had a baby and if I'd be willing to have a baby. I said I didn't know of anyone and laughed about me having a baby."

When she didn't hear from Robinson for several weeks,

Williams contacted Boothroyd because she had lost the piece of paper with Robinson's phone number. Though Boothroyd gave it to her, he also told her not to trust Robinson because "he could get [her] hurt." Calling him anyway, they met at the McDonald's next to the Laundromat where she worked. In the course of their conversation, she said, he offered to put her up in an apartment and take care of her financially if she would be his mistress. He also allegedly agreed to supply her with money and marijuana.

At the end of April 1985, Williams said, Robinson came to the Laundromat and handed her the keys to the Troost Avenue apartment, which by this time had been vacated by the two black women, and instructed her to leave work and never go back. "He told me our relationship must be kept quiet and wanted to always be sure that we were not seen together in public," she said.

There was at least one reason for Robinson's secrecy. After a long investigation, Johnson County had charged him in late March with felony theft by deception in the Back Care Systems case. After posting a $10,000 bond, he had been released on his own recognizance. Upon learning this, Haymes had written a second violation report, again recommending that Robinson's Missouri probation be revoked. Haymes, who kept hearing from Gaddis and other social workers about Robinson's continued attempts to find women with babies, had also asked Robinson on several occasions if he had gotten rid of the Troost Avenue apartment. He lied and said that he had.

Meanwhile, Robinson dropped by the apartment and asked Williams for a favor. Bringing out S&M equipment, he put roach clips on her nipples and asked if they hurt. He then told her that one of his customers in the escort business was into S&M and needed a girl for about a week. He brought out a whip made of cat-o'-nine tails and hit her with it on the leg so she could see how it felt. He also had some ropes and handcuffs that he demonstrated, saying his client might want to use them on her.

Robinson instructed Williams to dress entirely in black: nylons, skirt and blouse. He would have someone pick her up at the corner of the park near her apartment, about 7:00 P.M. that evening, and she should do whatever she was told. Sure enough, a stocky man with jet-black hair and a dark tan showed up in a dark four-door car at the appointed time and asked if she was Theresa. She said yes and he opened the door to the backseat; once inside, he put a cloth blindfold over her eyes and some money in her purse. He drove for about ten minutes, stopped and got out of the car. Someone—probably the same man, she thought—got back in the car and drove for another twenty minutes. Pulling into a paved driveway, he led her up to a house. He knocked and someone opened the door and let them in.

The driver brought Williams a glass of what he told her was orange juice. She drank from the glass, sat down on a couch and started to feel dizzy and very relaxed. He had obviously slipped something into her drink. Still blindfolded, she was led down a flight of stairs and put on a table, her hands tied above her head. A second man, with a deep voice, who sounded as though he were in his fifties, pulled her skirt up and her nylons down. "He put roach clips on my breasts and started to kiss me all over my body and talk dirty to me," she stated. "He then started to stretch me and I began to hurt pretty badly, especially under the arms. I started to yell and scream that the deal was off and to let me go. He slapped me on the ass and told me to shut up. By this time, I was crying and screaming."

The older man left and the driver came to release her from the handcuffs. She lay there awhile, then sat up and pulled down her blindfold. What she saw was a dungeon, with manacles for hands and feet attached to the walls and three red straight-back chairs. When she heard the driver coming, she put the blindfold back over her eyes. He helped her get dressed and they left the house. "When we were outside, I again pulled down the blindfold," she said. "I did not see streetlights and the house we had just left was off by itself; it was all dark around the area."

Back in her apartment, she counted the money the driver had put in her purse; there was $1,200. She went out to buy some booze and subsequently passed out. Meeting with Robinson the next day, she told him what happened and that she had spent some of the money. He let her keep another $50, she said, and told her not to worry about the incident. "He then consoled me for a while and left," she stated. "Before leaving, he said he would be out of town for a while."

Toward the end of May 1985, Robinson returned to the apartment and told Theresa he wanted to play a joke on his friend Irv Blattner. He told her to buy a diary and he would tell her what to write. "He gave me a manuscript that he had written with dates and entries for me to write in my own handwriting," said Williams, who started to work on her assignment.

When Robinson didn't return for ten days, though, Williams called an old boyfriend to bring her some food. While he was there, she said, Robinson appeared. The boyfriend hid in the second bedroom, but Robinson somehow figured out he was there and angrily told her he didn't want her seeing him until after 4:00 P.M. on weekdays.

Robinson let himself into Williams's apartment early the next morning, a Saturday, while she was sleeping. Entering her room, he grabbed her and put her over his knee to spank her, she said. "He said I had been a real bad girl and needed to learn a lesson." Apparently, he was still angry about her boyfriend's visit. While she yelled and screamed, he pulled her hair and threw her down on the floor. He took his gun, which Williams had seen him carry in a shoulder holster, and held it to her head. "I'll blow your brains out if you don't stop screaming," he threatened, then shoved the barrel of the gun in her vagina: "I'll bet you have never had a blowout before."

Telling her it was imperative that no one knew he was coming by the apartment, Robinson hit her in her face with his fist, she said. When she started to cry, he told her it was for her own good.

Despite the assault, however, they made up a few days later and Robinson promised he would take her on a Caribbean cruise on June 14. He also told her to get busy writing the diary. She worked late into the night making the entries, though for some reason she decided to deviate somewhat from Robinson's script. When he came by the next day and read the diary, he noticed the changes and grew very angry, hitting her and knocking her to the floor, she said. "He finally stopped hitting me and said he was sorry," Williams explained; she then went on to elaborate. Handcuffing her, she said, he stuck ice and a cucumber in her vagina before assaulting her with a ketchup bottle. He then tried to handcuff her feet, but the shackles were too small. "He said he wanted to hang me upside down," she stated.

Robinson returned with a new manuscript the next day, handed her a red spiral notebook and told her to start writing. He also had her sign three typewritten pages that had been notarized. "Robinson told me that Sandy [Boothroyd's wife] had typed them and I should not read them but just sign on the line above my typewritten name," she stated. He made her strip to the waist, photographing her as she held a sign in front of her that read, "I love you, Irv."

Finally he told her he had sold her car and needed her to sign over the title and that he planned to put her personal belongings in storage before they left for the Bahamas.

On June 6, Robinson came over and wanted to know if the diary was finished. In one of the smartest moves of her young life, Williams told him she needed more time.

The very next day, Lavin and Dancer, who had been

watching the apartment, paid a fortuitous visit. At first she lied and told them she worked for Robinson at Equi-II. However, after the FBI agents told her they believed her "boss" was involved in the disappearance of two women, she broke into tears and admitted everything. She told them about their upcoming trip to the Bahamas and how she was at that very moment fabricating a diary that accused Blattner of committing various crimes and threatening her life. The last entry in the diary was June 15.

The agents quickly suspected that Robinson somehow knew his partner (who would die of cancer in 1991) was about to testify against him and planned to use the fake diary to try and discredit him. Williams's life was most certainly in danger. To everyone's surprise, Robinson at that very moment unlocked the front door and entered the apartment. Holding up his draft of the diary, Lavin and Dancer identified themselves and asked Robinson if it was his handwriting. He admitted that it was, then beat a hasty retreat. The agents didn't attempt to stop him but insisted on moving Williams to a secret location. "I get a call from Lavin and Dancer, saying 'Get down here now,' " Haymes recalled. "They were at that moment realizing she was possibly within days of something happening to her."

By that point, Haymes just wanted to get Robinson off the streets to keep him from harming more women. Hearing Williams's story, too, helped him to clarify what had probably happened to Lisa and Tiffany. "There was no doubt in my mind that Lisa was dead," Haymes said. "My belief was that he had sold the baby to someone looking to adopt and had sold her into some sort of white slavery or S&M situation that already had or soon would result in her death. At the time, though, I still didn't believe—and I don't think anyone else did, either—that he would kill with his own hands. We believed he would have someone else do his dirty work."

Haymes drafted a third violation report against Robinson, asking the court to put him in jail for carrying a handgun, supplying drugs to Williams and lying to his probation officer. As soon as he made bail, however, Haymes said Robinson was on a desperate quest to find Williams, even going so far as to hire a private investigator to track her down. With some difficulty, the FBI kept her hidden, moving her from one motel to another until a July 1985 hearing that lasted two days. After she testified, the agents bought her a one-way ticket and shipped her out of town, never to return. Within weeks, the district judge ruled that he was revoking Robinson's probation, but he agreed to release him on bail pending appeal.

To the investigators' consternation, however, the Missouri Court of Appeals overturned the lower court ruling in the summer of 1986. Noting in his opinion for the court that hospital social workers had reported a mother and baby in Robinson's program missing, Judge David J. Dixon wrote, unbelievably: "There is not an iota of evidence in this record that [Robinson] had anything to do with the circumstance of the 'missing persons.'" Furthermore, he concluded that Robinson had not been allowed to depose his accuser, Theresa Williams, and hence his constitutional rights had been violated. "There cannot be the least doubt that the actions of the probation officer and the FBI agents denied [Robinson] due process of law," he said in conclusion, ordering a new probation hearing.

For the moment, Robinson had escaped justice in Missouri. He hadn't been so lucky in Kansas, however. In January 1986, he was convicted of felony theft in the Back Care Systems case. He was subsequently convicted of defrauding an Overland Park businessman in connection with a real-estate deal in Arizona. For those crimes, a Johnson County judge sentenced him to between six and nineteen years under the Habitual Criminal Act. After appeals had been exhausted, he began serving a four-year sentence in May 1987 in Kansas's Hutchinson Correctional Facility.

* * *

Shortly before Robinson went off to prison, however, a third young woman disappeared after telling her family she had found work with Equi-II. According to police records, Robert Bales had picked up his twenty-six-year-old stepsister, Catherine Clampitt, at the Kansas City bus station on a January night in 1987. She reportedly needed a fresh start after a life of drugs and drinking in Wichita Falls, Texas, and Bales and his wife had agreed to put her up in their Overland Park home.

Bales described his stepsister as a petite, intelligent woman with a wild streak. Born in Korea, she had grown up in Texas after being adopted by his mother, Jackie Clampitt. When she moved to Kansas, she left behind a son, Ryan, then three years old, in her parents' custody. Clampitt wasn't in town more than a month when she spotted an ad in *The Kansas City Star* for an executive secretary.

"Extremely busy CEO needs executive secretary /assistant," it read. "International travel required, long hours. Must be attractive, personable and able to devote complete energies to this position." Applicants were instructed to send their resumes to the Overland Park address of Robinson's Equi-II.

Upon landing the job, Clampitt told her stepbrother that her employer was "John Dawson." Once she started working, Bales said, she often traveled and would sometimes stay at local hotels between trips for several nights at a time. She was last at Bales's home between March 16 and April 2, when she left to stay at the Olathe Holiday Inn. She spoke to her stepbrother on April 4 and told him she was at the hotel to do research and would soon be meeting Dawson. They were supposed to drive a van to Chicago, where they would meet another secretary, and fly from there to New York.

Bales later said the job did seem a little far-fetched to him and his wife, but his stepsister was twenty-six and old enough to make her own decisions. "She's a grown lady; you don't lock her in a room and say you can't come out," he reportedly said.

When he hadn't heard from her for a month, Bales started looking through Clampitt's belongings and quickly grew alarmed. He found a receipt for a room at the Regency Park hotel. John Robinson and a company called Equi-II which had moved from Metcalf Avenue to College Boulevard in Overland Park, had paid for the room. Bales also found the advertisement in *The Kansas City Star* and a bizarre letter titled "Confidential," addressed from "Sandy" to "Cathy."

In the letter, "Sandy" informed "Cathy" she was writing to fill her in on "some of the neat things about your new position." As John's executive secretary for the past three years, she said she knew Cathy was in for "fun, work and great sex." She provided Cathy with a list of John's "dos and don'ts so you can have a leg up on things." She went on to describe how John loved blow jobs, back rubs, vibrators, bondage and taking photos and video. Regarding blow jobs, she said, "Swallow his cum, he gets really upset when someone spits it out." She also warned her not to "bug him about dumb stuff like money etc., he will take care of you really good, I should know."

Bales called Equi-II, and upon learning that there was no employee named John Dawson, he asked for Robinson. He told police that Robinson at first acted as though he didn't know Catherine but then said he didn't know where she was. Bales waited two more weeks before calling Robinson again. After leaving a message, his call was returned by a "Don Davis," who said that his secretary had seen Catherine two days earlier and she was fine. Davis also said that his secretary had just started maternity leave that day and could not be contacted for quite some time.

Two days later, Catherine's mother, Jackie Clampitt, received a letter from her daughter. By this point, though, Robinson no longer had his office on College Boulevard. Bales had called the building's leasing agent only to learn that Robinson was in trouble with the law—over the Back Care Systems fraud—and he should contact the DA's office. When he did, he was sent to the Overland Park Police Department to file a missing persons report. The police looked into the matter but ultimately couldn't find enough evidence to connect Robinson to Clampitt's disappearance. Bales became consumed with finding her on his own. After eight months, though, he, too, gave up. All the trails were dead ends.

Robinson made a good impression on prison officials during his four-year stay at the Hutchinson Correctional Facility in Kansas. The physical plant supervisor, J.E. Jestes, was reportedly very happy with Robinson's reorganization of the computer maintenance office and the new software program he developed, which Jestes estimated would save Kansas thousands of dollars each year. "Mr. Robinson performed his tasks well, accepted responsibility without question, and is an asset to this office," he wrote in a January 1989 report. "Because of his efforts, even when he leaves, this office should function well."

Inmate #45690 also left a relatively favorable impression with the supervising psychiatrist Dr. George Penn, who headed a team that clinically evaluated the 45-year-old Robinson while he was in Hutchinson. "Mr. Robinson has apparently used his time quite well and been a service to the state in the two years and four months that he has been incarcerated," Dr. Penn wrote. "Mr. Robinson has a very supportive family and says that he has supportive friends. He indicates that at such time as he is eligible for parole, he has been asked to teach X-ray nuclear medicine and medical laboratory procedures at K.U. Medical Center. He says he has been in contact with Dr. Walker and Dr. Peugh at the K.U. Medical Center." Dr. Penn, however, wisely qualified his comments: "This is not verified by this examiner."

Dr. Penn also stated that the inmate had told him about

his relationship with his wife, describing her as a loyal and loving person who had supported him through the whole ordeal of going to prison and who had been cooperative and eager to assist with the present evaluation. "The relationship, according to the inmate, is one in which he attempts to dominate the situation but, when his wife does not agree with his approach, she will not go along with it," he wrote. "This is not meant to cause arguments among them, because she does not make a big deal out of doing it her way."

Robinson's health had worsened while in prison and he had suffered three strokes, Dr. Penn noted. The residuals of the first stroke were hearing loss, low vision and weakening of the left side of his body. The second stroke left him aphasic and weak on his right side. "After three months, his speech improved, but he was left with a noticeable limp in the right leg," he wrote. "He now walks with the aid of the cane." The third stroke was less severe than the other two. "He has been examined by doctors outside of the prison facility and their most recommended preventative measure, according to the inmate, is to walk three miles a day. This is something he has not been able to do while being in prison."

When it came to Robinson's mental status, Dr. Penn and his team found him to be "alert and oriented . . . an articulate and bright man . . . a superior individual." They said they didn't find anything to suggest the presence of any major thought disorder or major affective disorder or that he was suicidal. "Mr. Robinson has been a man who has regrettably been involved in self-defeating, self-sabotaging behavior for a number of years," Dr. Penn and his team said. "He has a tendency to be grandiose and to be unconcerned with the feelings and needs of others, having deliberately exploited and stolen from them on a number of occasions." Robinson acknowledged to the psychiatrists that he was a confidence man and had continued with this behavior because he'd gotten off lightly each time. "He has no explanation for his repeated illegal behaviors except to say that he made many poor judgments and at one time was interested in making a lot of money and didn't really care how he went about doing it."

Based on their findings from the available data, Dr. Penn said that it was the opinion of the clinical team that Robinson had "shown some concrete signs of rehabilitation" and that it was "unlikely that further incarceration will be of any benefit to Mr. Robinson or society." However, Dr. Penn recommended that the inmate be restrained from entering into any future business arrangements. While Robinson didn't want to continue the illegal behavior that had been part of his life for such a long time, Dr. Penn said there was no guarantee he wouldn't were he given the opportunity. "He could once again begin by shading the truth and then moving into outright lies and be caught once again in a self-sabotaging, self-defeating situation," he said. "He is a man who is extremely convincing and those working with him need to be very careful less they be seduced by him, wittingly or otherwise."

In 1991, Kansas followed the recommendation of Dr. Penn's team and paroled Robinson, who was turned over to Missouri authorities to determine if he should be freed or face more prison time for violating his Guy's Foods fraud probation a decade earlier. Robinson, of course, claimed that his health had become so frail during his stay at Hutchinson that he should be released to go home to his family. His wife was now managing and living in a mobile home park called Southfork in Belton, Missouri, a south Kansas City suburb. Following her husband's incarceration, she had been forced to move out of her upscale country home in Stanley, Kansas, and single-handedly shoulder the responsibility of supporting herself and her family.

One of Missouri's physicians, Dr. Fred King, agreed with Robinson, saying that the inmate was "an extremely high risk medical patient." While Robinson was receiving his medications and had access to medical care, he noted that "the prognosis for this patient is extremely guarded. Due to the serious nature of his vascular disease, it is highly likely that he will suffer another stroke in the future. . . . It is my professional opinion that this inmate should be released without delay."

By now, Haymes was the lone voice speaking in opposition. "I believe him to be a con-man out of control," he wrote in a March 1991 interoffice memorandum to a colleague at the Moberly Correctional Center, which was responsible for evaluating Robinson in Missouri. "He leaves in his wake many unanswered questions and missing persons. I have observed from Robinson sociopathic tendencies, habitual criminal behavior, inability to tell the truth and scheming to cover his own actions at the expense of others."

Thanks, however, in large measure to the persistence of Haymes, who always believed that Robinson's medical problems were wildly exaggerated, the inmate lost his quest for freedom and was sentenced to spend the next three years in the Western Missouri Correctional Center in Cameron. In response, Robinson penned a long letter to the Clay County Circuit Court judge, blaming Haymes for his present situation and pleading for mercy. "This man has done everything within his power to keep me in prison and to assure that the hand fell heavy on me and my family," he wrote. "He has testified to falsehoods under oath, filed false affidavits with the Missouri Court of Appeals, provided false and misleading information to the Kansas Department of Probation and Parole and now, once again has repeated his actions with the Missouri Parole Board where he has power because of his position."

Robinson said he was not asking for the judge to release him but simply to order the Missouri Department of Corrections and the Missouri Parole Board remove all the "false and misleading information from my file, consider the information available from the Kansas Department of Corrections and all medical recommendations." Without such an order, he concluded, "I will remain in prison. If lucky, I will live long enough to get out but there will be little left. My illnesses are degenerative and, without proper rehabilitation, testing and long term treatment, will continue to get worse. Bruce [Houdek, Robinson's attorney], my family and I all realize that the decision made by the Clay County Court and the Missouri Parole Board amount to a sentence of death. Our only question: it [*sic*] this what is considered proportionate punishment for my crime in Missouri?"

Because of his alleged health problems, Robinson was finally released on house arrest in October 1992 and formally paroled in March 1993. By this point, Haymes was not as concerned about him as he had been back in 1986 and 1987. "No direct threat was ever made," said the probation supervisor, who had exercised caution after the defendant was convicted in Kansas. "But the probation officer that did the pre-sentence [report] in that case called me and said John blamed me for everything and he thought he might attempt to hurt me. So I got cautious. I was aware of who was in the car behind me. I had shown my wife photographs of him and his dark blue Dodge Diplomat. I had two young kids and I made sure they played in the back yard."

By the time he was released from Missouri, however, Robinson appeared to be lying low, supposedly disabled with multiple medical problems. "After he got out, he was supervised by our office in Belton where he lived," Haymes said. "I would check on him periodically but stayed out of it as I did not want to appear to have a personal agenda." After more than two decades of constant run-ins, Robinson would not get into any more trouble with the law until Suzette Trouten went missing seven years later.

When Overland Park detectives Greg Wilson and Scott Weiler began digging into Robinson's history in the spring

of 2000, they came across several references to Haymes in
the old court records. They decided to pay a visit to the probation supervisor to see if he could shed more light on their
suspect. Introducing themselves on April 13, 2000, the detectives explained why they had come. "You know, I have
had a lot of people come and go over the years," Haymes
replied. "Some people stick out in your mind and others
you quickly forget about. Usually we get rid of files after
a certain point. But I knew that eventually somebody would
come looking for this."

Their jaws dropped as Haymes reached into the bottom
drawer of his desk and retrieved a foot-thick file. It was
Robinson's.

Chapter 11

By mid-April 2000, Lenexa detectives had been working six and seven days a week trying to keep track of Robinson. Even with Wilson and Weiler on loan from Overland Park, the suburban police department was stretched to the limit and in dire need of additional forces and equipment. Sergeant John Browning's Directed Patrol Unit came up with the idea of renting dilapidated cars in order to blend better into the scenery during trailer park surveillance. Captain Keith O'Neal's Overland Park Special Investigations Section answered the call for help with surveillance. Beginning on April 17, they would take over most of the evening shifts.

The first night on the job, O'Neal's team followed Robinson and his wife to Toys "R" Us, JCPenney and back home. Given the experience of Lenexa's Directed Patrol Unit, they expected to watch them go to bed and call it a night themselves. But at 10:04 P.M., the white Dodge Ram peeled out of Santa Barbara Estates. "He was just flying down Highway 169," says O'Neal, who estimated his speed between 85 and 90 mph. "We could tell somebody else was in the vehicle with him, but we didn't know who it was. I was thinking, 'Oh my God, what is going on?'"

Waking Roth from a sound sleep, they decided that O'Neal and his team—including Detectives Mike Jacobson, Bill Batt, Jose Carrillo and John Clarke—would follow the Dodge Ram until they could figure out who was with him. Jacobson kept calling the Overland Park dispatch center in an attempt to get a phone number for the sheriff of the particular county they were speeding through. "By the time he could explain who we were and what we needed, [Robinson] would be in the next jurisdiction," O'Neal said. Finally, at 11:26 P.M., they reached an Allen County deputy in southern Kansas who managed to pull Robinson's Dodge Ram over in a construction zone. They were relieved to find Nancy in the passenger seat. The couple was on their way to Jenks, Oklahoma, to visit their son John junior, now married to wife Lisa, who had just gone into labor with their sixth grandchild.

Through trashings and plain old-fashioned police work, detectives by this point were dropping new subpoena requests on Morrison's desk nearly every day. Soon Robinson's financial records from banks, phone and credit card companies and service stations were pouring in. Among the most important for the investigation was Robinson's cell phone account with Sprint. Surveillance officers, who had noticed he was constantly talking on his mobile as he drove around the city, were amazed he never got into an accident. But they were absolutely flabbergasted when Detective Mike Lowther analyzed Robinson's records and found he had used his cell nearly twenty-five hundred times between August 17, 1999, and April 1, 2000, to call ten different women—including Suzette Trouten, Jeanna Milliron, Barbara Sandre, Lore Remington and Tami Taylor. He had called another woman, Katherine M. from Georgia, more than anyone else: 341 times.

It was immediately obvious to Lowther that Robinson used his cell phone much more frequently than the Monterey landline he shared with his wife. "You're talking about one or two pages of long-distance calls on his home phone versus stacks of pages for his cell phone that grew by inches," Lowther said. "You could see where he hit on a particular woman. Sometimes he would call that number literally dozens upon dozens of times. Other times he would call just once or the calls would end as quickly as they started."

One thing was certain: his calls always stopped by about

5:00 P.M. "The man was done for the day," Lowther says. "He was home with Nancy."

By Friday, April 21, 2000, Roth was frustrated. His team had made so many important discoveries in the first few weeks, but now he felt as though the investigation was losing momentum. Things weren't going well on the home front, either—it probably didn't help that he was always working—and he was about to leave town to attend a four-day training session with the Kansas Narcotics Officers Association. After joining the other detectives for "Fat Friday," a weekly tradition of doughnuts, reading newspapers and shooting the breeze, Roth took a very long drive. "The case was going very, very slow," he remembered. "Things at home were about as bad as they could get, and I was going to be away the following week. Could it get any worse?"

Back at the station, Dave Brown was waiting for Roth with a new development from Michigan. The detective had recently returned from his trip, where he had met with Suzette's mother, sisters and grandmother and broken the news about the dogs, which had been very difficult for the family. While he shared with the Troutens that Robinson had been convicted of a number of financial crimes, Brown withheld the fact that he had also been linked to three missing women and a baby. Amidst tears, the family reiterated their belief that Suzette was dead or being held somewhere against her will. Before he left, Brown had shown Carolyn Trouten how to record a phone call. They tried, without success, to reach Robinson.

After Brown's return to Kansas, however, Carolyn paged Robinson again and got lucky. When he phoned back a short while later, it was clear he didn't realize to whom he was speaking. She had caught him completely off guard. Knowing Robinson was aware of Suzette's promise to send her a doll from each exotic spot they visited, Carolyn told him a lie and said she had received one, when in fact she hadn't. She wanted to see how he would react. Roth was furious when he heard about the call, fearful that she had aroused

Robinson's suspicions. "I was about to blow a gasket," Roth recalled. But he changed his mind when Brown played him the tape, which would later be heard in court. "Carolyn did a great job. Robinson was so flustered."

After Robinson hung up with Carolyn, detectives picked up a flurry of cell phone activity on the PEN register as their suspect placed calls to several women scattered across the country. Later that afternoon, he dialed a number in Galveston, Texas, that the detectives had never seen before. Then he wired $100 to a Western Union in the same location. It looked like "Galveston"—whoever she was—was about to come to Kansas City.

Chapter 12

Vickie Neufeld was feeling lonely and down on her luck in the spring of 2000. The last five years had taken their toll on the blond Tennessee therapist, starting in 1995 when her husband of nineteen years asked her to move out. Busy raising two children and working towards her doctorate in clinical psychology, Vickie had ignored rumors that he was seeing another woman.

She moved by herself into a nearby apartment, saddened at having to leave behind her teenage son and daughter. She knew there was a good chance she would soon have to move out of town to find work, however, and she didn't want to up-root them. As Vickie struggled with her dissertation, her ex-husband remarried the other woman. "The grief was unbearable at times," she said.

Her $30,000 divorce settlement was almost gone by the time Vickie earned her doctorate in August 1998, yet she still needed to complete a one-year residency in order to become licensed. Vickie knew she couldn't afford to be choosy. That meant moving in late 1999 to Galveston, Texas, where she had been offered work counseling the elderly in nearby Houston. Vickie didn't care much for Texas and disliked the residency even more; the feeling apparently was mutual. She wasn't kept on at the end of a ninety-day probationary period.

Vickie filed for unemployment benefits, sent out dozens of resumes and even went on a handful of promising interviews. Nothing panned out. Then, in late March 2000, she was denied unemployment, which she had been counting on while she looked for a decent job. Crushed, she called her parents in rural Virginia and asked to go home for a while. But they thought her employment possibilities would be better in Texas, which only made her feel more abandoned and afraid. "I did not even have money for groceries," she said.

It was at that precise moment—when Vickie was feeling her most vulnerable—that Robinson waltzed into her life.

In Tennessee, the therapist had occasionally counseled couples who were having problems because one spouse was into alternative-lifestyle fantasies while the other was not. In order to provide them with intelligent feedback, Vickie said she began to research BDSM and soon realized that she had always enjoyed a spanking fetish, though her ex-husband had not been interested. She also found that she wasn't crazy or alone. There were others—hundreds of thousands, in fact—who shared her fantasies.

About a year before she moved to Galveston, Vickie began to place personal ads on Web sites in hopes of meeting Mr. Right. Some of the sites were BDSM oriented. Others were "vanilla," meaning they had nothing to do with BDSM or alternative interests. She corresponded with a number of men but met only a few. Most of the time they went to dinner and just talked.

Shortly after losing her Texas job, Vickie came across a new Web site called BDSMcontacts.com. She liked that it allowed her to create a profile of herself, indicating her likes and dislikes. In her ad, she said she was looking for a long-term, monogamous relationship with a man who liked to take control. "I was only interested in someone who enjoyed giving spankings for the intensity and erotic aspects of it," she said. "Outside of that fetish, I just wanted a normal, loving relationship. I was not into pain. I was not into going to swingers clubs. I was not into master-slave contracts. I was not promiscuous."

The Web site also asked her to list her employment and education. "I thought nothing about it when I checked 'unemployed' because I felt like that situation would be temporary," she said. But when no job materialized, she started to tell those who responded that she was out of work and might have to move in the next few months. "It's not a good time to get involved in a relationship with anyone right now," she wrote back.

Most of them replied: "I understand. Good luck."

But one man was different. Introducing himself as John Edwin Robinson (though his real middle name was Edward) and describing himself as a divorced Kansas City businessman, he seemed to take a keen interest in the fact that she was unemployed. "Tell me a little bit more," he wrote, signing his notes JR. "How long have you been looking for work?'"

An e-mail or two later and JR was suggesting that Vickie send him her resume and come to Kansas. He said he had a lot of contacts with psychologists and psychiatrists and could help obtain her license and find work. If there was sexual chemistry, he added, he would arrange for her to move with him into his five-bedroom house and be his full-time slave. He also gave her the e-mail addresses of two references: slavedancer@hotmail.com and KCSlave@email.com.

Vickie e-mailed the references and immediately got a response from a woman named "Izzy" at the address, slavedancer@hotmail.com. "She said she was a nurse, that her husband was a doctor and that [Robinson] had helped her a lot . . . and trained her husband to be a Master," Vickie later told detectives. "She was also very quick to say that . . . he was very wealthy and did not have to work if he didn't want to and that one of the things that he had done was to help professional women get started in the area."

Izzy also mentioned that JR liked to photograph his slaves but reassured Vickie that it was only for his personal use. She went on to describe him in glowing terms. "Fifty slaves," she gushed to Vickie, "would love to be in your shoes."

That JR never provided Vickie with phone numbers so she could call his references seemed strange. But in her eagerness to find work, Vickie didn't give it much thought. Not at the time, anyway. He certainly seemed convincing in other ways. He told her he'd given her resume to four psychologists and a physician. He also said his "secretary," whose name was "Sharon," was working on getting the necessary materials for her license.

They agreed to meet in Kansas City at 1:00 P.M. on Monday, April 24. In the meantime, he would send a slave contract for her to review, wire her money for the trip and arrange for her to stay in an Overland Park hotel. When she arrived, if all went well, she would sign the contract and he would pay her outstanding bills and the costs of her move to Kansas City.

JR called several times a day as the trip drew near and Vickie felt herself drawn to him. "Hello, beautiful," he'd say when she picked up the phone. He was charismatic and soft-spoken, but not wimpy, and his tone subliminally reduced the panic she was feeling about being unemployed. "I felt isolated and alone," she said. "I needed someone to offer me emotional warmth."

To be on the safe side, though, Vickie consulted Travis Wilson, a leader in the Houston BDSM community. He was instantly wary of JR's motives and told her to make sure she got his address and home telephone number before she left home. He also told her she should have a safe call—someone who would check in with her at agreed-upon intervals during her stay in Kansas City and make sure she was all right. Wilson agreed to be her safe call.

But JR told Vickie he was so prominent he didn't give his home phone number out to anybody. He also didn't want her safe call to be a man, so Vickie said she lied and told him it was a female friend. Only reluctantly did he agree to give her his cell phone number as well as the address and telephone number of his company, Specialty Publications, in Kansas City, Missouri.

Looking back, Vickie realized these weren't the only red flags.

For example, JR wired just $100 when he knew Vickie had
to drive seven hundred miles and planned to stop at a hotel.
She was grateful for any amount of money but perplexed that
he didn't wire at least enough to cover her gas and stay at a
decent motel. Since she thought it was to be primarily a professional encounter, she also wondered why he didn't offer to
fly her. The amount was so minimal for someone seemingly
so wealthy.

Then there was the issue of the slave contract, which JR e-
mailed the day before her departure. Though she'd heard of
them, she said this was the first time she'd ever read one and
much of the language really bothered her. "I pledge my master
my complete obedience and will never question his decisions
or commands," it began. "I hereby offer my master my entire
body to use as he wishes for his personal sexual pleasure. I beg
my master to use my breasts and nipples, asshole, pussy and
mouth to serve his needs. . . ."

The two-page contract included a list of twelve rules that
Vickie would be required to follow, concluding with: "I offer
this contract to my master of my own free will and beg my
master to accept me as his personal slut, whore and slave."
That last phrase was particularly loathsome to Vickie, who
did not want to be anyone's "personal slut, whore and slave."
She wondered if JR had any respect for her or was simply
planning to use her for sex but decided to wait until she arrived in Kansas City to take the matter up with him in person.

Following JR's instructions, Vickie packed her spiked heels
and a plaid bag full of her treasured sex toys, complete with
whips, paddles and riding crops. On Easter Sunday, she set
off in her Saturn with her Maltese, Mary Kate, arriving at
Overland Park's Extended Stay America that evening, a day
earlier than expected.

When the front-desk clerk found her reservation, JR hadn't
paid for the room as he'd promised. She tried to call him on
his cell phone. Reaching only his voice mail, she left a message for him that she'd arrived and needed to check in. After

an awkward moment, the clerk agreed to hold a personal check, with the understanding that Robinson would settle the account the next day. She booked Vickie into room 120.

As soon as Vickie left the motel lobby, the clerk paged Roth, who knew Robinson had recently used the motel for a liaison with Jeanna Milliron, also from Texas, and had asked the staff to notify him if anyone from Galveston checked in. When the clerk told Roth of Vickie's arrival, he immediately reserved two adjacent rooms for his detectives and made arrangements to install surveillance cameras in the hallway outside of her hotel room. Roth and the others working the case were all but certain Suzette was dead after a hotel encounter with Robinson. They wanted to make sure it didn't happen again.

Chapter 13

"So you arrived okay?"

JR sounded happy to hear Vickie's voice when he returned her call at eight o'clock the next morning, April 24. He told her he had been out of the country and had only returned late the night before. He assured her he would take care of the hotel bill and come to see her in an hour.

Wanting to make a good impression, she took her time getting ready, donning a loose-fitting burgundy dress that reached to her calves, taupe panty hose and black pumps. She also applied brown mascara, some soft brown eye shadow, face powder, powder blush and lipstick that matched her dress. She made a pot of coffee and waited.

At 9:30 A.M., Robinson stopped by the Extended Stay office and inquired how Vickie had paid. When he was told about the check, he asked for it back so he could pay for her entire stay through April 27. But the clerk told him that was impossible; Vickie's check had already been deposited. Upon hearing that, "Robinson became very angry," said Detective Perry Meyer, one of the detectives following him that day. "He threatened to place a stop payment."

A few minutes later, Robinson, carrying a black pilot's bag and a camera, knocked on Vickie's door. He was dressed casually, wearing blue jeans and a white dress shirt. She greeted him warmly and offered him some coffee. He said nothing about his problems with the front desk, she said, and they started off with small talk. "He was very well groomed in his own way," Vickie recalled. "He was very charismatic, and as

I look back, I think he was very intelligent. . . . He had a way of presentation that was convincing."

Detective Mike Lowther, standing out in the hotel hallway that April morning, thought Robinson seemed to dominate the conversation. He talked about his children, who were living with him while they built their own house, bragging that he could easily write a check to cover the cost but wanted to teach them about responsibility.

Robinson spoke in an instructional manner, Lowther thought, as a teacher might speak with a student. Robinson often referred to "the [BDSM] lifestyle," and told Vickie he was a member of a select group of masters that comprised doctors, lawyers, businessmen and truck drivers. He also said that admission to the group was closed and that one had to be recommended by a current member in order to gain membership.

Then Robinson started to talk about the darker aspects of "the lifestyle," including bad masters who abused their slaves, and slave auctions, in which slaves were sold, against their will, to other masters who might live in other parts of the country, or even overseas. Robinson told Vickie that his personal belief was that these aspects of the lifestyle were "a little extreme" and described himself as a caring and responsible master. He said he would treat Vickie with the same care and concern that she felt for her patients.

Vickie could be heard laughing at various times during Robinson's descriptions of the BDSM lifestyle, prompting him to ask her why she was doing so. Lowther heard her reply: "I love it. I just love it."

About this time, Lowther and Meyer also heard what sounded like a dog barking in room 120. "I thought he was trying to make her bark like a dog," Meyer said incredulously. It was only later that they found out that Vickie had actually brought her dog on the trip.

Vickie and JR began to discuss the slave contract. Vickie told him about her reservations with the wording and confessed that she wasn't ready to sign it. "Well, we can reword it if you want," said Robinson, insisting that "personal slut and whore" were affectionate, not demeaning, terms in the BDSM lexicon. They agreed upon some changes and she said she would have it ready for him later.

It was at this point that Robinson took off all his clothes and stretched himself out naked on the bed. "This is how we figure out if there's chemistry," he told her. "I want you to take your hands and rub me all over." He hugged her and told her he wanted oral sex. "I tried," she said. "He said I wasn't doing it right. That's when he pulled out a camera and he told me to look at him while I was trying to do that, and he started to take pictures."

While she had not given him permission, she didn't strongly object. "I protested, but not very much at that point," she later said. "I didn't want to do that right then because he told me that if I were going to be a good slave, that this was something that I was going to have to do and to do any less would be unsophisticated on my part."

Robinson moved from the bed to a rocking chair, pulling Vickie by the hair and forcing her to kneel before him. He continued to snap away, which she found offensive. Still gripping her hair, he grew physically excited, she said, as he thrust himself in Vickie's mouth and pulled her head back and forth until he ejaculated. Vickie gagged. "It was not enjoyable," she said. "He had wanted me to swallow it, and the taste was very, very sour, and I probably apologized for gagging."

"If I eat celery, it's going to change the taste," she said Robinson told her.

He gave Vickie about $50 for food and left the hotel about 3:00 P.M. He had handed Vickie his black pilot's bag containing sex toys, which she looked through later that day. Inside the bag were all kinds of floggers, chains, collars and leather restraints. "Even though I don't go to BDSM events very much, I had the opportunity to once go to a dungeon and I've probably seen everything that you can see," she later told detectives. "It was some of the most expensive, elaborate stuff I had ever seen in my life."

Vickie believed that sometime that day she checked in with Travis Wilson and told him she'd arrived safely and gave him her number at the hotel. She then proceeded to make a number of amendments to the slave contract, beginning with the following sentence: "As my master may change and/or add current or new rules as he desires, he will allow me to discuss with him any concerns about the potential changes and/or additions he intends to introduce."

She also spelled out her limitations: She would not tolerate knives, scat and water sports (feces and urination), blood, fire, suspension or foot worship. She allowed that "the gradual use of potential 'electrical' devices will be only used if tolerable to slave. . . . Lectures, humiliation . . . verbal attacks upon the integrity of the slave's personhood will not occur." Vickie also wrote that Robinson would "see her through a 2-month period" should he decide to terminate the contract at a time when she was unemployed. He would not impede her attempts to obtain permanent licensure as a clinical psychologist and "assistance will be provided to facilitate that goal." And lastly, she wanted him to promise never to hurt her beloved Maltese dog, Mary Kate.

Satisfied with her additions, she went to the hotel lobby and asked the front-desk clerk to make a copy. The clerk pretended the machine had run out of toner, crumpling up the first copy of the contract and throwing it in a nearby trash can. Then he acted as though he had replaced the cartridge and made a copy for Vickie. After she left, he retrieved the crumpled contract from the trash can and gave it to his manager, who turned it over to Meyer.

When JR returned the next morning, April 25, Vickie handed him the new contract, containing her signature and the date. He told her to put on her spiked heels and asked if she had seen any implements in his duffel bag that interested her. "You've got some really heavy-duty stuff here," she told him.

Robinson's response was to take off all his clothes again and sit in the rocker. Smiling, he told Vickie to do the same, but she didn't take him seriously. Then JR grew irritated and yanked off her shirt. Frightened by his aggression, Vickie took off her jeans and, following his instructions, got up on the bed on her knees.

Pulling one of the collars out of his bag, JR fastened it around Vickie's neck and tied her wrists behind her back. The collar and wrist restraints were connected by rope in such a way that Vickie would begin to choke if she moved her hands. "Owww, that's tight," she told JR. But he ignored her and kept on placing floggers and straps on the bed in front of her, as if he were about to start "playing" with her. Instead, he sat down in the rocker, with a wide grin on his face, and once again pulled out the camera. "Please stop," she pleaded as he snapped away. "I don't want you to do this." Laughing, he continued to ignore her; Vickie grew angry: "I'm going to go back to Galveston if you don't stop!"

It was JR's turn to get angry. Lowther, who had once again taken up his position in the hallway, heard him say, "I thought we got through the difficult part of this yesterday." Removing her collar, he told Vickie, "You're unsophisticated. If you were truly a slave, you would have no qualms about me taking pictures. If you want to go back: fine. If you don't, you have my number."

He put his clothes back on and packed up his toys.

Lowther, who suspected that Robinson was about to leave, started to walk back to room 122. Sure enough, he heard the door to Vickie's room suddenly open behind him. He did not run through his door and close it, fearing it would look suspicious. Instead, Lowther casually stood in the doorway while Robinson walked right by him, carrying the pilot's bag and looking down at the floor. He appeared upset.

Lowther returned to the hallway: there was no sound coming from room 120. Growing concerned for Vickie's welfare, he called her room.

"Is Tom there?" he asked when Vickie picked up the phone. Relieved to hear her voice, Lowther mumbled something about dialing the wrong number and hung up.

As Vickie sat in her room, she felt guilty remembering how she'd been warned of Robinson's penchant for photos and had just signed the contract giving him complete control. She wondered if she overreacted and weighed how badly she needed his help. "Am I gonna blow this?" she fretted, then called him to apologize. Once again, she got his voice mail and had to leave a message. "I'm sorry I freaked out," she told him.

He called back about an hour later. She remembered him telling her, "I want you to be my slave. But you will understand: I will take pictures."

He invited her to breakfast the next morning, April 26, but instead called about 10:00 A.M. and said he'd been delayed. He was having trouble with his company in Israel. He told her he'd be over that afternoon and gave her specific instructions: "I want my slave naked except for a housecoat."

She put on a fluffy robe and waited. When he arrived, she said, he was excited and his heart was beating fast. He wanted to have sex immediately—but because Vickie had her period it wasn't going to be intercourse. He laid her on the bed, arms behind her back, and removed her robe. "How does my slave want her sex?" he asked.

"I don't know," she replied, caught off guard by the question.

"My slave likes to have her face slapped, doesn't she?" he asked.

"Yes," she replied, closing her eyes as she anticipated the soft erotic slaps she had experienced with other men. Instead, Vickie was stunned by two of the hardest slaps she said she's ever received in her life. Her jaw tingled from the pain and she saw white. *This man is angry,* she thought to herself, petrified. *This man has rage.*

She quickly suggested oral sex in order to evade another blow. JR, who was aroused by the situation, had other ideas.

He put his penis between her breasts, squeezed them together and, thrusting back and forth, quickly ejaculated. Then he asked her to rub his semen all over her body.

"Taste it now," he commanded. "Can you tell that it's sweet? It's because of the celery."

Once again, JR put the restrictive collar and wrist restraints on her and took out some wooden paddles. He didn't seem to know how to use them, Vickie thought, hitting her five or six times before switching sides. An experienced master would have alternated blows, she said, beginning softly as a warm-up and waiting for his submissive to ask for more. With JR, there was no warm-up. Suddenly he hit her so hard she screamed out in pain.

Afterward, he left Vickie lying, still tied up and facedown on the bed. Any other "player" would have come over and taken off the restraints and comforted her. Instead, JR pulled out the camera and, looking through the viewfinder, commented: "Slave resting." Once again, he began to snap away.

Then, dressing quickly, he told her he had to fly to Israel that night. He wanted her to return to Galveston to pack and promised to send a North American Van Lines truck in two weeks to move her to Kansas City. He gave her $60 for the trip home and picked up her bag of sex toys. "You don't need these," he told her. "This is one way to get you back."

Vickie drove through the night and arrived home Thursday morning, April 27. That afternoon, she began a series of e-mails to JR that his defense attorneys would later play to their full advantage. She thanked him for inviting her to Kansas and said she was excited at the prospect of moving there permanently to be with him. She also apologized for her erratic behavior. "You saw me at my absolute worst," she wrote. "The stresses of the past year have been what those in our field call 'chronic.'"

Then, she said, there were the pictures. "While I'm not a prude, I'm not used to being naked in front of someone I've just met," she wrote. "Perhaps such encounters are a facet of the lifestyle—but I'm not used to it. I felt scared and (thankfully) I felt anger. I only regret that I reacted too strongly that way at a time that I know I would have otherwise enjoyed with you. . . . What happened on Tuesday, though, was not defiance. It was fear. It was just a 'bit much' a 'bit soon.' "

When she didn't hear back from JR that Thursday, Friday or Saturday, she e-mailed Robinson's friend Izzy for advice. Then she began to doubt he was in Israel and called to see if there were any connecting flights leaving Kansas City in the evening. She found none. She dialed Robinson's number at Specialty Publications and, to her horror, he answered.

Vickie hung up.

Feeling completely betrayed, she wrote Robinson the next day, April 30, and politely asked him to mail her sex toys, noting that some of them were gifts. It wasn't until Tuesday, May 2, that she finally heard back from him. When she did, he was very angry.

"I have just returned and I am one pissed MASTER," he wrote. "You called me when my phone was forwarded to another fucking country and then hung up? What was that all about?"

Robinson said he knew she was writing to others and trying to check up on him. "Yes, I got an email from Izzy's MASTER with a copy of your message," he explained. "He has punished her severely."

He added that he had also received her e-mail message, requesting that her sex toys be returned. If she wanted out, he said, that was fine but she shouldn't bother him again under any circumstances, adding that he would hold her signed slave contract, photos and resume just in case. "As far as your toys," he wrote in conclusion, "I will think about it and let you know!!!"

Vickie apologized and they continued to exchange e-mails over the next several days as she tried to salvage any hope of a job in Kansas. Softened by her promises of complete submission, he finally said the move was back on and he would call the next day to set the wheels in motion. After several more days of waiting, Vickie gave up. She couldn't put her life on hold any longer. She wanted to end the relationship once and for all.

On May 11, she sent him a very stern "buzz off" e-mail that had been crafted for her by an acquaintance in the BDSM community. She forcefully told him to keep away from her and that she did not want to hear from him or his "references" by e-mail, letter, telephone or in person. "I will not say or write this twice," she wrote. "KEEP AWAY FROM ME. If you do not abide by what I have asked, I will contact the police and report you for harassing me."

Her e-mail might have been the end of it all, had it not been for the fact that JR still had Vickie's sex toys. It continued to eat away at her that he hadn't returned them and she decided to write once more. "The toys I had were gifts and had sentimental value," she pleaded on May 22. "I want nothing from you—just to have my implements returned."

She unknowingly hit a nerve, for Robinson instantly shot back: "If you continue to harass me, I will go to the authorities. I will have my attorney handle any further contact by forwarding a copy of your [slave] contract to the state licensing board. Do not contact me again, ever!"

Completely rattled by this point, Vickie wasn't about to respond. Instead, she took a different course of action—one with ramifications she never could have imagined.

Chapter 14

Rick Roth had been out of town at a drug-training seminar during Vickie's visit to Kansas City. He returned on April 27 for what he thought would be an important meeting with FBI agents and the U.S. attorney to discuss a wiretap on Robinson's computer. Since state law concerning computers was vague at best, detectives were hoping the federal authorities might be able to help. But when Roth got back to the station, he discovered that the U.S. Attorney wasn't coming. Morrison didn't think they had enough evidence yet to support a wiretap. He wanted to go slow and keep building the case.

The sergeant struggled to contain his disappointment as he met with FBI agents John Brunell and Dirk Tarpley, who had been recruited to help the investigation with out-of-town leads. The two men mentioned they were headed to national headquarters in Quantico, Virginia, and wanted to bring copies of the reports on Robinson to their Behavioral Science Unit. *Why not,* Roth thought. *It couldn't hurt.*

Frustration with the investigation continued to mount. On May 2, the surveillance team followed Robinson to several locations and then to see Barbara Sandre. But instead of pulling into the driveway as he normally did, Robinson drove up and down the street for a full twenty-eight minutes. Officers felt he had been checking the area very carefully and were once again worried they'd been compromised. This time it was Roth's captain, John Meier, who decided to temporarily pull the plug on surveillance.

The detectives and the district attorneys held another disappointing meeting about wiretaps later that same day. ADA John Cowles, who was now helping Morrison and Welch with some aspects of the case, said they still weren't there yet. Then an argument ensued over whether to confront Robinson. Should they use the "dumb detective" method or hit him hard with everything they had? "Everyone was starting to show the stress," Roth said. "People were going back through the casebooks trying to see if something was missed. It had reached a point where people were looking for anything to jump-start the investigation."

On May 4, they got a small but important break when Meyer, filling in for Owsley, went through the trash and found a bill for Peoples Telecommunications, Inc., out of La Cygne, Kansas. They had no idea until that moment that he had a phone on his farm. Even more exciting was the fact that the bill showed someone placing a call to the front office of Santa Barbara Estates at 11:43 A.M. on March 1. "To us, this fit right in with the timetable we had created for that fateful day," Roth said. "It also gave us more indication that Suzette had been taken to the farm. Was the phone call to Nancy to say he'd be late for lunch?"

The following week, on May 9, as detectives began running down numbers that Robinson had called on his cell phone, they came across a man named Arthur Buschmann. It didn't take them long to figure out that the two probably met in the early 1990s when both were incarcerated at Western Missouri Correctional Center in Cameron, Missouri. Robinson had called Buschmann on numerous occasions over the years—including the periods when Izabela and Suzette went missing. Over the course of the next several days, detectives did a lot of digging into Buschmann's background, learning that he was a career crook with many convictions for forgery, burglary, drug dealing and fraud. For fear of jeopardizing the investigation, however, they held off contacting him. Interviews would have to wait.

Meanwhile, Owsley discovered two old typewritten notes in the trash that starkly illustrated how Robinson's infidelities had been playing at home. Known as the "wipe your dick" letter by detectives, Nancy's November 1999 note would later be read in court with devastating results. In it, she stated that she was aware of his affairs and the fact that he was receiving phone messages from women calling him "master." She referenced several of them, including Barbara, Isabel, or "byza." "This seems like an old song that I just play over and over," she wrote. "Why is it you just can't control yourself? . . . You know you can only push a person so far . . . or rub their face in shit so many times."

Nancy also accused her husband of being a pathological liar and of having an unhealthy obsession with what she called his "games."

"You look me in the eye and lie about every thing even things that are not important," she wrote. "You haven't gotten very far with job hunt, but working would interfere with your games. You want me to work so you can do whatever you want during the day. . . . I hate it when you talk to me like I'm stupid. I do appreciate the fact that before you have sex with me after being with someone else you do wipe your dick off, all though it is a turn off."

Robinson drafted a letter of his own a few weeks later, protesting that she was wrongly accusing him of stealing. "All of a sudden, out of the blue, you become angry," he wrote on November 23, 1999. "I will say this one last time. I took nothing from your purse, was not near your purse and the fact that at the drop of a hat you begin accusing me bothers me a great deal." Robinson, who helped his wife by performing odd jobs around the trailer park, breezily concluded that he was off to the store to purchase a thermostat for the maintenance office and metal to make feet for benches. He said he told maintenance man Carlos Ibarra that it was too wet and cold to work outside.

In the same trashing, Owsley found Robinson's Sprint bill. Two very important phone calls stood out: Monday, March 27, 2000, at 1:48 P.M. to San Jose, California, and a second call placed the next day to the same number. Was it just a co-incidence that he made the calls at the same time the cards and letters had been postmarked to the Troutens? Detectives didn't think so.

Robinson's subpoenaed American Express records sent Detectives Beyer and Dougan over to the Guesthouse Suites on May 15, 2000, to check out an old transaction for $331.52. Tim Herrman, the assistant manager, checked Robinson's name in the computer and could find no record of the charge. However, that changed when he plugged in his American Express number. The room registration card indicated that a woman named Alesia Cox had checked into room 223 on April 30, 1999, and stayed a week. The card, however, did not provide any personal information for Cox. Was she alive? They'd have to wait for the answer.

That same day, the pace of the investigation once again picked up. Robinson called the Extended Stay in Overland Park. Browning went down to talk to the clerks, who confirmed that Jeanna Milliron was expected back in town the next day. By this point, they were familiar with Robinson's habits and knew that with a woman en route he would soon pay a visit to the locker at Needmor Storage to retrieve his black pilot's bag of sex toys. Sergeant Browning had playfully dubbed his bag the "ACME Spankmaster Kit."

Detectives were still pulling out the stops trying to get a look inside the locker. Roth and Brown came up with the idea of sending Detective Dawn Layman to pose as a damsel in distress with car trouble. However, storage facility workers told them Robinson always parked his truck right in front of the locker door and had hurriedly closed it on one occasion when they approached. So instead, detectives decided to borrow a lift truck from the city, park it on the street by a power pole and station two of their men in the cherry picker. They had just gotten it all lined up when Needmor called; Robinson had already shown up. As luck would have it, too, detectives hadn't even gotten there in time to change the VHS tape. They decided to go ahead with their plan, though they realized it would probably be a waste of time.

All the players gathered in the Lenexa training room the next morning for an important meeting. Morrison, Welch and Cowles were there from the DA's office, as were Reed and O'Neal from Overland Park and the usual contingent of detectives working the case. Up for discussion was whether or not they now had enough for a wiretap on his cell phone or his computer. At this point, the cops were ready to go to war for the wire and thought they had plenty of ammunition. "I argued for the phone," Roth said. "Others argued for the computer and I believe all of us wanted both if we could get them." Morrison, Welch and Cowles seemed to sense that the detectives' patience was about gone. After some heated discussion, the district attorney relented. They would go for the wiretap on his cell phone.

While the meeting was in progress, Officer Casey Flack and Officer Rick Dougan had come in on separate occasions to let Roth know that Robinson had called a second motel in Overland Park and then booked a room at the Guesthouse in Lenexa. There were now three hotels where he was possibly putting women. On top of that, they had also discovered a travel receipt in Barbara Sandre's trash, indicating she had flown to Canada on May 6 but was expected back on May 21.

Roth took Reed, O'Neal, Wilson and a few of his own detectives out for lunch that day to talk shop at The Woks, a Chinese restaurant in Lenexa. He still couldn't get over how much help his department had received from Overland Park. "I know there were the '80s cases, but when it came right down to it, it was our investigation," he said. "We were running the show and Overland Park—a much bigger department—was helping us. Considering how many detectives they had tied up for weeks with us, it was quite a contribution. It's not easy for the big kid on the block to help the little guy, but OP bent over backward."

Dougan called Roth while they were eating to let him know

that Robinson had just checked Milliron into the Guesthouse Suites. Milliron, wearing a T-shirt and shorts, drove up a little while later and disappeared inside room 124. Her white Chevy Corsica, Dougan reported, was packed solid. Once again, they'd need two surveillance teams—one for Robinson and one for the lady in town. Roth arranged with O'Neal to set up the Overland Park van in the Guesthouse Suites parking lot; he stationed a couple of his own guys in the room next door. They watched as Robinson showed up at the hotel in the afternoon and stayed about an hour. The walls were thick, however, and surveillance officers couldn't hear a thing.

Meanwhile, Beyer and Bussell sat up in the cherry picker outside Robinson's Needmor Storage locker all day, the only result being a good argument with a power company official who protested loudly about them working on a city utility pole. The officers finally flashed their badges and told the official to get lost.

Robinson did not visit Milliron over the next two days, instead calling her several times from home. In the much-needed lull, Roth and his crew worked on preparing the wiretap. After a lengthy talk on Friday, May 19, 2000, he and Brown decided to ask the DA for a minimization meeting on Monday before going live with the wiretap on Tuesday. Of course, Morrison would make the final call.

Several officers were sitting in the wiretap room when the phone rang for Dougan, who quickly put the call on speakerphone. It was the clerk from the Guesthouse Suites. Milliron had just come to the front office, crying and shaking, and asked for the name of the man who had checked her in. When the clerk told her it was John Robinson, she grew hysterical.

Milliron, at the clerk's suggestion, called police a few minutes later. In response, Brown and Browning threw on police uniforms and drove to the hotel. Roth also dispatched Layman and Beyer to keep an eye on Robinson at his Monterey Lane address. They soon called to report that he had left the house, wearing a suit and tie, with Nancy. It looked as though they were headed out for a night on the town. The surveillance team followed them to the home of Nancy's mother before Roth called them off. What they didn't know at the time was that the Robinsons' youngest daughter, Christy Shipps, now married to a Prairie Village detective, was graduating from Johnson County Community College with an associate of science degree in emergency medical science. The ceremony was scheduled for 7:30 P.M.

Meanwhile, Brown and Browning brought Milliron back to the station to take her statement. Watching the interview from the privacy of his office, Roth couldn't help but feel sorry for the woman. *What a pathetic sight,* he thought. She'd quit her job, gotten rid of her stuff, spent most of her savings—all to come up to work for and live with a man she knew as Jim Turner. She was upset that he had taken pictures of the red welts his floggings had left on her body. When he left that afternoon, he had taken his camera with him. He was supposed to return at 3:30 P.M. but had instead called at 3:20 P.M. to let her know he had to leave for Europe—and she had to get out of the room by the next day. He told her he had left $100 in a drawer. That's when she paid a frantic visit to the front office.

That Friday night, Brown and Layman checked Milliron into the Days Inn in Lenexa at the department's expense. Roth took $50 out of the station's drug buy account and gave it to her for food. The detectives tried to impress upon her the importance of not contacting Robinson. Although she shed no light on what had happened to Trouten, her story sounded very similar to what they could gather from Suzette's family and it helped to establish a pattern of behavior. The fact that he continued to use the alias of Jim Turner in Kansas City when Jim Turner was supposedly sailing around the world with Suzette was bewildering. "This guy was so sure of himself," Roth said. "If it worked once, it would work again."

With Sandre in Canada and Milliron at least temporarily out of harm's way, Roth decided to call off surveillance for the weekend. Robinson would not be doing anything but playing husband and grandpa. The plan was to bring Milliron back into the station Saturday morning, May 20, for a lengthy taped interview. Then either Monday or Tuesday, they'd have her call Robinson and ask for some money to get back home. *I hope he turns her down,* Roth thought. *It would play good for a jury.*

Brown called Roth at home the next morning to tell him Boyer was en route to pick up Milliron and bring her into the station. Brown, who planned to attend one of his kids' soccer games later that afternoon, showed up in sweatshirt and shorts. He and Boyer walked Milliron through her entire relationship with Robinson, eventually approaching the subject of sex. Milliron explained how Robinson had instructed her over the phone to strip naked and kneel by the bed until his arrival. When he discovered she'd gotten up a couple of times, she said, he struck her. That had happened during the first visit in April and again this time around.

When Brown asked her what she called Robinson, she told them she used to call him JT but that he made her switch to "master" or "sir" soon after they met. At that point, Boyer walked out of the interview and down the hall to Roth's office. He leaned over his sergeant's desk and pointed a finger in his face. "I hate Mr. Robinson," Boyer told him, "that arrogant son of a bitch."

Roth could certainly relate to Boyer's anger and disgust. The interview on Saturday morning only underscored their belief that Robinson had plans for Milliron, but not the ones she had in mind. She had given police the slave contract she had signed and allowed them to retrieve the e-mails she had exchanged with Robinson; he had all her personal and financial information. "I'm quite sure he was setting her up for the great demise," Roth said. "Milliron seemed an excellent victim that a jury, if she got there, should really find believable and feel for her. What Robinson had done to her was, to me, so damned degrading. And then when you sat and read the slave contract, you wanted to strangle him."

The next day, Barbara Sandre flew back into town. Then a

clerk at the Extended Stay called with news that both amazed and horrified detectives. Katherine M., from Georgia, had called to check on a room that Robinson was supposed to have reserved for her. All they knew about Katherine M. was that Robinson had called her hundreds of times over the last several months. Extended Stay didn't have a reservation for her, but, sure enough, Robinson made one the next day. *It's getting crowded,* Roth thought. How was their suspect possibly going to keep juggling so many different women?

The minimization meeting went forward as hoped on Monday morning, May 22, in the Lenexa Municipal Court. Once again, everyone involved in the case was there. Welch went over the wiretap order with the officers while O'Neal, Reed, Brown, Roth and Overland Park Captain Jeffrey Dysart met outside the courtroom to discuss Katherine M.'s impending visit. All agreed that Overland Park would watch her while Lenexa kept tabs on Robinson.

Over lunch at The Woks, Welch, Roth and Brown discussed their authority to keep or detain Robinson if he should start driving to the farm with Katherine M. Welch was going to talk to Morrison about it, but they were in agreement: they'd pull the plug on the investigation. They also decided to begin the wiretap as soon as possible. Back at the station, they scrambled to get the equipment ready and to line up the officers who would monitor his cell phone conversations.

That afternoon, Reed called to report some good news: Vickie Neufeld had contacted their department to file a complaint against Robinson. They decided Wilson, as Overland Park's representative, would be assigned to make the call since the alleged crime had taken place at a hotel on their turf. Boyer, Brown and Roth hovered over Wilson as he dialed Neufeld in Galveston. Soon Agent Tarpley, of the FBI, arrived. During the call, the eager detectives bombarded Wilson with questions to ask the therapist, writing them down on yellow sticky notes. As Vickie recounted her story, they saw that there were a lot of similarities between what she and Milliron had experienced. They decided Boyer and Wilson should meet her face to face.

The next day, May 23, Wilson and Boyer found themselves driving to Little Rock, Arkansas, to intercept the psychologist, who had just left Texas and was moving to Virginia. The long drive was a good opportunity for the two detectives to get to know each other better. "Jake and I found that we had a lot of the same likes, dislikes, hobbies and think the same way about a lot of things," said Wilson. "[For example,] we both enjoy golf, the mountains and cool weather versus the heat. We are both kind of type "A" personalities. And when we were driving to Arkansas, we even learned that we got married on the exact same day. The biggest thing that came out of the drive was the respect and trust that we both garnered from the other. When I first went to Lenexa, they treated me very well but they needed to get to know me. Once they did, it was like I was one of their own."

Over the course of a four-hour interview the next afternoon, the detectives heard all about Vickie's encounter with Robinson and the graphic world of BDSM. "She had taken pretty good notes and kept copies of her emails," Wilson said. "She did want to play it off like she was completely naïve and a novice about this whole BDSM thing but it got to a point where she told us stuff in such detail that I finally told her it was apparent she was a step or two above being a novice."

Discussion about her wide array of stolen sex toys, alone, was an eye-opener for the detectives. She told them that the plaid mesh bag Robinson had stolen from her contained, among other things, a strawberry-flavored dildo worth $30 and a blue butt plug that cost $60. "Now, I'm no prude," quipped Boyer, "but I was shocked to learn that a butt plug could be worth more than a flavored dildo."

Despite the inevitable jokes, however, the detectives believed Vickie to be a very credible witness. She was articulate, intelligent and well educated—"After all, she had a Ph.D. in psychology," noted Boyer. Unlike some other women who had hotel encounters with Robinson, she would never waver when it came to testifying against him in court. Paul Morrison showed his appreciation to the psychologist by later characterizing her decision to step forward as "manna from heaven."

Meanwhile, surveillance crews witnessed yet another bizarre scene at the Extended Stay. Katherine M., driving a purple Lincoln Mark VIII, had checked in on the afternoon of May 22. Minutes later, the blond-haired woman had donned a bright red bikini and walked outside to lie down on a blanket in a little grassy area near the parking lot. The air was chilly, and the hotel was located right next to the I-435—hardly optimal conditions for sunbathing. "It had to have been set up," said O'Neal, who was on duty that afternoon. "She had only been there a few minutes and [Robinson] drives through the parking lot, circles slow, looks over at her and then drives off. About five minutes later, she gets up and goes into her room."

Robinson drove over to the Extended Stay twice the next day—going home for lunch with Nancy in between visits with Katherine M. As soon as he left the second time, surveillance officers watched her check out of the hotel and begin the long drive back to Georgia.

By then, detectives had their hands full with Milliron, who had shown up unannounced at the Lenexa station that morning. She spent four hours telling the detectives she wanted to get back together with Robinson. She hadn't done a thing about finding someplace to go. Brown was concerned about her, but Roth was no longer sympathetic. "What an ignoramus and lazy person," he said. "She basically wanted someone to take care of her because she was too lazy to do anything herself."

Roth ordered Milliron to vacate her room at the Days Inn by noon the next day. "If she wants to get back with Robinson," he told Brown, "so be it!" Instead, they checked her into a woman's shelter, where she would stay for several days before eventually leaving Kansas City.

Thursday, May 25, 2000, was full of important developments. Detectives opened the subpoenaed records of Specialty Publications and found that Robinson had written checks to two women. One of them, Alesia Cox, they recognized from the Guesthouse Suites registration records. But they had never heard of the second: Izabela Lewicka. As Roth flipped through the pages, he noted that Robinson had written numerous checks to Lewicka, totaling thousands of dollars, including one that was made out to Izabela Lewicka Robinson. She was obviously important to him, he realized. He came across an August 1, 1999, check in her name and then an August 23, 1999, check to a moving company called Two Men and a Truck. Turning several more pages, he saw there were no more checks to Lewicka. Roth showed the records to Brown, grimly stating: "This doesn't bode well for Izabela."

That day, saying it had gone very well, Boyer and Wilson returned from Little Rock with Neufeld's complaints of aggravated sexual battery, felony theft and blackmail against Robinson. Detectives were pumped to also pick up Lore Remington on the wiretap, capturing a conversation between her and Robinson that would be played later in court. They grew disturbed, however, when they also listened to an unidentified Tennessee woman telling him she was packed and ready. She would be traveling to Kansas City with her eight-year-old daughter the next week. "Sandre was back in town," Roth said. "Milliron was flip-flopping on us and now we had a woman bringing her eight-year-old daughter into the fray. This phone call caused unity in the police ranks. That woman and child would not meet Robinson."

Roth went to see Meier early the next morning, finally confiding in his good friend that his wife of twenty-five years was leaving him. He hadn't yet come to terms with the news himself and it wasn't an easy conversation. "Me and John went back over twenty years," Roth said. "He knew my wife very well. She took care of his two boys for a while. He was very sorry about it."

The men dropped the subject to go into a Fat Friday powwow that included Morrison, Cowles and Welch from the DA's office, Tarpley from the FBI and the usual suspects from Lenexa and Overland Park. Brown brought the group up to date on Milliron, and Boyer briefed on Neufeld. Then the detectives told Morrison about the unknown woman coming up from Tennessee with her daughter. With the complaints from Milliron and Neufeld and the strong circumstantial evidence pointing to Robinson's involvement in Suzette's disappearance, Paul Morrison finally agreed that they had what they needed to arrest him and execute search warrants for his trailer, his Needmor storage locker and his Linn County farm. The detectives, needless to say, were thrilled.

Morrison initially wanted to arrest Robinson on Wednesday, May 31, 2000, but decided to move back the date to Friday, June 2. The biggest reason was to give Welch enough time to make sure the affidavits were squeaky clean. It would also give them the cover of weekend to quietly execute the warrants. There had been no media attention and they wanted to keep it that way for as long as they could. "A huge caravan of police vehicles heading for rural Linn County during a normal business day would raise all kinds of eyebrows," Roth said. "Early Saturday morning we just might go unnoticed."

Chapter 15

Roth and his detectives had their hands full. While Brown worked with the DA's office to prepare affidavits for the search warrants, the sergeant doled out assignments: Boyer and Wilson would confront and arrest Robinson. As the designated search team, Lowther, Layman and Owsley would collect evidence at Robinson's Olathe home and storage locker. Missouri K-9 Search and Rescue, Inc., with their highly trained handlers and dogs, would have first crack at the Linn County farm. They would be joined by dozens of investigators, agents and crime scene specialists from multiple jurisdictions.

That Wednesday, Owsley went through Robinson's trash for the last time. Roth didn't know whether to laugh or cry when the detective found a note, apparently penned by their suspect, which read as follows: "Picking up peoples' trash from in front of their homes is an illegal activity!!! A videotape of you, your vehicle license plates will be turned over to the police. Have a nice day." Robinson had signed off with a smiley face. "Did he see us?" Roth asked. "Did the trashman alert him? We were never to know the answer. After a few minutes, though, we pretty much thought, 'What the hell, what can he do now?'"

Meeting on Thursday for hamburgers and grilled-chicken sandwiches at Chili's restaurant, Roth went over the final arrangements with Reed and O'Neal. Among other things, they agreed that Overland Park would safeguard the Raymore, Missouri, storage lockers through the weekend while Lenexa searched the Kansas sites. The Overland Park investigators believed the Raymore lockers—particularly the one that Nancy didn't know about—were their responsibility. "We felt that locker was our best hope of finding evidence linking Robinson to our missing women from the '80s," Reed said. "We had officers watching it 24 hours a day starting Friday morning."

All three men were confident the Johnson County District Attorney's Office would give them the warrants they needed to search Robinson's properties in Kansas. But they were concerned whether they would find enough to go across the state line for the Raymore warrant. "At the time," Roth said, "we didn't have any hard evidence that we could put on paper that showed the link between what we were doing in Kansas and [Robinson's] storage locker in Missouri." Added Reed: "The DA's office would give serious consideration to obtaining a search warrant for [the lockers] after we found out what else we had at his house, the Olathe locker and his farm."

Their mission was given added urgency on Thursday afternoon when Robinson was heard on the wiretap calling a seventeen-year-old mother who lived at Santa Barbara Estates, offering to put her up on the farm with her baby if she would become his mistress. Detectives, already aware of the Tennessee woman and her eight-year-old daughter coming into town, were understandably worried. "We felt we had to move quickly," Roth said.

Friday dawned, sunny and warm. Brown headed to the courthouse about 8:00 A.M. to finish up the warrants, while most of the detectives took up positions north of Santa Barbara Estates, smoking cheap cigars in the parking lot of the Ridgeview Amoco. Wilson, Boyer and a few other detectives waited in a strip mall across from the trailer park entrance. The Directed Patrol Unit was inside the park watching Robinson to make sure he didn't leave. The plan was to catch him at home before his wife left for work—in hopes that she might become an ally after hearing about his escapades with Vickie Neufeld and Jeanna Milliron.

It would prove to be a nerve-racking morning. Reed was late; his car wouldn't start. *A bad omen?* Roth wondered, nervously puffing away. Then Nancy Robinson left for work. When Reed arrived shortly thereafter, they decided that Overland Park's detectives Bill Batt and Bobbi Jo Hohnholt would interview her separately from her husband. But what was keeping Brown? To their relief, he finally called at 9:30 A.M.; the judge had just signed the warrants.

Wilson hadn't eaten much all week, his stomach in knots as he contemplated what it would be like to put handcuffs on Robinson. "By this time, we had a pretty good feel for what this guy was and I just didn't want to do anything to blow it," he said. Boyer, the old-timer, was chomping at the bit: "All the hard work we had done on this case was about to pay off."

Just after 9:30 A.M., the two detectives pulled up to the Monterey Lane address and knocked on the front door of the tidy gray-and-white double-wide. Sheba, the family dog, barked loudly as Robinson, dressed in a worn T-shirt, blue jeans and slippers, answered the knock and invited them in. Walking into the living room, Wilson was struck by all the photos on the wall. "There he was with the kids, with the grandkids, growing up through the ages," he recalled. "As I thought of my daughter and the way she loves her grandpa, I couldn't help but wonder what this was going to do to his family. To this day I feel sad for them."

The detectives, wearing dark suits, sat opposite Robinson, who sank into a recliner near the door. "We want to visit with you a little bit," said Wilson, handing him his card as Boyer quickly got down to business and explained that they were responding to complaints from Vickie Neufeld and Jeanna Milliron. Turning beet red, Robinson acknowledged that he had engaged in BDSM sessions with the women. But he insisted that they were consensual and the rest was a misunderstanding. He was happy to return Vickie's sex toys if she would send him postage. He had never tried to blackmail either one of them, insisting he had destroyed their photos. He also denied telling Milliron his name was Jim or James Turner or that he had ever used that name with anyone. "Why would I do that?" he asked.

The detectives asked if his wife was home and he said that she was not. "Why would I want my wife here now?" he asked. "'Cause it's a very embarrassing situation, okay? . . .My son's [*sic*] a police officer on the . . . on the Prairie Village Police Department. My daughter is a paramedic for Johnson County Med-Act. . . . It's a very embarrassing situation."

Boyer and Wilson began querying him about the level of his involvement with BDSM. "So what's the deal with the [slave] contract?" Boyer asked. "I mean, what does that do for you?"

"It's part of the lifestyle," Robinson replied. "Part of the game."

He claimed he'd been involved with BDSM for only about a year and seemed to imply that Milliron and Neufeld were the first women he'd ever met. "There's people on the Internet all the time," he said, fumbling for words. "I—I've chatted with people all the time but these are the only two that, that, you know, whatever . . ."

"What do you do—talk dirty to 'em or something?" Boyer asked.

"No, I don't," he insisted. "I just basically answer their ad . . . and, and, you know, sometimes you click and sometimes you don't."

When asked how he ranked himself in the BDSM hierarchy, Robinson admitted to the detectives that he was a "dominant."

"There are guys out there who, who entice women just so they can abuse 'em," he said, ". . . abuse 'em and force 'em to do anything and, and, you know, 'cause I don't believe in that kind of stuff."

Wilson remembered Robinson becoming aggressive as they plied him with questions. "Jake is a little bit older than I am and I kind of felt like Robinson was kind of shying away from him a little bit," he explained. "But he would lean toward me and raise his voice, like he thought he was going to intimidate me or something."

It was about this time that Jake Boyer grew tired of listening to John Robinson lie to them, like he had done to so many other people. Having heard more than enough, he told him they would like him to come down to the station and give a statement. Robinson stalled, saying he wanted to change his clothes and shave first. "I want to keep my wife out of this," he added. "She has no idea about the lifestyle. This is compromising a thirty-six-year marriage."

Suddenly Robinson jumped up, saying he needed to call his lawyer. At this point, the detectives moved in to block him from getting anywhere near his computers and told him he was under arrest. "What for?" Robinson asked. Sexual battery, blackmail and theft, Boyer told him.

Robinson appeared surprised but sat quietly. Boyer, on the other hand, started pacing the floor like a caged tiger. "I was going over the case in my head and thinking of all of the women that Robinson had conned, stolen from and probably murdered," he said. "I thought how much I despised this man for the way he treated these women."

As he continued to pace back and forth, Boyer told his prisoner, "Don't be surprised if we charge you with murder." Robinson, with a confused look on his face, leaned forward in his chair and asked, "Murder?"

"Yes, murder," Boyer replied. "Five counts."

The veteran detective started rattling off the names: Suzette Trouten, Paula Godfrey, Catherine Clampitt, Lisa and Tiffany Stasi. At the mention of Suzette, Robinson fell back in his chair and all the color left his face. At Lisa and Tiffany, he took off his glasses, wiped his brow, glanced at Wilson and muttered, "Jesus Christ."

"You could see him kind of crumble in this recliner that he was sitting in," Wilson remembered. "He was hyperventilating and he kept taking his glasses off and wiping his brow. The guy was imploding."

After placing him in handcuffs, the detectives led Robinson out through the screened-in porch attached to his trailer home. By this time, police were pulling up in unmarked cars and several neighbors were gathering. Wilson, guiding Robinson by his left arm, felt his prisoner stiffen as he faced the onlookers. Regaining his cocky demeanor, he suddenly smirked and said, "You're making quite the production out of me, aren't you?"

The detectives had a surprise waiting for Robinson back at the Lenexa station. Wilson instructed the shackled prisoner to say nothing as they escorted him into a police conference room. "We are going to respect the fact that you have asked for your attorney," he told him. "But I want you to understand how much work we have done and how much we know about your activities."

On the conference room table lay photographs of several women Robinson had recently met for sadomasochistic sex, including Vickie Neufeld and Jeanna Milliron. On another table were seven black binders, containing hundreds of pages from the exhaustive ten-week investigation. On the bulletin board was a picture of Suzette Marie Trouten, her police case number scrawled beside it, grainy surveillance photos of Robinson and his wife and a hand-drawn map with directions to the Linn County farm.

With his hands cuffed in front of him, the balding, innocu-ous-looking grandfather slowly and silently walked around the conference room table, pausing for several seconds at each photo to stare intently.

Returning to the booking room, detectives removed his shackles and allowed him to phone his attorney, Ron Wood. He explained he'd been arrested on charges of aggravated sexual battery, blackmail and felony theft. Bond, he calmly added, had been set for $250,000. "Yes, I'm *sure* that is all they have charged me with," he insisted when Wood appar-ently expressed surprise at the shockingly high amount.

Then Robinson dropped an even bigger bombshell. "They're talking about charging me with murder," he con-tinued in a cocky tone, as if he hadn't a care in the world, "and they have a bunch of pictures of women that you and I need to talk about."

Chapter 16

As soon as Robinson was escorted to a waiting police car, the designated search team—Dawn Layman, Dan Owsley and Mike Lowther—moved into the Monterey double-wide and got down to work. "We didn't expect to find much at his home, but we were wrong," Roth said. In fact, there was a treasure trove of incriminating evidence. "We started finding stuff right away," agreed Lowther. "Every five seconds, it was like, 'Hey, come look at this' or 'Oh my God, look what I found.' "

Specialty Publications checks were lying out on the kitchen table. The master bedroom yielded a collection of eighteen adult videos. A second bedroom had been converted into an office that Robinson shared with his wife and—after three desktop computers, two laptops, a printer and a fax machine had been hauled away for examination by forensic experts—the search team found files dating back years. Unbelievably, an expandable folder in the closet contained the 1985 receipt for Lisa Stasi's stay at the Rodeway Inn, as well as a single blank piece of paper bearing her signature and an envelope addressed to Stasi's brother.

Also in the closet inside a black soft-sided briefcase was a checkbook containing the names of account holders Barbara L. Sandre and John Robinson, Social Security benefit statements from 1999 for a Debbie L. Faith and Sheila D. Faith and pieces of paper with e-mail addresses scribbled all over them. Several were eerily familiar to detectives: midwestmaster, eruditemaster, preipo, slavedancer and KCslave.

The black soft-sided bag also contained Robinson's passport,

e-mails containing the name Barbara Robinson and slave contracts containing the names of Katherine M. and Linda G.
There were also a whole host of personal effects relating to
Katherine, including her W2 forms, Georgia driver's license
and other ID cards, her resume, her signature on a document
granting Robinson power of attorney and a $16,908 check she
had made out to Specialty Publications.

On the top shelf of the closet were seven adult videotapes,
which would later be reviewed by Lowther and Weiler. Though
some were of very poor quality, they appeared to be mass-pro-
duced professional adult videos dealing with BDSM. They all
included scenes of bondage and sadomasochistic sex, including multiple scenes of women being chained or tied up, then
whipped, flogged and subjected to various other painful or hu-
miliating acts, including fisting, simulated rape and golden
showers.

James A. Turner's name turned up on all kinds of paperwork. So did the name Beverly J. Bonner. In a brown wallet
found in the master bedroom was a store credit card in
Turner's name. In Robinson's desk drawer was a manila envelope containing a typewritten page with his signature, as
well as an application by Bonner for an employee identification number. There were Missouri articles of incorporation for
Hydro-Gro, Inc., containing both names. There was a sheet of
computer-generated business cards for the same company that
listed James A. Turner as vice president of finance and John
E. Robinson as vice president of international operations.

Detectives found stationery in Robinson's office that contained fake letterheads from the CIA, the White House, Drug
Enforcement Administration, Department of Justice and State
Department. In addition, they came across two books offering how-to guidance for one of Robinson's favorite illicit
pastimes: *New ID: How to Create a Foolproof New Identity*
by Anonymous and John Q. Newman's *The Heavy Duty New
Identity.* They also recovered a red address book belonging to

Robinson. Under *B,* they found listings for Beverly Bonner and BJB. Both names had been crossed out with a big X.

While the search team was processing Robinson's home, Overland Park detectives Bobbi Jo Hohnholt and Bill Batt had gone to the Santa Barbara Estates front office to speak to Nancy. When asked if there was a quiet place where they could talk, she suggested they step outside. Out in the parking lot, they informed her that her husband had just been arrested for sexual battery, blackmail and felony theft. The petite blond-haired woman clutched her chest. "I can't believe my husband would do something like that," she answered, gasping.

Nancy agreed to accompany the detectives back to the Overland Park police station for a lengthy taped interview. According to police records, the detectives informed her on the way over that her husband had run up more than $50,000 in charges on just one of his credit cards. Visibly blanching, she told them she would be in a coma if she had known they were in that much debt.

Robinson's wife told the detectives that her husband had been consumed with the Internet ever since he bought his first computer several years earlier. She acknowledged that she was aware of his interest in BDSM, but she couldn't comprehend it. From time to time, she noted that he left BDSM "material" lying around, but she refused to read any of it or view his collection of sadomasochistic sex tapes.

She also admitted she had recently found out about Barbara Sandre and had driven by her address Grant Avenue. She knew her husband had an affair with Sandre in the 1970s but had had no idea how they had recently become reacquainted; she was getting ready to confront him once again. "Guess that makes me feel really silly!" Nancy exclaimed to detectives. "When did that woman move back to Grant?"

Though she would later acknowledge knowing more, Nancy told detectives she knew "Iza," "byza" or "Izzy" Lewicka to be her husband's friend who had done work on his manufactured modular home magazine. Questioned about

Lisa Stasi, she said she remembered that police in the 1980s had talked to her husband about a missing person, but she could not recall any of the specifics.

Nancy also said she only knew that they were renting two lockers, the one at Needmor Storage and locker 23 at Stor-Mor For Less in Raymore. She gave them her consent to search the latter. When they did later that day, they found nothing of evidentiary value. She seemed overwhelmed to learn that her husband kept a second locker at Stor-Mor. She was also shocked that detectives had been following her and her husband for more than two months. "We really live boring lives," she protested.

After five hours at the mobile home—where they carted out more than a dozen boxes and ultimately towed away Robinson's Dodge Ram—the search team drove to nearby Needmor Storage on North Kansas City Road in Olathe. Using heavy-duty bolt cutters, Lowther cut the metal hasps to open B18, the 10' x 15' locker that Robinson had been renting for two years. Right out in front were Suzette's Compaq Presario computer, several Big Boy boxes and three bags of sex toys, including the plaid bag Robinson had allegedly stolen from Vickie Neufeld.

There were also several briefcases in the locker that would prove to be extremely valuable. Inside a black hardcover case was a red box, and inside the box, Owsley found a Kansas driver's license belonging to Izabela Lewicka, as well as her Social Security card, passport, resident alien card and high school diploma. Besides several pieces of jewelry, there was a document indicating that Izabela had given Robinson power of attorney. There was also an Olathe Public Library card in the name of Izabela Lewicka Robinson.

Also inside the hardcover case were several nude photographs of Izabela, tied to a table and in various other positions, and her six-page contract that specified 115 "Basic Slave Rules" of sexual conduct. The same briefcase, moreover, contained slave contracts for Alesia Cox and Vickie

Neufeld, more Social Security benefit statements for Sheila D. Faith and Debbie L. Faith, and two 1997 Social Security checks, for $582 each, made out in their names.

Layman opened a brown leather briefcase that contained a number of Suzette's personal effects, including her Michigan driver's license, Social Security card, birth certificate and application for a passport. It also held forty-two preaddressed envelopes to various members of the Trouten family and thirty-one sheets of pastel colored stationery, blank except for the signature "Love ya, Suzette." There was also her yellow legal pad listing the names and home and e-mail addresses of friends and family, her slave contract containing 128 rules and an unlabeled videocassette.

In a black pilot's bag—the one that Robinson carried with him when he met the various women coming into town —were a variety of floggers, pieces of rope, clothespins, several golf balls and the harness he had used on Vickie. A blue nylon bag with black handles in the locker contained several nude photos of Suzette, as well as a number of her sex toys, including a collar, dildos, butt plugs and a metal speculum, electrodes and a battery-powered electrical device called a TENS unit. Recovered from a Hyvee grocery bag was Suzette's journal. In the various cardboard boxes were many of her knickknacks, jewelry and anatomy and physiology textbooks. "There was just a ton of stuff," Lowther said.

After several hours, they transported all of the property to the Lenexa Police Department, where Morrison, Welch and Cowles joined them. "Everyone was excited with the results of the two searches," Roth remembered. "[The detectives] worked well into the night and still hadn't finished booking property." It was past midnight when the last detectives, tired but pleased, headed home for some much-deserved rest. Saturday morning would be the farm.

Chapter 17

The conference room was packed for the Saturday morning briefing at the Lenexa police station. Everyone was there by 7:00 A.M., from the detectives working the case to several members of the Johnson County District Attorney's Office, Overland Park Underwater Rescue and Johnson County Sheriff's Department. Roth brought everyone up to date on what they had found Friday and outlined their various responsibilities for the day. When Overland Park captain O'Neal pointed out that the search warrant contained an incorrect address, Brown went scurrying back to the courthouse. The rest of the investigators hopped in unmarked vehicles and, in caravan fashion, headed south to Robinson's farm. By now, several of them had become familiar with the route.

A Linn County deputy and members of Missouri K-9 Search and Rescue met the investigators out on the gravel road at the end of Robinson's dirt drive. There they waited, patiently, for about forty-five minutes until word came from Brown that the updated warrant had been signed and they were finally free to search. Roth sent in the K-9 teams first, about 9:00 A.M., instructing the handlers to begin by having their dogs sniff around the trailer. Next to go in were Keith Kerr, Dan Rundle and Harold Hughes, the crime scene investigators from the Johnson County Sheriff's Department who began processing the trailer's interior. "It looked like it was going to be a disappointment," noted Roth, who had to force the trailer door open with his pry bar. "The inside was a wreck . . . and the only item of significance that I could see initially was a Big Boy box matching the ones Suzette had brought with her from Michigan."

Besides killing a snake with a shovel, in fact, Roth felt as though the entire morning was a disappointment. The K-9 teams worked east to a collapsed building and a nearby concrete foundation, then south to the pond near the back of the property. Once they had cleared the area, Overland Park's five-member underwater team began a hand search of the snake-infested pond, looking for bodies, weapons, clothes or anything else that might point to evidence of foul play.

The rest of the investigators began combing other areas of the farm, including a jumble of metal and plastic barrels and lawn equipment in undergrowth next to the shed. By lunchtime, they had covered a lot of ground but had little to show for their efforts. "It was very hot and humid, the chiggers were in legions and I, for one, was rather glum when we broke for lunch," Roth said. "So far, we had found nothing in the trailer that stood out and nothing remotely close to a grave site."

Lenexa had done a good job of planning ahead in the eating department, however, packing grills, chips and coolers filled with hamburgers, hot dogs, soda and bottled water. While Roth was munching on a freshly grilled hamburger, K-9 handler Petra Stephens approached and asked if he could have someone move some barrels away from a small shed that stood a stone's throw from the trailer. One of her Border Collies, Wolf, had shown some interest, she added, but there was so much other junk in the way she couldn't get them in there for a good sniff. "Since I'd seen the handlers down there earlier actually leaning on the barrels, I didn't give the finding much hope," Roth remembered.

Strolling to the shed a few minutes later, he found Stephens working her collie around two yellow eighty-five-gallon metal drums. By this point, she had also removed the small plug from the top of one of the barrels and reported that it "smelled kind of bad." Roth threw a few items out of the way and began rocking one of the yellow drums from side to side as he pulled it backward. When he hit an area of grass and bushes, he laid the barrel on its side, rolled it a few feet to a clearing and stood it back up. That's when he saw it: a single bead of reddish liquid that began a very slow roll from the edge of the lid down the side of the barrel.

"Is that blood?" asked Reed, who had walked up with Overland Park captain Jeff Dysart. Roth replied that yes, it certainly looked like blood. "Or transmission fluid," offered Dysart. No sooner had the captain uttered the words than a gigantic black fly landed and began to feast on the reddish liquid. No more doubts. Turning to Officer Rick Dougan, his designated crime scene photographer, Roth asked him to snap a close-up of the fly. Then he directed one of his detectives to summon the investigators from inside the trailer.

Within minutes, Harold Hughes had used a pair of pliers to loosen the bolt on the seal of the first yellow drum. Blood started running down the sides as the veteran detective removed the band that secured the lid. Lifting the lid, he peered inside. Sure enough, he was looking at a decomposing body, unclothed, curled up in a fetal position and immersed in about fourteen inches of its own fluids. The stench of death was overwhelming. "Bingo," he said matter-of-factly.

While a crime scene videographer captured the moment on tape, investigators moved the second yellow barrel out from the brush. Hughes opened it in the same manner as he had the first. Inside was another decomposing body, this one partially clothed in a nightshirt and covered by a pillow. It, too, was curled up in the fetal position and floating in its own fluids. Hughes quickly resealed the barrels and, using a black Magic Marker, labeled them UNKNOWN NO. 1 and UNKNOWN NO. 2.

By this time, investigators were congratulating one another, shaking hands and exchanging high fives. "We felt sad for the fact that two people were dead—murdered," Reed said, "but at the same time, since we suspected that was the case, we felt relief that we had found the evidence that would bring John

Robinson to justice." They had hoped to find Suzette and were already convinced she was Unknown No. 1, but the discovery of a second body came as something of a shock. "It immediately reinforced the belief that we were dealing with a serial killer," Reed said. "It also raised the question: exactly how many more victims were we going to find?

While Assistant District Attorney Sara Welch spent her Sunday at the courthouse in Cass County, Missouri, securing the search warrant for Robinson's Raymore storage locker, Dr. Donald Pojman spent his at the Shawnee County Coroner's Office in Topeka, Kansas, performing autopsies on Unknown No. 1 and Unknown No. 2. After an all-day session observed by Detectives Hohnholt and Boyer, who took careful notes, the deputy coroner concluded that both were females who had been viciously bludgeoned to death by a weapon consistent with a hammer.

Unknown No. 1 had died instantly after being dealt a single blow to the left side of the head that left a quarter-size hole in her skull. She wore nothing but a black cloth blindfold that appeared to be held in place by a soft nylon rope encircling her face and neck; the only other article in the barrel was a plastic Price Chopper bag. Her long hair had been pulled back into a ponytail and she had several piercings in her ears, nipples and genitalia. Mildly decomposed, she had been dead a few months to a year. Using dental records, a forensic odontologist would soon confirm what detectives already knew in their hearts. Unknown No. 1 was Suzette Trouten.

A turquoise diamond-shaped patterned pillow partially covered Unknown No. 2, who was wearing a dark short-sleeve nightshirt. Three pieces of gray duct tape, found floating loose in the barrel, could have been used to bind or muzzle her. Bludgeoned twice on the left side of the head—and judging by the blood that had collected in the subdural region of the brain—she may have lived fifteen minutes. Moderately decomposed, she had been dead for six months to two years. It would take a week to obtain the dental records that would be used to identify her. Several of the detectives were already speculating that she was Izabela Lewicka.

Meanwhile, back in Linn County, the news had finally leaked that police were onto something big. As Overland Park captain Keith O'Neal and his crew were wrapping up at the farm on late Sunday afternoon—they would continue the search for evidence for several days—the first news chopper circled overhead. The media frenzy was about to begin.

Chapter 18

Roth and Reed hadn't even left the Linn County crime scene on Saturday afternoon, when, sitting in a police cruiser, they decided it would be a good idea to form an official joint task force to continue their investigation, as it undoubtedly was about to send them in countless directions. The next day, Sunday, June 4, 2000, they met with their respective chiefs, who put Captain Meier in charge and appointed Reed as the lead officer and Roth as the report officer. The task force, it was determined, would be jointly controlled by Lenexa and Overland Park but continue to operate out of Lenexa.

Lenexa's technicians worked feverishly over the weekend transforming the large police classroom on the station's top floor into the new task force headquarters. Phone and power lines dropped from the ceiling tiles and four computers—to be used for entering police reports—were stationed in the middle of the room. Long tables were banked around the computers and phones with recorders were positioned every few chairs.

As the room started to fill on Monday morning, June 5, the makeup of the group now working the case took on a new look. Investigators from Linn County and the Kansas Bureau of Investigation joined the Lenexa and Overland Park detectives. Though technically not on the task force, members of the Directed Patrol Unit were also there, along with a few detectives who had been sent back to work the daily cases. There were also seats for Morrison, Welch and Cowles from the DA's office, Lenexa's chief Ellen Hanson and other important guests.

The biggest change, however, was that the lead investigators were no longer in the same positions. Boyer, who had become very ill with lower back problems, barely making it through the autopsies of Unknown No. 1 and Unknown No. 2, would be out for more than a week. Brown was now the designated press officer. Roth was the report officer. "Joe and I would share the 'lead officer' role, since his familiarity with the case was behind [mine]," Roth said. "As it would work out, the titles assigned to the two of us were pretty meaningless. We got beyond them."

The room was packed as Meier addressed the investigators and told them how the case would be worked. Reed had a few comments on how leads would be distributed, followed by Roth who had some housekeeping tasks surrounding report narratives, logging of property and the computer system.

Mike Lowther was somewhat disappointed that he had been selected to help with the Monday morning search of Robinson's locker at the Stor-Mor For Less facility just over the state line in Raymore, Missouri. For some reason, the bald-headed detective thought it was going to be a waste of time. "I recall thinking that Raymore was the end of the earth," he said, "and all of the action was taking place back in Johnson County." Scott Weiler, who went with him, jokingly threatened to quit if they discovered any more barrels.

Needless to say, neither detective was prepared for what lay in store for them—literally. When Douglas Borcherding, an evidence technician with the Overland Park Police Department, opened the door to E2 about 10:00 A.M., the 10' x 15' locker appeared to be about halfway filled with an odd assortment of junk, including books, magazine racks, boxes and tools. There were also three garment bags, all of them with tags that contained Robinson's name. In the rear left corner was a particularly large stack of items, many of which could not be viewed from the doorway. "You could smell a strange but faint odor—a mix of decay and mold," said Weiler.

A group of about eight investigators from Overland Park, Lenexa and Raymore slowly and methodically began to make their way to the back of the locker. After about ten minutes, Lowther heard someone say, "Are those barrels under there?"

Sure enough, in the rear left corner, they could barely make out a black metal barrel standing by itself and two blue metal barrels that appeared to be covered by a heavy opaque plastic tarp. Newspapers, a crib mattress, a dog carrier and a brown tent were stacked on top of the barrels in an apparent effort to hide them from view.

Removing the items, they realized that the blue barrels were not only covered in heavy plastic but also individually wrapped in plastic and secured with copious amounts of gray duct tape. A bag of gray kitty litter had been spread on the floor around the blue barrels to soak up fluid that was leaking from them.

At this point, Kevin Winer, an evidence technician from the Kansas City, Missouri, Crime Lab, was called to the scene. He decided to open the black barrel, which was sitting by itself in a back corner with the words "rendered pork fat" on the label. Looking inside, investigators saw an amorphous mass halfway filling the barrel. Winer grabbed a stick and began poking around in the barrel, identifying a brown sheet, a pair of glasses and some dark shoes. He lifted up one of the shoes. There was a leg attached.

No sooner had the newly formed task force begun to chase the leads they had sat on for weeks when Lowther called about 10:30 A.M. from Raymore, Missouri, to report the discovery of the three barrels in Robinson's storage locker. "'Now we might have to switch gears,'" Roth remembered thinking upon hearing the news. "Although they hadn't opened the barrels, he said there was kitty litter and a bad smell. We knew our case had just escalated."

Reed and Roth, who were supposed to be running the day-to-day operations, instead spent the first day just trying to keep up with the phones. Lowther called back a little later and confirmed that one barrel had been opened at the scene and it did, indeed, contain a body. Raymore investigators were buying three plastic wading pools to set the barrels in, since they were obviously leaking, he said, and from there they would be taken to the Jackson County medical examiner in downtown Kansas City, Missouri.

Missouri would soon send two detectives each from Raymore and Cass County to join the task force. There would now be thirty-five investigators working the case—and that didn't include the various personnel from Johnson County and Kansas City, Missouri, crime labs who would spend the next two years processing and analyzing fingerprints, DNA, blood and other biological material.

That same Monday morning, Paul Morrison also called the first of many press conferences. Flanked by Captain Jeffrey Dysart of the Overland Park Police Department and Linn County sheriff Marvin Stites, the Johnson County prosecutor solemnly provided dozens of print and television reporters with sketchy details about the two-month investigation that had preceded Robinson's arrest and the subsequent discovery of two bodies in barrels on his farm. "Mr. Robinson is a suspect in the deaths of the two women found in the barrels in Linn County," said the genteel DA, who added that Robinson was their only suspect and he would be facing homicide charges within a few days.

While he did not name Suzette Trouten, Morrison acknowledged that one of the bodies was believed to be an out-of-state woman missing since March 1. He said they did not yet know the identity of the second victim, but he thought she would be identified in the next few days. He also refused to elaborate on the cause of either of their deaths.

Robinson was being held on charges of sexually assaulting two Texas women after meeting them separately for sadomasochistic encounters at hotels in Lenexa and Overland Park, Morrison explained. Both women involved in the criminal charges told police that they had voluntarily agreed to act as his "slaves." But they said he had photographed them without their permission and brutalized them in a way that went beyond what they intended. One of the women also claimed that Robinson had stolen more than $700 worth of whips, paddles, riding crops and other sex toys.

Morrison told reporters that Robinson allegedly had used the Internet to develop relationships with these and other women interested in sadomasochism. He was apparently known to use the screen name "slavemaster" in his computer correspondence and sometimes called himself James Turner in person, he reportedly said. "This case has to do with the suspect having numerous contacts throughout the United States who share similar interests over, among other things, the Internet," Morrison said.

(Forensic experts analyzing Robinson's computers would later determine he never actually used the "slavemaster" handle, but the media immediately seized on the apt and catchy description and, not surprisingly, it stuck.)

Stites also said that about twenty investigators, including some from the FBI and the Kansas Bureau of Investigation, were continuing to search Robinson's farm in rural Linn County. "We are ground searching every bit of land involved and there is also a pond involved," said the laid-back country sheriff as he stepped up to the podium. "There's a possibility that we may drain that pond."

Shortly after the press conference, Robinson was led into the Johnson County Courthouse to face charges of aggravated sexual battery and felony theft. Wearing a prison standard-issue orange jumpsuit, he tried to shield himself from a barrage of waiting photographers by holding a large manila envelope over his face.

Robinson asked for a court-appointed attorney and District Judge William Cleaver appointed the public defender's office to represent him. Ted Baird, one of Morrison's assistant district attorneys, told Cleaver that prosecutors considered Robinson an extreme flight risk with previous felony convictions for theft, stealing and fraud. By the end of the hearing, the judge had increased the $250,000 bond set in his arrest warrant to $5 million—the largest in county history.

That evening, Lowther and Weiler accompanied the bodies they had found in the Missouri storage locker to the Jackson County morgue, where Dr. Thomas Young and his assistant were waiting. "I still recall the young medical examiner that night," said Lowther. "As he opened each lid, he would peer inside and then close the lid and look at us with a grin on his face, enjoying our anticipation of learning what was inside."

Young and his assistant had to shake the barrels vigorously to release their contents, which wanted to stay stuck to the bottom. At first only a trickle of thick fluid emerged. Eventually each of the bodies let go with a loud sucking sound and spilled onto a plastic sheet on the floor. Lying there, they still didn't look at all like bodies—just amorphous masses. Once they were cleaned up, Young was able to confirm that all three were females and that they, too, had been bludgeoned to death by a weapon consistent with a hammer. Judging by the state of decomposition, he added, it was conceivable they had been dead six years.

The body from the "rendered pork fat" black barrel was fully dressed, wearing dark-laced ankle shoes, size 14 black pants with stirrups, knee-high hose, panties and bra, a sweater blouse, a multicolored scarf, a pair of knit gloves and a second set of grayish blue gloves. Attached to the right collar of her jacket were two pins. One was the letter *B* and the other a letter *J.* She was also wearing ornate earrings, rings and a Bulova watch with hands frozen at 1:22. She had received multiple blows to the left side of her head, causing several eggshell-like fractures to the skull.

In the second barrel was the body of a woman wearing blue jeans, white tennis shoes and a T-shirt with CALIFORNIA, A STATE OF MIND printed on it. She also had on green socks, a black belt, bra and panties, a couple of rings and a gold watch. She had received multiple blows to the back of her head, causing numerous eggshell-like skull fractures. Unlike the others, she had also sustained a fracture on her right forearm that was consistent with a defensive injury.

In the third barrel was the body of an overweight teenager who was dressed in a pair of green ribbed knit pants and a green knit pullover blouse. She was wearing an adult disposable diaper and, in what was left of her straight brown hair, a silver-colored barrette. She, too, had been bludgeoned several times on the back and right side of her head.

On Tuesday morning, June 6, 2000, Kansas City residents awoke to the news that a brazen serial killer had likely been operating in their very midst. POLICE NAME SUSPECT IN DEATHS OF WOMEN," blared the headline in *The Kansas City Star*, which would devote many front-page stories to the barrel murders in the coming weeks, months and years. While the *Star* focused on the two bodies found on Robinson's farm, it also mentioned that police in Raymore, Missouri, had found three suspicious fifty-five-gallon drums in Robinson's Stor-Mor For Less storage locker. After looking inside one of them, they had sent all three barrels and other evidence to the Jackson County Medical Examiner's Office and the Kansas City, Missouri, Crime Lab for analysis, Police Chief Kris Turnbow said. While Turnbow refused to divulge what police had seen in the barrel, the paper noted that Cass County prosecutor Christopher Koster had scheduled a news conference for 1:30 P.M.

The *Olathe Daily News*, the paper of record for Robinson's suburban community, reported the same day that the suspect known online as "the Slavemaster" was believed to be involved in sadomasochistic activity over the Internet and would soon be charged with murdering at least two women found on his farm. By this time, too, Kansas City's four main TV stations were all over the story, bringing its viewers the latest developments in the case. It was the biggest news to hit Kansas City in years and the media's appetite for details was insatiable.

Thanks to the trove of paperwork found in Robinson's Olathe storage locker and his home office, Roth and a handful of those detectives most familiar with the case files were pretty sure they knew just who was in the barrels. But since they hadn't yet been positively identified, police had to keep their mouths closed and were therefore inundated with calls from other departments and families all over the country passing on the names and descriptions of missing persons. "The leads were pouring in," said Roth. "We had a file that contained nothing but reports or calls from people concerning missing people. We had detectives going all over the two states."

Dave Brown, fielding many of the calls, was going nuts. Suddenly there was constant press interest not only locally but also nationally and worldwide. In the first live broadcast of his life, Brown spoke to London's BBC and was astonished to learn that his voice was carrying all the way to Asia. *Wow!* Brown thought.

"It was overwhelming," he said of working with the press in general. "It was very difficult to keep up with what was going on. I was getting calls from all over, saying, 'What about this? What about that?'"

That Tuesday afternoon, June 6, Brown was happily given a break from his press duties and assigned to follow an important lead that had long intrigued him and the other detectives: Barbara Sandre, the woman at Grant Avenue. Brown was forced to conduct the interview over the phone because Sandre had once again gone back to Canada.

Reaching the middle-aged woman in Toronto, she told an unbelievable story: In May 1963, when she was just fifteen, she said, she had become involved in a Toronto production of the Boy Scouts' *Gang Show*. On the last night of the show, there was a cast party and Robinson, who had come from Chicago with several other Scouts to see the production, was among those invited. The two immediately hit it off and agreed to keep in touch.

Sandre said she and Robinson wrote each other until he told her he had been drafted for the Vietnam War and was leaving to join the fighting. When he returned from Vietnam, in early 1967—about the same time his and Nancy's first daughter, Kim, was born—he wrote again and told her he wanted to get engaged. However, Sandre had just gotten married to her first husband and declined his proposal. She did not hear from him again for several years.

In 1969, Robinson somehow got her telephone number, she said, and called her out of the blue in Toronto. They occasionally spoke on the phone after that and in 1971 he flew to Toronto on business. She met with him and the relationship turned romantic; she even introduced him to her mother. Then Robinson left Canada, telling her he would not be able to contact her for a few months. During that time, she moved to Germany, she said. She did not hear from him for more than twenty years.

The next contact came in July 1993, she told Brown, when her mother received a letter addressed to Barbara that had purportedly been written by John Robinson's adopted son. Barbara's mother forwarded the letter to her daughter in London, where she was now living with her third husband. "Henry Robinson" explained that John Robinson was his biological uncle who had taken him and his three siblings under his wing after his father and mother had been killed in a car accident. Henry described him as a good father who never missed any of the kids' sporting events or school activities.

Now that they had grown and established themselves, Henry explained that he and his sisters and brother wanted to write the letter to Sandre as a favor to Robinson. He said that his adoptive father still carried Barbara's photograph in his wallet and cared for her. He also said that Robinson frequently spoke about her and that he and his siblings thought it would be nice if the two of them could talk again.

Barbara told Brown that at the time she and her parents were not suspicious of the typewritten letter and felt that it was genuine. Writing back to the address that had been included, Barbara once again started a correspondence with Robinson. This time, they stayed in touch by mail and by telephone. In the summer of 1994, Barbara returned to Canada, and while she was there, Robinson bought her a ticket to Chicago. It was during this meeting that Robinson told her that the CIA had recruited him upon his return from Vietnam. While he did not explain what he did for the CIA at that time, he later told her he was an assistant director who traveled between Denver, Houston and Washington.

Besides his employment with the CIA, Robinson told Barbara that he also ran a business called Specialty Publications and it produced a magazine for mobile-home dwellers. She said the magazine was free to the public at area stores and Robinson told her he was in the process of publishing it on the Internet. (Apparently, this was one of the only factual parts of their conversation.)

Barbara told Brown that she moved to Kansas City in July 1999 and lived briefly in a furnished apartment on West 117th Street. She moved in August when the unfurnished duplex at Grant Avenue became available. While Robinson's name was also on the lease and he had a key to the duplex, she said he never stayed the night, preferring to visit her in the mornings once or twice a week. She said they also held a joint checking account at the Bank of America, even though he never deposited or withdrew any money. The only money in the account was hers.

Barbara also maintained that the sexual relationship she shared with Robinson was normal. When Brown first asked her about BDSM, she didn't know what it meant. She said she didn't have that many intimate encounters with Robinson, and could count the number of times on one hand. But he never asked her if she wanted to try anything BDSM-related and he never talked about possessing any sexual aids or toys.

While her new apartment was unfurnished, Robinson told her he could provide her with all the furniture, artwork, bedding and books that she needed. On August 23, 1999, a moving company brought the large items over to her new apartment on Grant Avenue, which Robinson paid for using a Specialty Publications check. He also brought over a number of smaller items a little at a time, saying he bought them at estate sales or that they belonged to his grandmother and had been kept in storage.

At the time of Brown's call to Barbara in June 2000, Robinson had recently told her he was handing in his resignation to the CIA and their lives were in danger as a terrorist group had recently tried to kill him by planting a bomb in his car. She was in Canada hunting for a place for them to live, she said, and Robinson was supposed to follow her up there at the end of the month.

Brown was blown away by the magnitude of Robinson's lies to Barbara. "That was a tough conversation," he acknowledged. "I felt really bad telling this woman that the person she planned to live the rest of her life with was nothing but a fraud—and very likely a murderer. She was stunned, truly stunned."

Over the ensuing weeks, Brown would speak to Sandre many more times over the phone. He and his new task force partner, Bobbi Jo Hohnholt, would conduct a lengthy interview with her in person when she came back into town. By the end of their first conversation on June 6, 2000, however, Barbara had agreed to let detectives search her apartment on Grant Avenue. All they needed was for her to sign and return a form giving them her consent. What they would ultimately find there would prove to be almost as valuable as her shocking testimony.

Meanwhile, Hohnholt was chasing down a separate lead of her own. From Robinson's storage locker, detectives had recovered numerous pieces of identification belonging to Izabela Lewicka, including her passport and high school diploma. By 10:30 A.M. Tuesday, June 6, 2000, the Overland Park detective was on the phone to the West Lafayette, Indiana, Police Department, where she asked a detective if they had a missing persons report on file for the young woman. While the answer was no, the Indiana detective ran a check and found that she had surrendered her driver's license to Kansas in September

1997 and had a listed address on Metcalf Avenue, Overland Park, Kansas. He was also able to provide Hohnholt with Lewicka's prior address and telephone number.

By that afternoon, Hohnholt had reached Izabela's father, Andrew Lewicki, a Purdue University instructor whose last name is spelled differently from the women in his family because the suffixes of Polish surnames depend on gender. Lewicki acknowledged that he had not seen his daughter since she left home in 1997 to move to Kansas City for a summer internship. He said that Izabela had cut all ties when she left and that three months later he and his wife visited Kansas to try and locate their daughter and bring her home. It was then that he discovered her address was a post office box for Mail Boxes Etc., but workers there refused to give him any information about his daughter's whereabouts.

Lewicki said he had kept in loose touch with his daughter through e-mail. While she never initiated contact, he said, she was pretty good about responding. She had written in one e-mail that she had a new husband who had bought her a new computer. Lewicki couldn't tell Hohnholt how Izabela had met her husband but said she did have access to the family computer before she left home. She referred to him as John only once, claiming he was wealthy and they often traveled to exotic foreign countries. Lewicki said the last message he received from his daughter was in April 2000, when she told him she had just returned from a trip to China.

By this point in the conversation, Hohnholt asked Lewicki for his daughter's dental records. He agreed to send them, as well as Izabela's e-mails, which he had saved. He also had Purdue University, where Izabela had a second e-mail account, forward her records. Even though the information found in Robinson's Needmor Storage locker and from her father suggested that Izabela was probably one of the victims, Hohnholt tried to remain optimistic. "There was still hope," she said.

Chapter 19

Leads continued to pour into the task force. One of the first was a tip from a local couple who recognized Robinson from the news and wanted to report that he was renting a post office box from them at their Olathe mail facility. Greg Wilson and Rick Dougan were assigned to investigate, and on the morning of June 6, they headed over to the Mailroom on East Santa Fe Street, which was just down the road from the Johnson County Courthouse and not far from Robinson's home on Monterey Lane.

Randy Davis, the owner of the Mailroom, explained to the detectives that he and his wife had been watching the news coverage of the homicide investigation when they saw the suspect on television. Both immediately recognized him as a six-year customer they knew as James A. Turner. He also said that Robinson had been picking up what he believed to be Social Security benefit checks in the names of Sheila D. Faith and Debbie L. Faith since June 1994. In fact, they mentioned that two checks had arrived the Friday before—the day of Robinson's arrest—and were still sitting in box 215.

Colleen Davis, Randy's wife, told the detectives she thought it was strange that Turner always arrived to collect the checks and had asked him once where the Faith women were. Out of the country, she was told. She was pretty certain he mentioned Australia. Dougan excitedly phoned Welch and requested a search warrant.

Up to that point, Wilson said, detectives had been very puzzled as to where Robinson was getting the money to bring all his women into town. "When we saw the checks, it all fell into place and was a major score in identifying who was in the Raymore locker," he said. "It was kind of like the fog immediately lifted and everything started becoming clear. This guy was such a mystery, yet when we started finding all of the pieces, it was so simple."

Meanwhile, Alan Beyer and a detective from Raymore, Jim Wilson, had been assigned to try and locate Beverly Bonner, whose name had appeared on several of Robinson's business records and been ominously crossed out in his little red address book. Her driver's license, which had expired in 1996, showed that she had once resided in Cameron, Missouri, about fifty miles northeast of Kansas City. They also had information from Robinson's storage locker that Bonner had once worked at the Western Missouri Correctional Center, also located in Cameron.

When they had no luck at her last known address—someone else was living there—the detectives paid a visit to the prison. There they learned that Bonner had worked as a librarian from September 1989 to May 1992. They also found out that she had been married to a former physician at the jail, Dr. William R. Bonner. None of the prison officials, however, had any idea where either of them could be found. But the Cameron police chief then told them he thought Dr. Bonner was living and working somewhere in the Ozarks, in the southwest part of Missouri.

Luck was on their side. Through directory assistance, Jim Wilson found Dr. Bonner's number in Stockton, Missouri, and spoke to him while they were driving back to Kansas City. He explained that they were trying to locate his ex-wife. "The cell phone connection was bad and we didn't get to talk to Dr. Bonner very long," said Beyer, "but he confirmed that he had been married to [Beverly] and he told us he hadn't spoken to her in over five years."

Following their divorce in February 1994, Bonner also said his ex-wife had hired a moving company to deliver all of her belongings to a storage locker in Raymore, Missouri. As part of his settlement, moreover, the doctor said he had mailed a number of $1,000 checks to his ex-wife at a post office box in Olathe, Kansas. Back at Lenexa, Beyer quickly ran Beverly's Social Security number, which he had obtained from her driver's license, through TransUnion. The credit-reporting agency spit out three previous addresses for the missing woman. The last one: East Santa Fe Street, Olathe, Kansas.

Beyer, who was aware that similar checks for the Faith women at the same address had been found in Robinson's Needmor Storage locker, knew right away that something was up. "The mail drop in Olathe had been a common denominator in this case," he said. "[Dr. Bonner] also told us that Beverly had hired a moving company to move all of [her] property to a storage locker in Raymore. When Jimmy told me that . . . I pretty much knew at that point that Beverly was going to be one of the bodies in the barrels."

That same afternoon, June 6, a joint press conference with Chris Koster and Paul Morrison was taking place at the Cass County Courthouse in Harrisonville, Missouri, where it was obvious (in hindsight, anyway) that detectives were staying several steps ahead of the news. Koster confirmed that the three barrels in Robinson's Raymore storage locker had each held a female body. He added that the badly decomposed remains had probably been in the barrels for several years. Though they did not reveal their cause of death, the prosecutors also confirmed that all five victims—the two in Linn County and the three in Cass County—had suffered severe blows to the head.

Because investigators were dealing with victims who may have met Robinson on the Internet, the investigation promised to be vast and laborious, Morrison said. Detectives were busy gathering and sifting through hundreds of pieces of evidence, including pictures and names of people Robinson corresponded with online. "In some cases, we have names but no photographs and in others we have photographs but no names," explained the Johnson County prosecutor.

Morrison also said that Robinson appeared to use two purportedly international companies—Hydro-Gro and Specialty Publications—to make his contacts. He used his real name and an alias, James Turner, interchangeably. The prosecutor asked anyone who had come into contact with the suspect using his own name, his alias or his companies to call the task force. "This started out as a missing person investigation," he said. "But now this case has taken on a life of its own."

On Wednesday, June 7, Dougan and Wilson returned to the Mailroom armed with a search warrant, where they collected the two Social Security checks. They also obtained the rental agreement, which was signed by James A. Turner, who listed his firm as Everblooming Enterprises, which apparently specialized in "agricultural products." He had also given a phony address and phone number in Kansas City, Missouri. The driver's license number provided on the form did belong to Sheila Faith.

Before detectives had a chance to inquire, Davis also told them that he and his wife had remembered seeing Robinson retrieve mail from another rental box years earlier. Checking their records, they had found a rental agreement, which had been opened in January 1994 and expired in April 1997. The name on the agreement was none other than Beverly Jean Bonner.

At a Lenexa news conference the same day, Morrison finally confirmed that one of the bodies found in barrels on Robinson's farm was that of Suzette Trouten of Newport, Michigan. In addition, he acknowledged that Robinson had been the last person seen with nineteen-year-old Lisa Stasi and her four-month-old infant Tiffany Lynn before they were reported missing in 1985. Both stories had appeared in the *Star* that morning, June 7.

For the first time, too, Morrison revealed publicly that there could be as many as nine victims—the five victims found in the barrels and a total of four people reported missing in the 1980s. Besides Lisa and Tiffany, he said, Robinson was connected to the disappearances of two women named

Paula Godfrey and Catherine Clampitt, both of Overland Park, who had vanished after going to work for him in 1984 and 1987, respectively. Morrison also said that Izabela Lewicka, a Polish immigrant who had dated and worked for the suspect until 1999, could not be found. Morrison admitted that one of the bodies in the barrels might be Lewicka, who had originally been living around the Westport neighborhood of Kansas City. "This is one of those cases that continues to unfold every day and I think it's impossible for anyone to speculate where it will end," the prosecutor said.

The district attorney also told reporters that police did not believe the bodies in the Raymore barrels were those of the missing women from the 1980s. "We're talking about a guy here who has lived in a lot of different places and has had a lot of contacts," he said, refusing to elaborate further. What he didn't say was that at least two of the three women found in the Raymore lockers were physically much heavier than Godfrey, Stasi or Clampitt.

Overland Park Captain Jeffrey Dysart explained to the press that in the 1980s Robinson was presenting himself as a businessman and philanthropist who wanted to help unwed mothers and other young women who needed a hand. "It appears as if all these women [Godfrey, Stasi and Clampitt] were just getting started in their lives," Dysart said. Morrison added that the Overland Park police had worked hard to solve the old cases but never gathered enough information to charge Robinson with a crime. They had reopened their investigation in March 2000, he noted, when Trouten vanished after telling relatives she had met him on the Internet and was moving to Kansas City for a job.

Lead No. 164 had come in at 10:52 A.M., June 7. Morrison's assistant, Terri Issa, reported to Roth that she'd received an anonymous phone tip from a caller—identified by sources as a close relative of Robinson's wife, Nancy—who said the suspect had helped his brother and sister-in-law Don and Frieda Robinson adopt a baby back in the 1980s. But as this would involve an out-of-state inquiry—the family lived in Illinois—he handed the lead to Agents Tarpley and Brunell, from the Kansas City field office of the FBI, who would co-ordinate the follow-up investigation through their Chicago field office. It wouldn't take them long to get some answers.

On Thursday, June 8, Sergeant John Browning located Arthur Buschmann, who was sitting in a Missouri jail after being arrested for writing bad checks. According to police records, a sickly Buschmann revealed during the course of three interviews that he had indeed met Robinson when both served time at the state prison in Cameron, Missouri. They began their friendship with talk about one day opening up a car dealership, he said.

Buschmann acknowledged that Robinson knew Beverly Bonner in prison and that they had gotten romantically involved after he was released. "A ball of fire," was how Robinson described Bonner, Buschmann said. He added that the couple had met at a motel on at least one occasion. In later conversations, Robinson told him that Beverly had taken a job overseas.

In July or August 1999, Robinson asked him to sell a 1988 blue Hyundai with a sunroof, Buschmann said. A girl who worked for Robinson was leaving the city and no longer needed the car. Buschmann explained that he had picked up the Hyundai from Robinson at an apartment, which he subsequently identified as Izabela Lewicka's Edgebrook residence. He said he went into the first-floor apartment and saw that there were computers in one room and bedroom furniture and women's clothing in another. It looked lived in and there was food in the kitchen.

When Browning informed him that police knew he had forged a signature to obtain a duplicate title, Buschmann admitted as much and explained that Robinson had told him he wanted nothing to do with the car. He also acknowledged this time that Robinson had told him he had to "get rid" of the girl because she wasn't working out. Buschmann said he assumed

Robinson meant he had fired her. He emphatically denied having any knowledge of Robinson killing anyone or helping him to dispose of any bodies.

Roth was somewhat reticent when it came to talking about Buschmann, who would die in custody of natural causes. He acknowledged that the police had asked the Johnson County Crime Lab to go over the Hyundai, which they were easily able to recover since Buschmann had sold it to an acquaintance. "We went after Art real hard," Roth said. "We really thought he was going to be involved somehow. Although we had our eyes on him, none of it ever panned out." In the final analysis, the sergeant said, Buschmann was nothing more than "a lifelong crook who got rid of [Izabela's] car."

While Browning was interviewing Buschmann, Bill Batt and Mike Bussell drove down to Jenks, Oklahoma, to talk to Nancy Robinson, who was hiding out at her son's house in order to escape the press hordes that had descended upon her home in Santa Barbara Estates. According to police records, John junior first met the detectives by himself at the local Arby's, telling them that he had talked with his father shortly after his arrest. "I got involved with some really bad people," he said his father told him. "You don't know how really bad they are. I'm fucked!"

He also told police that from what he had heard on the news and from what his mother told him, there was not much doubt in his mind that his father had committed several of the murders. The question both he and his mother had, he said, was whether Robinson had acted alone. He also said that if push came to shove, he thought his father would confess the truth about what he had done, if he had killed people and where the remains were.

John junior also told the detectives that the man suspected of such heinous crimes was not the father he knew. When he was growing up, he recounted, he had been spanked when he did wrong but was never physically abused. According to what John Jr. told police, his father had not been so lucky. On more than one occasion, he said, his father told him he had been mentally and physically abused by his mother, Alberta, who was now dead.

Because his father had always taken care of financial matters, he said, his mother had no idea before his arrest that he was in debt for a total of nearly $100,000. He said that what little his mother had left, she probably would lose. Things were so bad she didn't even have enough cash to make the next payment on her Mercury Moutaineer.

Nancy soon joined John junior and the detectives. Mother and son spoke about how they were aware that Robinson had helped his brother and sister-in-law adopt a baby in the 1980s. However, they had recently logged on to a Web site for missing persons and did not feel that Heather, as the adopted girl was called, looked anything like Tiffany Stasi. At the time of her adoption, the baby appeared to be only about two months old—not five months as the newspapers had reported, Nancy said. Heather had just finished her freshman year in high school, they said, and she had bright red hair and blue eyes.

Nancy acknowledged to the detectives that she knew her husband had been unfaithful on many occasions. She specifically admitted that she was aware of her husband's affair with Izabela Lewicka. Though she never met the young woman, she said she had confronted her husband about providing an apartment for her on Mur-Len Road in Olathe and he soon said he had resolved the problem. But a few weeks later, she realized that her husband was spending a lot of time on the west side of town. One day she followed him and watched as a woman she believed to be Izabela met him in the parking lot outside an apartment building. She confronted him again.

Asked about Beverly Bonner, Robinson's wife acknowledged to police that her name was familiar, but she did not know her whereabouts. She recalled that she and her husband had received a set of bedsheets from Bonner for Christmas one year. "Is this one of the girls that's dead in the barrels?" she asked, seemingly horrified.

Nancy also said she was not aware that her husband was receiving any Social Security checks from Sheila or Debbie Faith. "Who are these people anyway?" she asked. When told that her husband was believed to have cashed numerous checks over the last several years, she countered, "What has he done with this money?" The detectives reportedly told her they had no idea, unless he had spent it on other women.

Batt and Bussell also showed Nancy pictures of several women, some of whom she could identify. But others, such as Neufeld and Milliron, she did not recognize. "Who are these women anyway?" she reportedly asked. "John has basically no self-esteem. I don't know why he was looking for women with less self-esteem than him."

Upon further questioning, Nancy said she wasn't familiar with Mark Boothroyd but acknowledged that her husband had met Arthur Buschmann in prison. She commented that she didn't think they were still in touch. "I told him to stay away from [Buschmann]," she said. "He is nothing but bad news."

That same afternoon, the family released their first public statement about the "surreal events" that had overwhelmed them since Robinson's arrest. "We, as a family, have followed the events of the last week in horror and dismay along with each of you," they said in a written statement, which Overland Park attorney Kelly Ryan, who was acting as the family's spokesperson, read at a news conference. "While we do not discount the information that has and continues to come to light, we do not know the person whom we have read about and heard about on TV."

The family described Robinson as a "loving and caring husband and father, the type of parent who has never missed a sporting event, a school function, or missed an opportunity to be there with his family. We have never seen any behavior that would have led us to believe that anything we are now hearing could be possible."

They also criticized what they said was the "utterly irresponsible" behavior of the news media and asked that their privacy be respected. "Whether any allegations are proven or not, we had had no involvement and can offer no insight," they said. "We wait with each of you for the cloud of allegations and innuendo to clear, revealing, at last, the facts."

Robinson's new court-appointed attorney also made his first public statements to the press, saying his client denied the allegations against him. Regional defender Byron Cerrillo questioned whether the saturation news coverage made a fair trial possible. "One cannot go to the grocery store now without hearing about Robinson and the bodies that were recovered," he growled to reporters. "I resent the fact that people are now claiming that Mr. Robinson, either directly or indirectly, is a serial killer. There hasn't been one fact produced in the courtroom."

Robinson would plead not guilty to the current charges of aggravated sexual battery and felony theft at the appropriate time in court, Cerrillo said. If prosecutors brought murder charges, he added, Robinson would plead not guilty to them as well. Cerrillo acknowledged that he had been in contact with the Kansas Death Penalty Defense Unit, which would take over the case if capital murder charges were filed. He also argued that the $5 million bond was excessive and authorities were simply using the system to hold Robinson. "Wouldn't [murder charges] be filed already if they thought they had the right person?" he asked.

But at a separate press conference with Sheriff Marvin Stites at the Linn County farm earlier the same day, Morrison said the high bond allowed authorities to develop carefully what was proving to be an extremely complicated case. "[It] gives us the luxury of being able to take our time and not be stampeded into filing charges when we're just not ready," he said.

He said that investigators had talked to Robinson's family and some of his known associates but that no one else had emerged as a suspect in the women's deaths. Investigators had found no evidence that his wife or children knew about or were involved in any crimes. "We continue to believe that he's operating alone," he told reporters.

Morrison also said the crimes had possibly been connected to a moneymaking venture that he would not describe. One of the difficulties prosecutors faced, Morrison noted, was that Robinson had been connected to numerous businesses—at least some of them sham operations—over the years. "This case has a lot of angles," he said. "There's a sex angle; there's an Internet angle; there's also a developing financial angle that ultimately will be a very large part of this case."

Stites, for his part, said investigators had finished looking through the pond, which they had drained, and checking under the trailer on Robinson's property. They had also dug up parts of the farm in places where it looked as though the ground had been disturbed, under brush piles and around spots where dogs indicated something might be buried. They had made "no major discoveries," he concluded. That night they planned to search the barn with luminol, a substance that makes blood spots glow under a special light. They had already conducted the same process on Robinson's rural trailer.

On Friday, June 9, 2000, Johnson County judge John Anderson III—the son of a former Kansas governor, he was assigned to hear the sexual assault case pending against Robinson—met in his chambers with Morrison and regional defender Byron Cerrillo before issuing a gag order. The court also received Robinson's signed affidavit showing that he qualified for a court-appointed attorney. According to the affidavit, the suspect had been unemployed for at least the past twelve months and received $1,021 a month in Social Security benefits. It also stated that he owned land valued at $28,000, later identified as his Linn County farm.

On the same day, Brown received the consent-to-search form from Barbara Sandre, but when the detective was busy with another assignment, Roth sent Layman, Wilson and Ron Frazier to complete the investigation of Grant Avenue. Inside, they found a number of items that provided further evidence that Robinson had killed Izabela Lewicka and that it was her body in the second yellow barrel on his Linn County farm.

There in the living room were dozens of books about paganism, vampires and the occult, as well as several fiery impressionistic paintings and drawings. There was also a handwritten journal that contained several ink sketches inside. While detectives were pretty certain they knew who had created them, they would have to wait until later for confirmation. "We knew about [Lewicka's] Gothic leanings and that she was supposed to be a very good artist," Roth said. "And from the handwriting and content in the journal, we thought it was hers."

Those key findings, however, paled in comparison to what they discovered inside a Rubbermaid trash barrel in the dining room. Detectives had already recovered several photos of Lewicka from Robinson's locker and computer, which showed her very much alive, lying on sheets and pillows that matched the pillowcase found in the barrel of Unknown No. 2. Inside the trash barrel were the matching sheets, which Sandre later confirmed came from Robinson. Even more damning was the single pillowcase missing from the set. Layman called Roth to tell him the news. It was a "good end" to the task force's first week, the sergeant thought.

It was about to get even better. A little later that afternoon, Tarpley called Roth to let him know that FBI agents had just paid a visit to the home of Robinson's brother in suburban Chicago. A thin-faced teenage girl with dark black hair had opened the door. This didn't jibe with the description provided by Nancy, who had told detectives that her adopted niece had bright red hair. But to Roth, it matched the physical appearance of the women in the Stasi family. "Looks like we found our girl," Roth wrote in his journal that night. "Looks like the sick bastard gave the kid to his brother—but at least she is alive. The agents said the family wanted to talk to a lawyer so they didn't learn much. Their gut feeling was that they were ignorant of the nature of the adoption."

That same evening, having just received word from the Jackson County medical examiner that one of the bodies in the Raymore storage locker had been positively identified as Beverly Bonner, Alan Beyer, called Lowell Heath, Bonner's older brother, in Mississippi. The detective gently broke the news, saying the identification had been made using dental records. Beyer asked him if he should contact the other family members. The brokenhearted Heath replied that he would prefer to notify them himself.

Chapter 20

For more than two months, the detectives investigating Robinson had managed to operate under the cloak of secrecy. Even Morrison, Welch, Cowles and Terri Issa went out of their way to travel to the Lenexa police station whenever they needed to discuss the investigation. They didn't want a bunch of detectives showing up in Morrison's expansive office on the fifth floor of the Johnson County Courthouse—a true indication that something "big" was going on.

Tony Rizzo, the Johnson County courts reporter for *The Kansas City Star* had an office in the courthouse and was constantly roaming the halls and stopping by the DA's office. He was a friend to many and an astute reporter. It was hard enough to keep the details of the investigation from him and nobody wanted to be put in the position of having to say, "No comment," which would only have spurred him on. So the detectives had stayed away. Mum was the word pounded into their heads.

But with the discovery of the bodies on Monday, June 5, everything changed. For the first couple of days, the press was so busy catching up on the emerging details that they weren't clamoring for inside information. But soon the identities of victims not officially released and the names and accounts of people whom investigators had just interviewed were ending up on the nightly news with alarming frequency. "We had gone for two months without [a leak], and the first week of the task force, there was a flood," Roth said. "It seemed that the media knew everything we were doing."

Paula Godfrey disappeared from Overland Park, Kansas, in August 1984. *(Courtesy of Lenexa Police Department)*

Lisa Stasi and her four-month-old daughter vanished in January 1985. *(Courtesy of Lenexa Police Department)*

In 1987, Catherine Clampitt became the third woman with a known connection to Robinson to drop out of sight.
(Courtesy of Lenexa Police Department)

Beverly Bonner told family and friends in early 1994 she was moving to Kansas City to begin an exciting new job, but she was never seen again.
(Courtesy of Lenexa Police Department)

Sheila Dale Faith took her 15-year-old wheelchair-bound daughter, Debbie Lynn, on vacation in the summer of 1994 from their home in Pueblo, Colorado, never to return.
(Courtesy of Lenexa Police Department)

Debbie Lynn Faith (left) with her best friend Suzanne Lawrence at their 1993 graduation from Nicolas Junior High School in Fullerton, California.
(Courtesy of Deborah Lawrence)

Purdue University co-ed Izabela Lewicka disappeared after telling her family she was going to Kansas City for a summer internship in 1997.
(Courtesy of Douglas Studios)

In February 2000, Suzette Marie Trouten left her home in Michigan and drove to Kansas City, telling her family she had taken a job with a man she'd met on the Internet.
(Courtesy of Lenexa Police Department)

Robinson grew up in this nondescript home in the working-class
Chicago suburb of Cicero. *(Author's photo)*

As a 13-year-old,
Robinson met
actress
Judy Garland
backstage at the
London Palladium.
*(Courtesy of
Chicago Tribune)*

Robinson's 1961 senior photo at J. Sterling Morton East High School in Cicero.
(Courtesy of John Fleck)

In 1977, Robinson lived in the Kansas City area with his wife and four children and had gone into business for himself.
(Courtesy of The Kansas City Star*)*

Surrounded by family in January 1985, Robinson holds four-month-old Tiffany Lynn Stasi on his lap. He was later convicted of murdering Tiffany's mother and arranging the baby's fake adoption to his unsuspecting brother. *(Courtesy of Lenexa Police Department)*

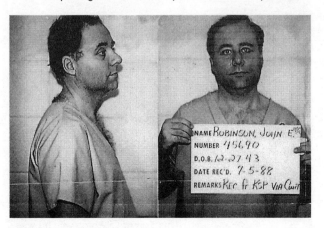

Robinson served time for fraud at Kansas Hutchinson Correctional Facility in the late 1980s. *(Courtesy of Kansas Department of Corrections)*

The investigators from the Lenexa Police Department assigned to the Robinson case in March 2000. Front row, from left: Det. Brad Hill, Det. Mike Bussell, Det. Perry Meyer, Det. Dawn Layman. Back row, from left: Det. Alan Beyer, Det. Dave Brown, Det. Mike Lowther and Sgt. Rick Roth. *(Author's photo)*

Lenexa detective Jake Boyer. *(Courtesy of Lenexa Police Department)*

The investigators from the Overland Park Police Department assigned to the Robinson case. Front row, from left: Det. Bobbi Jo Hohnholt, Det. Jose Carrillo, Det. Ron Frazier. Back row, from left: Det. Scott Weiler, Sgt. Joe Reed, Det. Greg Wilson, Det. Mike Jacobson and Capt. Keith O'Neal. *(Author's photo)*

Liberty, Missouri, probation supervisor Stephen Haymes suspected Robinson as early as 1985 and aided detectives when they reopened the investigation in 2000. *(Courtesy of Jim Barcus/ The Kansas City Star)*

Johnson County District Attorney Paul Morrison and Assistant District Attorney Sara Welch prosecuted Robinson for the murders of Trouten, Lewicka and Stasi. *(Author's photo)*

Before she disappeared, Trouten stayed at the Guesthouse Suites hotel in Lenexa, Kansas. *(Author's photo)*

After a sadomasochistic encounter with Robinson, Vickie Neufeld accused him of aggravated sexual battery and felony theft and testified against him at his 2002 trial. *(Courtesy of Mark Fisher)*

At the time of his arrest in June 2000, Robinson lived with his wife in this trailer at 36 Monterey Lane in Olathe, Kansas. *(Author's photo)*

Detectives discovered that Robinson was using the Internet in his home office to troll for victims. *(Courtesy of Lenexa Police Department)*

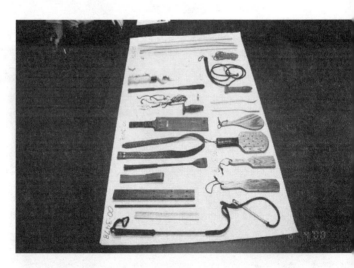

Searching Robinson's storage locker in Olathe, Kansas, investigators found an assortment of whips, paddles and other sex toys, some of which belonged to his victims. *(Courtesy of Lenexa Police Department)*

Aerial view of Robinson's 16.5-acre La Cygne, Kansas, property, where authorities discovered the bludgeoned bodies of Trouten and Lewicka. *(Courtesy of Shane Keyser/The Kansas City Star)*

The twin yellow barrels on Robinson's rural property contained the bodies of Trouten and Lewicka. *(Courtesy of Lenexa Police Department)*

Robinson's storage locker in Raymore, Missouri, where investigators found three barrels containing the bludgeoned bodies of Bonner and the Faiths. *(Author's photo)*

Morrison held a photo of the missing Lewicka at a press conference shortly after Robinson's arrest. *(Courtesy of Rich Sugg/ The Kansas City Star)*

Investigators theorized Lewicka was murdered in her apartment in Olathe, Kansas. *(Author's photo)*

The first day of Robinson's preliminary hearing, February 5, 2001. He would later fire his defense team, from left, Ron Evans, Mark Manna and Alice Craig White. *(Courtesy of Jeff Roberson/The Kansas City Star)*

Morrison and Welch at a press conference moments after Johnson County District Judge John Anderson III sentenced Robinson to death January 21, 2003. *(Author's photo)*

Relatives of Trouten and Stasi at the same press conference. *(Author's photo)*

Robinson arrives at the maximum security El Dorado Correctional Facility near Wichita after being sentenced to death. *(Courtesy of Kansas Department of Corrections)*

Besides the local press, the "Slavemaster" serial killer story
was all over the Associated Press wires and heavyweights such
as the *New York Times, USA Today,* and *Time* magazine were
weighing in. Soon they would by joined by television news-
magazines *Primetime* and *Dateline,* each eager to provide a
unique angle. Several of them agreed with *USA Today*'s assessment on June 9, that, should Robinson be charged and
convicted in the killings, "he would prove to be one of the worst
murderers in state history and the first documented serial killer
in the nation to use the Internet to recruit potential victims."

The media attention was overwhelming to the investigators, who had their hands full just trying to do their jobs.
On Saturday morning, June 10, several of the task force
supervisors—Morrison, Welch, Cowles, Meier, Roth, Reed
and Brown—met behind closed doors to discuss how to
stop the leaks. With the recent development out of Chicago,
there was even more cause for concern. "We were worried
about it leaking to the press before we could investigate,"
said Roth. "The Robinsons were cooperating with the FBI
up there and the last thing we wanted were a bunch of
reporters camped out on their doorstep."

Roth said the group suspected they knew who was dish-
ing to the media. While the sergeant declined to elaborate,
other sources in the investigation pointed to Christopher
Koster, the young and enthusiastic prosecutor from Missouri
who had a reputation among the local media for being a publicity hound. The supervisors questioned why they even
needed to continue the task force, since Robinson was already
in jail, the identification of bodies would soon be complete
and murder charges forthcoming. While they didn't set a date,
they agreed that the investigation would soon be restricted
to Lenexa and Overland Park. "The work was slowing," Roth
said. "It would seem the perfect time to disband."

Their concern was only reinforced by an article in the *Star*
that day, which mentioned that police were investigating the
1994 disappearance of Beverly Bonner, a former Cameron,

Missouri, woman who, they believed, had met Robinson
when she worked in the prison library at the local Western
Missouri Correctional Center. The article quoted Koster as
saying that one of the leads investigators were following involved a statement Robinson had reportedly made to a worker
at Stor-Mor For Less that he was storing furniture for Beverly. In addition, the storage facility worker reportedly said
Robinson had mentioned that he was renting the space for his
sister and that she was enjoying herself traveling so much she
might never return. Robinson, the *Star* noted ominously, "has
two sisters, but neither is named Beverly."

William Bonner also told *Star* reporters that he had been
contacted by investigators from the task force and said he suspected that Beverly came to know Robinson well when the
two worked together in the prison library. "He was very gre-
garious, outgoing, friendly," Bonner reportedly said. "He
came across well-spoken grammatically. He seemed like a
businessman."

Meanwhile, the article noted that upon his release from
prison in 1993, Robinson had moved to Belton, Missouri,
where his wife, Nancy, managed the Southfork Mobile Home
Communities. Their children grown and out of the nest by
this point, the couple had resided in the community on Valeen
Lane until moving to Santa Barbara Estates in Olathe three
years later.

On Sunday, June 11, a meaty three-page profile of Robinson appeared in *The Kansas City Star,* asking: "Who is John
E. Robinson Sr.?—Eagle Scout. Businessman. 'Man of the
Year.' Habitual Swindler. 'Slavemaster.' Serial Killer? The life
of the man suspected in one of KC's most notorious murder
cases has taken one extraordinary turn after another." The
news feature chronicled John Robinson's beginnings as an
Eagle Scout and promising young student at Quigley to the
dizzying array of scams that he had perpetrated in the 1960s,
'70s and '80s. It also detailed the investigation by Stephen
Haymes, the FBI and Overland Park Police into the three

women and a baby who had gone missing, as well as Robinson's frighteningly abusive relationship with Theresa Williams. Finally it noted that Beverly Bonner had disappeared after telling friends she had a wonderful job lined up, one that involved foreign travel.

The next day, June 12, Koster officially announced that Beverly Bonner was among the victims found in Robinson's Raymore locker. He acknowledged that her identity had been confirmed late Friday, using dental records, and said he had spent more than an hour talking by telephone to her relatives about the case. "Her family is obviously grief-stricken," Koster told the *Star*. "They still had hope in their hearts it might come to a better ending."

By this point, Hohnholt was getting ready to deliver some bad news to Izabela's family in Indiana. She had received a faxed report from Dr. Daniel Winter that said he had compared the dental records sent by Izabela's father with those of the body in the barrel marked Unknown No. 2. There was a match. The deceased was, in fact, Izabela Lewicka.

Hohnholt said she found it "very difficult" to call Izabela's father to break the news. "That was the hardest thing I had to do in the investigation," she said. "To do it by phone, rather than in person, makes it even worse. You keep thinking, how would you want your parents to find out?" Lewicki took his daughter's death as well as could be expected under the circumstances. "He expressed guilt over not doing more to locate his daughter," Hohnholt said. "I think he felt like they were part of the scam and he was ashamed they never recognized it."

Chapter 21

At 1:30 P.M. on June 13, Morrison and Koster held a joint press conference at Lenexa to charge Robinson formally with capital murder in the beating deaths of the five women found on his farm and in his storage locker. Morrison began by saying his office was charging Robinson with the premeditated deaths of Suzette Marie Trouten and Izabela Lewicka. They had also filed an aggravated kidnapping charge involving Trouten, alleging that he had taken her "by force and or threat and or deception with the intent to inflict bodily injury."

Although the bodies were discovered in Linn County, Kansas, Morrison noted, under Kansas law, murder charges could be brought in Johnson County if it could be proved that the two women were killed there or the "chain of events" that led to their deaths began there.

Morrison explained that the charges also stated that Trouten and Lewicka were killed as "part of a common scheme or course of conduct in which another human being was killed in a premeditated and intentional manner." The premeditated killing of more than one person is one of the limited number of scenarios in Kansas in which capital murder charges can be filed, Morrison said, adding that he was not required to file a death notice until after Robinson's arraignment, which was still months away.

Then Koster took the floor to announce that he was charging Robinson with the premeditated murder of Beverly Bonner, Jane Doe 1 and Jane Doe 2. He said he had already sent Robinson's court-appointed attorney in Kansas a registered letter saying he would seek the death penalty. To support his execution request, Koster said he intended to prove Robinson had committed multiple murders to receive money or something of value from his victims; and that the murders were committed in a manner outrageously or wantonly vile, horrible or inhuman, involving torture or depravity of mind.

Morrison and Koster agreed that the case would first be handled in Johnson County, where the investigation had originated and where Robinson had been held under a $5 million bond for the sexual assault and theft charges involving the two Texas women.

Koster also said he would pursue the death penalty in Missouri, even if Robinson was sentenced to die in Kansas. The families of victims found in Cass County had the right to see separate convictions for the murders of their loved ones, he said. "Unquestionably, even if the death penalty is successfully prosecuted in Kansas, we will transfer him back," he told reporters.

Returning to the task force headquarters after the news conference, Roth received a call from FBI's Tarpley, who excitedly told him he'd probably want to put him on speakerphone. Roth replied that he'd prefer to hear what he had to say first—and was soon glad he had been cautious. Tarpley told him that one of the agents in Chicago had just been talking to the attorney for Robinson's brother and sister-in-law Don and Frieda Robinson. As the agent was leaving the office, the couple had shown up and she was invited back in and given the scoop.

The couple had been trying to adopt for several years. At a family reunion in 1983, his brother in Kansas City had told them he might be able to help. After a couple of attempts, where things didn't work out, Robinson called in January 1985 to tell them he had found a baby. They immediately flew to Kansas City, stopping by his office at Equi-II to sign the paperwork. Robinson had also said his attorney Doug Wood was handling the private adoption and they saw that Wood's name did, indeed, appear on the adoption papers. From there, they went to Robinson's home in Stanley, Kansas, they told the agent, and picked up their beautiful new daughter. They had named her Heather, but her middle name was Tiffany. Her hair was naturally red—she was dying it black.

Roth, hardly able to contain his excitement, summoned Meier and Cowles into a private office and they called Tarpley back to hear the story again. Afterward, they went into a closed-door meeting with Morrison, who was just coming back from the news conference. Lenexa police chief Ellen Hanson soon joined a small group that now included the prosecutor, Cowles, Meier, Dysart, Reed and Roth. After they were filled in on the amazing turn of events, Morrison said he wanted the task force to fold quickly. He wanted a tight lid on the new information.

On the night of June 13, in response to the murder charges that had just been announced, Robinson's family released their second and final statement to the news media, saying they were done talking—at least until the suspected serial killer had his day in court. "Our ultimate goal is for the truth, no matter what that may be, to come to light," the family said in a release issued through their lawyer and spokesperson, Kelly Ryan. "The proper place for the presentation of information and evidence is in the courtroom. This is a place where rules of evidence apply, and imagination, rumor and innuendo are eliminated from the process."

The family pleaded with the media for privacy while they struggled to deal with a situation that they said had devastated them. They insisted they would continue to offer any help they could to investigators and they expressed sympathy to the families of the women whom Robinson was accused of killing. "To the families and friends of the victims," they said, "no matter what the outcome, you are in our prayers each and every day."

By the next evening, June 14, Dave Brown had managed to track down Mary Kathleen Norman in Canton, Texas, obtaining the first sketchy details about Sheila and Debbie Faith. Kathy Norman, who was one of Sheila's two sisters, said they had last spoken in 1994. Sheila had lived in California with her daughter for many years but moved to Colorado not long after her husband had died in 1991. While in Colorado, Sheila told Kathy that she had met a man who was very wealthy and liked to travel. She talked about moving to work on this man's ranch, which Kathy thought was in Oklahoma. While she didn't know how Sheila had met this man, she told Brown her sister was "big on using the Internet."

Kathy also acknowledged to Brown that sometime ago she had found some BDSM-related literature at Sheila's residence. Based on this literature, she said, she believed Sheila was involved in BDSM and had a spanking fetish. However, she added, they had never spoken directly about the taboo subject. She also said that she and her other sister, Michelle Fox, had each received a letter from Sheila around Christmas 1995. Both were typewritten, postmarked in the Netherlands and bore Sheila and Debbie's signatures at the bottom.

Brown didn't waste any time. The next morning, the task force put out a press release asking for the public's assistance in locating the Faiths. Anyone who knew the mother and daughter were asked to call a toll-free number with information. "According to family members, Sheila and Debbie are believed to have left Fullerton, California, in 1994 to move to Colorado," the press release stated. "After spending a few months in Colorado, they again moved to the Kansas/Oklahoma area. Family members have not had contact with them since. Debbie Faith has been restricted to a wheelchair since birth. Sheila and Debbie have known connections with John Robinson."

That same day, about sixty people packed the courtroom for Robinson's first court appearance since his arrest. The defendant, now represented by the Kansas Death Penalty Defense Unit, was not required to enter a plea. His new attorneys—Ron Evans, Christian Zoller and Mark Manna—received a copy of the charges against him and waived their reading in court. He spoke only once, nodding his head and saying yes when Judge Pro-tem Earle Jones of Johnson County District Court asked if he understood what was happening and if he would be available for a preliminary hearing on October 2, 2000.

Security was tight for the five-minute hearing—four officers stationed themselves inside the courtroom—but Robinson wore no restraints. Ever the natty dresser, his dark suit and tie would become standard attire for his many courtroom appearances in the months and years to come. After the hearing, his attorneys left the courthouse without commenting to reporters.

That afternoon, detectives hit a snag. They were already convinced that Sheila and Debbie Faith were Jane Doe 1 and Jane Doe 2. Besides the information provided to them by Kathy Norman, they had also been sent proof from the Social Security Administration that Robinson had been cashing their government checks. But then the medical examiner's office called to inform them that the dental records didn't match. There was no positive ID. "We were all stunned," Roth said.

In an incident that only strengthened the task force's resolve to disband, the press suddenly began calling to ask whether the detectives were going to issue a statement about being wrong with regard to the mother and daughter. Someone had obviously leaked the information about the dental records—though nothing of the sort had come from the task force. Since Brown had left for the day, Roth took over the calls. "It was easy—when your pet answers are 'No comment,' or 'That didn't come from this office,' or 'I can't confirm that,'" Roth said, "the conversations ended quickly. It wasn't our mess."

Meanwhile, on June 16, Detective Scott Lininger of the Raymore Police Department followed up on an article that had appeared in *The Kansas City Star*, which featured a close friend of Sheila Faith's in Pueblo, Colorado. Nancy Guerrero had met Sheila about eighteen years earlier in Santa Ana, California. Her daughter, Melissa, and Debbie both had cerebral palsy and had attended the same school. In 1989, Nancy's family moved to Colorado. Sheila, very lonely after her husband's death in 1991, had followed her friend to Colorado in 1993.

Nancy Guerrero said that Sheila was very vulnerable and attempted to meet men through personal ads and the Internet. She said that around 1994 Sheila mentioned meeting a "well-to-do" man named John. He had promised to take care of them financially. "He told her he was going to take her on a cruise, that he would take care of her daughter, that she'd never have to work, that money was no problem," Guerrero said. "He promised her the world."

In June or July of that year, Sheila told Nancy she was going to visit her parents for a couple of weeks and asked her friend if she could pick up her mail. Nancy had been with them the night before they left, helping them pack for the trip, and said Sheila had talked only about visiting her family in Texas. When she went back the next day at 9:30 A.M., they were gone. Sheila drove a white 1978 Chevy Van, Nancy said, with a lift in the middle to load Debbie up in her wheelchair.

Guerrero told Lininger that she became suspicious when she went to the Faiths' home and there was no mail in the box. She went to the post office and learned that her mail had been forwarded to a post office box in Olathe, Kansas. Nancy's daughter, Melissa, also said that Debbie had mentioned they were possibly going to stop in Kansas on the way. When she called Sheila's family, she learned that they never showed up in Texas. About a month later, Guerrero called the Olathe Police Department and reported what she knew, but she never heard back. She never heard from Sheila and Debbie, either, which was highly unusual because of their close friendship.

On Monday, June 19, the investigation was scaled back to twelve detectives from Lenexa, Overland Park and Raymore. Boyer had returned to work, Brown had been relieved of his press duties and Wilson was still on board. Reed and Roth brought them—as well as Hohnholt, Batt and Beyer—into the police department's library and told them what they knew about Tiffany. "A tight lid was still on the news," Roth said.

Finally the detectives would have a chance to catch up on the voluminous case files that had accumulated in just two weeks. Since June 5, they had been heading in so many different directions that none of them knew what their colleagues were doing. They needed to make sure they hadn't missed anything. "Reed and I took home a volume of the case files every night," Roth said. "I was trying to keep up. Joe was trying to catch up."

The next day brought a new development from Agent John Brunell, who had gone with Tarpley to help coordinate efforts in Chicago. He provided copies of the adoption paperwork and family pictures that Don and Frieda Robinson had given him. "Seeing John Robinson surrounded by his family, holding Tiffany with his big shit-eating grin, made me want to puke," Roth wrote in his journal. "Several others had the same feeling."

On Thursday, June 22, Koster announced that a second woman found in the Missouri barrels had been identified; she was Sheila Faith. Earlier tests, which compared old dental records and X rays, seemed to indicate that she was not one of the bodies, he said, but Sheila had undergone extensive dental work since 1981, which included numerous extractions. When the Jackson County medical advisers took additional X rays, they were able to make a positive identification. Koster also said that he expected to be able to identify Jane Doe 2 within a week. Asked whether he thought she was Faith's daughter, Debbie, Koster responded that it was "certainly a distinct possibility."

Friday, June 23, was the final day of the modified task force. On Monday, Reed and Batt would go back to Overland Park. The Raymore detectives would return to their department to continue investigating leads pertaining to the Missouri women. Wilson and Hohnholt would remain for a while longer to concentrate on the missing women from the 1980s. That afternoon, Roth took a call from Richard Espinoza of *The Kansas City Star*, who asked if there was anything to the fact that Tiffany Stasi was referring to Robinson as her uncle. "I refused to comment," Roth said. "But the cat was coming out of the bag!"

The story hit the newspaper the following Tuesday, June 27. CHILD MISSING SINCE 1985 MAY BE ALIVE, trumpeted *The Kansas City Star*. Scott Canon reported that police were investigating whether Tiffany was living under another name in the suburbs of a Midwestern state. Contacting the household, the *Star* had been told "no comment" by a woman who had come to the door. A lawyer who had been retained by the family would say only that they were "cooperating fully with law enforcement."

The paper noted that the case presented legal and ethical issues because the 15-year-old girl, who had recently finished her freshman year in high school, was still a minor. It also quoted sources knowledgeable about the investigation as saying that she could have been raised by a couple that Robinson knew without ever being legally adopted.

Only the day before, Roth had received the FedExed footprints of Don and Frieda's daughter from the FBI and dispatched Wilson to Truman Medical to pick up Tiffany's records. They sent both sets of prints to the lab for comparison. At 7:00 P.M., June 29, Roth was at home when he received a page from Wilson. "Bingo, it's Tiffany," Roth wrote in his journal that night.

On July 5, Morrison called a meeting at the DA's office to discuss what they had on the old cases. Reed and Wilson were there from Overland Park; Meier and Roth came from Lenexa; Gary Dirks and Keith Kerr from the Johnson County Crime Lab; Brunell from the FBI and Frank Booth from the Kansas City, Missouri, Crime Lab. Kerr had bad news. They had all hoped there would be a match on the typing from Tiffany Stasi's doctored adoption papers with those on the letters in the Clampitt and Godfrey cases. But it wasn't to be. There was no match. The group then asked Kerr to examine letters that several of the women (including Trouten, Bonner and the Faiths) had purportedly written to their loved ones and compare them with correspondence known to have been authored by John Robinson. Their big hope, with the earlier one dashed, was to link him by either the handwriting, typewriting or DNA on the envelopes.

Debbie Faith's body was finally identified on July 14. She had a hip deformity, authorities said, and had undergone surgery that required insertion of staples in her abdomen area. Ultimately, the Jackson County Medical Examiner's Office had wound up using X rays taken within one year of her disappearance to make the identification.

The news hit Suzanne Lawrence particularly hard. Lawrence, Debbie's best friend from Nicolas Junior High School in Fullerton, California, had met her in 1991 when they were assigned to sit next to each other in the school choir. "We started talking," Suzanne recently recalled. "She was a very funny person, very outgoing, and already I could see she was a very loving person."

For two years straight, she and Debbie were inseparable, Lawrence said. They walked and wheeled the few blocks from their homes to the mall, where Debbie's favorite pastime was challenging others in wheelchairs to a race and happily slurping down root beer floats made with strawberry ice cream. They also hung out in the park near where Debbie lived, where she was always getting into water fights. Then there were the countless sleepovers at Debbie's house, where they'd laugh for hours about nothing, and watch their favorite TV shows, *American Gladiators* and *All My Children.* "I practically lived at their house," said Suzanne, who still resided in California.

Debbie deeply mourned her father, who had died of cancer in 1991. "She talked about him a lot," Suzanne said. "She talked about how much she missed him and what a good guy he was. She was so close to her father." She was close to her mother, too, whom Suzanne described as her second mom. "Her mom was just a wonderful person," she said. "She was hilarious. She would always have me laughing. I would be teasing her and she would be chasing me around the house."

Two weeks after graduating from eighth grade in June 1993, however, Debbie and her mother picked up and moved to Santa Cruz, California. Her mom had met somebody, Suzanne said. The last day before she left, Debbie broke into tears as she gave Suzanne a crystal necklace. "It's beautiful," Suzanne said, her voice cracking with emotion ten years later. "She was always wearing it around her neck. She said, 'This is a reason for me to come back to you.' I still keep it in a black suede bag in my jewelry box at my mom's house."

Debbie and Sheila didn't stay in Santa Cruz for long, Suzanne said. The relationship with the man didn't work out and they decided to follow their friends the Guerreros, who had moved to Pueblo, Colorado. Suzanne kept in constant touch with Debbie by telephone, however, running up monstrous telephone bills as they chatted about everything under the sun.

By the summer of 1994, Debbie told Suzanne that her mother had met a new man. "She said she was going to drive out to Kansas City to meet up with a guy named John that her mom had met through the Internet or newspaper," Suzanne said. "She said he had a farm and she was finally going to be able to ride horses. This guy made her mom happy and she couldn't wait to meet him."

But Suzanne instantly had a bad feeling about the trip. "I can sense when something is wrong," she said. "I had a feeling that she should not go there and I said, 'Try to talk your mom out of it.' But she said, 'Oh no, it's fine. He seems like a very nice guy. My mom is happy.' She said, 'I'm leaving tonight and I'll call you tomorrow as soon as I get there.' But no call ever came."

Though she didn't want to believe it, Suzanne was certain her friend was gone long before she saw pictures of Debbie and Sheila plastered on the news in June 2000. "I started getting worried the next day when she didn't call," she said. When others tried to comfort her by saying Debbie was probably just having too much fun to call, Suzanne knew otherwise. "I said,

'No, no. That's not her. She'd call.' When you're best friends like that, there's just a connection," she said.

Debbie, who dreamed of being a teacher to the deaf or blind, had gone to a wheelchair sports camp at Saddleback College in Mission Viejo, California, and Suzanne went with her in the summer of 1992 as a helper. It inspired her to want to become a physical education teacher for the physically challenged. "She got me started in it," said Suzanne, who continued to attend even after Debbie moved out of state. "I enjoyed helping people out up there and it just seemed like an excellent career choice."

Though Debbie had cerebral palsy and was confined to a wheelchair, she never seemed to let it get her down. "She was very able to get around," Suzanne said. "Her disability didn't stop her at all. She was so full of life and seemed content the way she was that you just looked past the wheelchair. She lived her life, as short as it was, to the fullest, and I'm a better person for having known her."

Mike Jacobson, a high tech crime investigator for the Overland Park Police Department, had spent weeks analyzing the three desktops and two laptops found in John Robinson's office. Ably assisted by Lenexa's Brad Hill, they quickly determined that Robinson's grandchildren had used the first desktop primarily to play games. The second belonged to Nancy Robinson but showed signs of having once been used by Barbara Sandre. Of the two laptops, there was evidence that John Robinson occasionally logged onto one and Izabela Lewicka had used the other for a short period of time.

But it was the third desktop computer belonging to John Robinson that yielded literally hundreds of relevant files, including slave contracts, nude photos of women and numerous references to BDSM. Of special significance, Jacobson said he found test fragments showing that Robinson had logged onto Web-based e-mail as Suzette and sent messages to her family.

He also came across a message fragment from Robinson to the Michigan woman, demanding her usernames and passwords, and Suzette's reply, providing all she had.

Because Robinson reportedly had been using the online handle, "The Slavemaster" and the name had garnered such widespread media attention, Jacobson felt obligated to check it out. He ran a "Grep string search" on the computers using EnCase from Guidance Software. "A grep string search includes all of the known files, contents of deleted files and any other area on the hard drive," Jacobson said. "If 'Slavemaster' was used recently by JR, grep probably would have found it. Not to mention the lack of any plain view communications to him or from him, using that name. In all the months I worked on those computers, I never once found any evidence he used that handle."

The origination of the erroneous "Slavemaster" handle would remain a mystery. "I'd like to know myself where the name came from," Jacobson said. "I'm almost certain it's a result of people calling in to the media saying they'd talked to someone online who called himself 'The Slavemaster'— thinking it was JR. It's a great name, but he never used it. Factoid: If JR did use 'Slavemaster,' in the BDSM world, that would be about as original as calling yourself 'Smith.' JR liked to think he was rather clever."

On the contrary, Jacobson said he was not convinced that Robinson was all that savvy about computer technology. "JR is a liar and a con man," he said. "The computer was just another tool to that end and he used it well in the context of a con. He was not good enough to cover his tracks, nor did he really understand how the Internet works. Ultimately, that was his fatal mistake. I would say his computer knowledge was approximately a seventh grade level of expertise."

Of all the incriminating material recovered by Jacobson and Hill, however, arguably the most intriguing find was the pager software discovered on a floppy disk near Robinson's desktop. "I found 30+ pages of pager messages to a person I thought was Izabela," explained Jacobson, who noted that a file of this sort would not normally be saved to a floppy. More than likely, Robinson had deliberately copied and moved the messages. "Like all good serial killers, he kept everything needed to put him in jail," he surmised.

The pager messages, which Jacobson had extracted by mid-July 2000, helped to illuminate not only Robinson's delusions of grandeur but also the bizarre two-year relationship between the married con artist and the young woman from Indiana. To begin with, he told her that he worked for the government and she was under constant surveillance by the Feds (or the "Putz's," as he called them). "Tim (a Fed) just left," he messaged her in October 1997. "He was on your detail last night . . . said that some guy almost got taken down after he put his hands on you in what they considered a potential threatening jesture [*sic*]."

He also sent her messages suggesting he was in tight with the president and his wife. "Leaving DC in a few minutes," he wrote on January 1, 1998. "Bill and Hillary send New Year's Greetings. We will have a private dinner with them in the White House the day we leave for China. Miss you!" Moments later, he referred to her as his wife. "I'll call in the morning," he added. "Sleep tight, think about your hubby! Hugs and Mugs."

Robinson also spoke about his friendship with Al and Tipper Gore and his many interactions with prominent world leaders. He was always holding negotiations with the Russians, the Chinese and the Poles. "Have not died, forgot that Lec Walenska [*sic*] was going to be in town for a briefing," he told her on April 3, 1998. "He sends his best wishes."

A few days later, Robinson said that Clinton was about to make him an ambassador. "At 3 P.M. today, there will be a news conference," he wrote to her. "Billy Bob will announce my appointment as a special roving ambassador. Tomorrow an article will appear in *The Washington Post* about me . . . the article will also contain information about you, our age difference, your parents, etc. I will be receiving a copy of the article by e-mail later and will forward it to you."

Robinson demonstrated effusive affection toward his girlfriend on many occasions. "Happy Birthday to you, Happy Birthday to you! You're 20 years old and I love you," he gushed on April 11, 1998. At other times, however, he expressed frustration or anger when she apparently exercised some independence. "It really pisses me off when I have to hunt for you," he lectured her a few months later. "I have beeped you five fucking times and told you to call. My anger is building by the moment! I am tired and do not have patience for this shit!"

In the middle of all these messages, Robinson would receive a reality check in the form of pages from his wife Nancy, telling him to come home or to fix something around Santa Barbara Estates. One time, she said the county had called and was offering him a job as a meter reader. Detectives were left shaking their heads at the absurdity of it all.

The pager messages, however, helped to resolve one mystery: the blank stationery in Robinson's office containing fake letterheads from the CIA, White House, Drug Enforcement Administration, Department of Justice and State Department. "After reviewing the 'pages,'" Roth said, "we had no doubt that Lewicka had been the proud recipient of several letters from the leaders of government extolling the virtues of John Robinson."

Brad Hill also made some key discoveries in his analysis of Suzette's computer. First of all, he investigated the Web site that Suzette was supposedly developing for Robinson about a secret BDSM society called the International Council of Masters. "Like everything else in JR's life, it was a figment of his overactive imagination," Hill said. "Although there were several references in Suzette's computer, my opinion is that he had her build this Web site to keep her busy while he got her ready to go on her 'trip.'"

Hill also created a profile of Suzette's computer in the final hours of her life. He was able to see that she had spent some time on March 1 browsing various Web sites, searching for people (John Robinson) and places (Olathe, Kansas) and checking out Robinson's new online magazine, *Manufactured Modular Home Living*. "I suspect from what she was searching for that morning that she may have been suspicious of him and looking for ways to do research and find out more information," he said. Hill also found the ICQ message she had sent that morning to her friend "ahsa" in Australia, where she mentioned going to the farm.

The Lenexa detective was able to determine that Suzette's computer had been on until 2:51 P.M. CST. As Hill noted, the computer was not actually shut down at that time but unplugged as if someone was in a hurry. "There is a bit on the hard drive that is used to tell the operating system when the computer did not get a successful shut down," Hill said. "You may have seen this if your computer ever lost power while on. When it restarted, it either displayed a message or started a scandisk program to check the drive for errors. In my opinion, JR came back and pulled the plug on her computer before he checked her out of the hotel."

Hill's profile of Suzette's computer, Jacobson said, "told a story only a geek could love." More importantly, he noted that it also bolstered the investigators' timeline of events for March 1.

Morrison called Roth on July 21 and said he was getting ready to go with the Stasi charges. Overland Park had borne the brunt of trying to reinvestigate the old cases in hopes that charges could at last be filed. However, more than fifteen years had gone by and memories had faded, other witnesses couldn't be found and still others were no longer living. It was a daunting task and the detectives had gone as far as they could in Lenexa. That day, after a farewell dinner, Hohnholt and Wilson officially headed back to Overland Park.

On July 28, Morrison called a news conference in Overland Park to announce new charges against Robinson for the first-degree murder of Lisa Stasi and aggravated interference with parental custody in brokering the phony adoption of her infant daughter, Tiffany. Morrison told reporters that the child was now living with a Midwestern couple who had illegally adopted her fifteen years earlier.

The couple knew Robinson before they adopted the girl, he said, and gave him money that they thought was to cover legitimate adoption fees. He added that investigators did not believe the couple, whom he refused to name, had any knowledge that the adoption was not legal. "There is paperwork that would appear to be genuine if you didn't know any better," the prosecutor said.

Morrison said that Tiffany was now a teenager, aware of the investigation and struggling to come to terms with the situation. He said he wanted to try and limit her involvement in the case and that his office might help to arrange a meeting between the girl and her blood relatives, who maintained that they had no intention of seeking custody. "I think everybody wants what is best for this kid," he stated.

The prosecutor also said that detectives in Overland Park and Lenexa were continuing to investigate the disappearances of Catherine Clampitt and Paula Godfrey. While they had also investigated Lisa and Tiffany's disappearances in the 1980s, Overland Park police chief John Douglass said, "It wouldn't have been possible to prosecute then, with much less evidence."

Tiffany's family—still unnamed—released a statement through Agent Tarpley, who read it aloud after Morrison had announced the new charges: "We love our daughter very much. Since her adoption, which was never kept from her, we have always assumed that as she became an adult, she would be curious about her birth family. Because we were unaware whom her birth family was, it was our intention to assist her in any way possible in her efforts in identifying and locating them."

The couple, through Tarpley, also appealed for the media's continued cooperation in protecting the girl from publicity: "The circumstances surrounding the investigation of John Robinson are as distressing to our immediate family as they are to the other families victimized. Our daughter is aware of the investigation and we are doing our best to help her through this difficult time. We hope our daughter's privacy, and ours, will be respected. As her parents, we will protect her right to a private life as best we can. We only hope that the media will also respect the need to keep this matter private."

Stasi's sister-in-law Kathy Klinginsmith, who had reported Lisa and Tiffany missing in 1985, was among the girl's relatives who attended the emotional news conference. She said she was relieved to learn that Tiffany was still alive. "I've thought about [Tiffany] every day," she reportedly said afterward. "It's something you carry with you. I'm just glad that my niece is alive and I just want to see her." Klinginsmith, who was with her fourteen-year-old son, Paul, said she wanted Tiffany to know she had a big extended family and "we all love her."

On August 23, the *Star* finally broke the story that Tiffany Stasi had grown up as Heather Robinson, the adopted daughter of Robinson's brother and sister-in-law. The newspaper acknowledged that it had sat on the shocking development for two months out of respect for the teenager's privacy. However, it argued that her identity had become public when "Tiffany Stasi, a.k.a. Heather Robinson" was one of more than 300 names added to the DA's endorsed witness list. The newspaper noted that Heather Robinson's adoptive parents had also been added to the list but did not name them.

At the time, Morrison was quoted as saying that prosecutors probably were not required to list both names for the girl but would not say why they had. Much later, however, he confirmed that his assistant district attorney John Cowles had added Tiffany's adopted name to the list by mistake. "I know it was inadvertent," Morrison said. "But there's no doubt about the fact that it created a bit of a stir because we had been hypersensitive about trying to protect that kid's identity. There wasn't any reason at that stage to endorse her."

Indeed, Carl Stasi was not pleased when the *Star* called

for his reaction to the news. Under a tentative agreement brokered by Morrison, he had only recently consented to a blood test which proved that he was Tiffany's father. In return, her adoptive parents had said they would allow him to get in touch with her for a possible meeting. "I'm just upset, okay? . . . You can't even imagine how I feel," Stasi reportedly said.

And Karen Moore, Lisa Stasi's aunt, appealed to the media to respect the child's privacy. "She's fifteen years old," she said. "She's got to be having a really tough time with this. School is getting ready to start and it's got to be very hard for her. I'm hoping everyone will be just as delicate with her now as they have been for the past couple of months."

Over the fall, Lisa and Carl's relatives attempted several times to contact Heather Robinson. Tiffany's biological father wrote to the girl on her sixteenth birthday. His sister, Kathy Klinginsmith, also wrote several times, sending gifts and a flower basket for Halloween. But there had been no reply. "The only thing I can assume is that they are trying to stall and delay all they can," Seth Shumaker, Carl Stasi's attorney in Kirksville, Missouri, told *The Kansas City Star*. "It's frustrating. You believe people are telling you the truth and dealing with you in a gentlemanly manner, and then their promises don't hold up. It pushes you to an adversarial position."

Her maternal grandmother, Pat Sylvester, had better luck. She had received a card from the family but refused to disclose whether it was from Heather or her parents and what it had said. She noted that she was just trying to be patient and hoped one day to meet her granddaughter.

Chapter 22

The preliminary hearing would be postponed twice, first from October 2, 2000, to November 13, 2000, and again—once and for all—to February 5, 2001. Over the course of five days in the midst of particularly harsh winter weather, prosecutors called fifty witnesses and outlined a strong circumstantial case against Robinson, who was ably represented by attorneys Ron Evans and Mark Manna of the Kansas Death Penalty Defense Unit, along with attorney Alice Craig White.

On March 2, 2001, Johnson County district judge John Anderson III ruled that prosecutors had established probable cause to proceed with trial on seven felony charges, including two counts of capital murder in Trouten and Lewicka's deaths and one count of first-degree murder in Stasi's death. Robinson avoided a capital murder charge in Stasi's case because Kansas did not have capital punishment at the time of her disappearance in 1985.

The capital murder charges involving Trouten and Lewicka were based on the allegation that their deaths were part of a common scheme or course of conduct involving Stasi and the three women found in Robinson's Missouri storage locker. Despite the absence of a body, Anderson noted, there was enough circumstantial evidence to establish probable cause that Stasi was dead and Robinson was responsible.

Anderson also ruled that there was probable cause for one count of aggravated kidnapping involving Trouten, one count of aggravated interference with parental custody involving

Stasi's adoption and one count each of aggravated sexual battery and felony theft involving his encounter with Neufeld. The judge sided with defense attorneys in only one instance, dismissing the aggravated sexual battery charge involving Milliron whose testimony at the preliminary hearing did not convince the court that her sadomasochistic encounter with Robinson was nonconsensual.

Defense attorneys had maintained in legal filings that the evidence was insufficient to show that any crimes occurred in Johnson County. But Anderson agreed with prosecutors that virtually all of the evidence showed Robinson's involvement with the women was in Johnson County and that Linn County was nothing more than a dumping ground for bodies. "The court is convinced that the venue is proper," he said.

Anderson entered pleas of not guilty on Robinson's behalf after defense attorney Ron Evans said his client would "stand silent" to the charges. Morrison then handed Robinson's attorneys written notice that he would seek the death penalty if Robinson was to be convicted. The defendant only spoke once at the Friday-morning hearing. When asked by the judge whether he agreed to waive his right to a speedy trial within ninety days, Robinson said, "That's right, Your Honor."

The judge's ruling coincided with an event of momentous significance to those involved. ADA Sara Welch had been prosecuting an aggravated robbery case out of Lenexa and one of Roth's detectives was scheduled to testify. However, he had a family event he wanted to attend that, as luck would have it, was right in the middle of her trial. The detective had gone to Roth to solicit his help in the matter. Roth called Welch, and after complaining a little bit, she said she'd do what she could.

"I went out of my way to get one of Rick's detectives on and off the stand so he could attend some music function at which his daughter was performing," Welch remembered. "It was a hassle, but I did it. I was none too gracious about it. You have to understand that when I am in a jury trial, nothing else matters.

Sick kids, wives in labor, natural disasters and world war all take a backseat to one of my jury trials. So working my witness schedule around to accommodate a band concert was above and beyond the call of duty as far as I was concerned."

On March 2, 2001, Welch sent Roth an e-mail, saying she felt he owed her a thank-you for helping out his detective. Roth, whose divorce had become final two months earlier, immediately responded with an offer of lunch. She replied that DA Morrison was already taking her to lunch along with the rest of the "Dixie Chicks" (Roth's nicknames for Sara, Terri Issa and Linda Carter, who would later serve as witness coordinator for the trial). However, she agreed to have a drink after work, which turned into a nice evening meal.

"I should point out how horrified I was when Sara asked me to take her to the restaurant in my vehicle," Roth said. "I had an old beat-up truck with a muffler about to fall off. I was also worried about how she would crawl up in it. There were no running boards and she still was not getting around real well (due to her back surgery a year earlier). But she was a trouper and climbed up and off we went. I tried to head out slowly so my muffler didn't sound too bad."

And that, they both say, was how romance blossomed between the police sergeant and the assistant district attorney.

Four months later, in July 2001, John Robinson took the unorthodox step of hiring rookie attorney Bob Thomas. Thomas had only graduated from law school in May 2000 and had served previously as a police officer in the Kansas City suburb of Prairie Village (where he worked with Robinson's son-in-law, Kyle Shipps). The team of lawyers who had been representing Robinson subsequently filed a motion to withdraw from the case, saying that since he had hired his own attorney, he was no longer considered indigent and eligible for the services of the state-financed Kansas Death Penalty Defense Unit.

Concerned that Thomas's lack of experience would be certain grounds for an appeal, Paul Morrison insisted that Thomas be provided some assistance. Even though Thomas was a "fine young attorney," Morrison said he was taking on an assignment that would be overwhelming for any single lawyer—even one who had substantial experience with capital cases. Thomas had only a few jury trials under his belt and never had defended anyone facing the death penalty. "I don't want to try this case twice and I know he doesn't, either," Morrison argued.

Judge Anderson called the situation a head-on clash between the two parts of the Sixth Amendment. Robinson had the right to hire any lawyer he wanted, the judge explained. But he also had the right to be represented by a lawyer with the necessary qualifications for a complex capital murder case. He asked Evans whether he or other lawyers from his office would be willing to remain on the case as co-counsel to Thomas, who had insisted on being the lead attorney. Evans, however, repeated his earlier stance that it was not a "workable situation," since Robinson had hired his own attorney, which made him ineligible for representation from the state-financed office. "I don't see any statutory mechanism that allows you to keep us," Evans told the judge.

After meeting privately with Robinson and his new attorney a few days later, Judge Anderson said he had determined that the defendant was "partly indigent"—in that there was no way he could afford to pay for effective representation—and therefore qualified to receive appointed legal assistance. He allowed the Kansas Death Penalty Defense Unit to withdraw from the case. The fact that Robinson could have kept the unit's services for free but chose to hire a private lawyer "speaks for the relationship between Mr. Robinson and our office," Evans told the judge.

Because Kansas had only reinstated the death penalty in 1994, only a few lawyers in the state had even handled capital cases. So it wasn't terribly surprising that Judge Anderson appointed on August 1 two Missouri attorneys, Sean O'Brien and Patrick Berrigan, to assist Thomas in the complex case.

Both men had extensive capital trial experience in Missouri,
where the death penalty had been reinstated in the 1970s. "I
have met both Mr. O'Brien and Mr. Berrigan," Thomas said
at the time. "I'm extremely happy with the judge's decision
and I think we'll work very well together."

Robinson became only the second capital murder defendant
in the state to hire a private attorney. The first was Debora
Green, the Prairie Village doctor charged with killing two of her
children in 1995. Ironically, O'Brien had been the one called in
to that case to assist Kevin Moriarty and Dennis Moore—
Morrison's former boss and now a U.S. congressman. O'Brien
was considered one of the best in his field, a truly superb
attorney who was passionately opposed to the death penalty.

Berrigan had equally impressive credentials. At the time of
his appointment to the Robinson case in the summer of 2001,
he was defending Keith Nelson, the man charged in the high-
profile kidnapping and death of a young local woman,
Pamela Butler. He had also argued successfully against capital punishment in a recent federal case in which two other
defendants were sentenced to death, going so far as to travel
to South America to record statements from the man's family
and friends, which he then played for the sympathetic jury.

Of course, Robinson's new attorneys could hardly be expected to digest the twenty-five thousand pages of court
documents in time for a previously scheduled January 14,
2002, trial, and within a few weeks Judge Anderson reluctantly agreed to postpone once again. Robinson's Johnson
County trial was now slated for September 16, 2002, and authorities predicted it would last about six weeks—including
jury selection. The judge was adamant there would be no
more delays. "I will consider this date locked in," he said.

That didn't stop Robinson from trying to postpone the proceedings, however. On February 21, 2002, seven months after
he'd agreed to take on the case, Bob Thomas asked the judge
for permission to withdraw, citing a potential conflict of interest. According to court documents, he argued that one of

his previous clients who had been in jail with Robinson could be called as a witness because he was claiming that the defendant told him crime details no one else knew.

Thomas was referring to a convicted thief named Marvin Ray. In a letter to prosecutors in the summer of 2001, Ray apparently had offered to testify about his conversations with Robinson while the two were incarcerated at the Johnson County Jail. However, a subsequent search of Ray's cell turned up a three-page handwritten letter in which Ray allegedly admitted he had helped a woman and a man—not Robinson—take the bodies of two women from Topeka to a farm in Linn County, Kansas, in exchange for two pounds of crack cocaine.

In the February 21 hearing, Thomas complained that prosecutors had turned the letter over to him only the week before, and he said he felt he could not continue to represent Robinson and maintain his ethical obligation to his former client. Based on his withdrawal request, Berrigan and O'Brien, the two defense lawyers who had been appointed to help Thomas, asked the judge to postpone the trial by yet another four months because they would have to shoulder Thomas's workload.

However, Morrison said the state had no intention of calling Ray as a witness. Robinson had made veiled allegations that others had information about the women's deaths, but authorities didn't believe him. "We absolutely believe Mr. Robinson manufactured that evidence," Morrison said of the letter found in Ray's jail cell. When Morrison said he wanted to file written objections to the motions, the judge agreed to take up the matter on Thursday, February 28, 2002.

The following week, after reading Morrison's objections, Judge Anderson agreed to dismiss Thomas from the defense team, but only after Robinson had agreed.

"Do you, then, discharge Mr. Thomas as your attorney?" the judge asked the defendant.

After conferring with Thomas, Robinson replied, "Yes, sir, Your Honor."

Berrigan and O'Brien then asked again for more time to prepare for trial, noting that they had been planning to conduct only the sentencing phase of the trial. "We're not lazy fellows," Berrigan argued. "We're willing to work hard on behalf of Mr. Robinson. But we also think we need to be prepared."

However, Anderson denied their motion for a continuance, echoing the argument Morrison had made that there was still plenty of time for the defense attorneys to prepare in the seven months before the trial. But he appointed Jason Billam, a young redheaded associate of Berrigan's, to replace Thomas, since neither Berrigan nor O'Brien was licensed to practice in Kansas. "The division of labor that occurred was something that occurred among counsel," the judge said. "It was my expectation that appointed counsel were going to be involved in all phases of the case."

In the following months, the defense tried unsuccessfully to change the venue of the trial and throw out evidence that had been gathered from Robinson's trash, property searches, his computers and from the wiretap on his cellular phone. They also tried several times to convince the judge to grant them more time to prepare a defense adequately.

After four hours of such arguments on July 25, 2002, in which the defense requested an eight-month delay and argued that the mountain of evidence made it impossible for them to be ready, the judge replied that he knew it would not be easy, but he thought they could do it. By this time, Joseph Luby, O'Brien's associate, had also joined the defense team. In again denying their request, the judge called them "four extremely good" lawyers who made up "probably the finest capital defense team in the Midwest, if not the nation."

About six weeks before trial, Robinson's defense attorneys quietly approached Morrison and Welch to talk about the possibility of a plea bargain: life in prison in exchange for a confession. "They indicated that they'd try to produce the bodies [of Stasi, Godfrey and Clampitt], but they didn't know if they were producible," Morrison said, reiterating the belief among law enforcement that Robinson had disposed of bodies in a location that had been excavated and covered over by concrete. "They didn't make any admissions, but I think they were all talking about theories."

In the discussion that the prosecutors held with the defense, it was not clear that Robinson had admitted any crimes even to his own lawyers, who steadfastly refused to comment on the case. But as Morrison knew, top-notch lawyers like Berrigan and O'Brien were adept at establishing a relationship with clients in which they could talk hypothetically. "It might very well be that he hadn't per se admitted anything to them," Morrison said. "But they had to at least have said, 'Hey, without you admitting anything to us right now, do we have permission to lay a hypothetical scenario out to prosecutors?'"

It was a moot point, in any case. Morrison and Welch were not interested in cutting any deals with Robinson. They held several discussions about how they would like to bring closure for the families of the three women and even discussed it with Bill Godfrey and other family members. "Frankly, I think they were surprised we didn't take [the offer]," Morrison said. "I felt pretty good about saying no. It was repugnant that someone like John Robinson thought he could continue to use [these women] as if they were bargaining chips."

Morrison also said that Robinson had been lying his entire life and he didn't believe for a minute that he was suddenly going to turn over a new leaf. Even if he actually told them what he'd done and where the bodies were located, "how would you know what to believe?" Morrison asked. "He's a guy who would take great joy in misleading us and feeding a line of BS to these families and laughing about it inside. He had no credibility with us."

By the end of August, Robinson's court-appointed attorneys had grown even more insistent, asking the judge the next month to delay the trial or else remove them from the case. They accused Anderson of being insensitive and unresponsive to their pleas for more time and said they could not and would not be ready. Proceeding as scheduled would present them with troubling ethical questions, they argued, "including whether it is moral to participate in a trial where counsel's mere presence would only serve to sanitize the execution of John Robinson."

In asking a second time for another eight months to prepare, the lawyers said they needed more time to conduct independent testing on evidence such as DNA and fingerprints, investigate Robinson's background and have him undergo a psychological evaluation. In their "unskilled attempts" to investigate, they argued, "we have stumbled across several possible indicia of mental disease. . . . At times, Mr. Robinson appears to lack a rational understanding of the evidence and charges against him."

They noted that numerous death penalty convictions had been reversed because of attorney failure to investigate social and mental history adequately. "A trial of this case on September 16, 2002, is exceedingly unlikely to produce a valid outcome," they wrote, "leaving the distinct probability that the court will have to try Mr. Robinson a second time."

They also reminded the judge that a year ago they had answered his call for experienced death penalty attorneys and suggested that they had come to regret the decision. "Had we known at that time how events would subsequently unfold, the court would have received a firm, resolute and resounding NO! in response to its request," they wrote.

But Judge Anderson was not swayed. Whether the lawyers were ready or not, he ruled on September 5 that the trial would proceed as scheduled. He denied their request for further delay and refused to allow them to withdraw. He also upheld his earlier ban against television cameras in the courtroom. He had allowed a video camera, a still camera and a microphone in Robinson's preliminary hearing but had barred the equipment earlier in the year while he considered the issue. He now said that the court had operated more smoothly without them and he didn't see the need to change.

In another move that upset the media, Anderson also ruled that jury selection would be closed to the public. He argued that potential jurors should feel free to answer personal questions candidly and said he was concerned they might be influenced by the presence of the media. In response to his ruling, however, several local outlets voiced their displeasure and quickly filed an appeal to the Kansas Supreme Court.

On September 11, as part of their progressively preposterous pretrial motions, Robinson's lawyers asked the judge to dismiss the entire panel of twelve hundred prospective Johnson County jurors that were supposed to begin reporting to the courthouse in five days.

Earlier in the year, the defense had presented a survey showing that 94 percent of the county's residents knew of the case and 67 percent of those thought Robinson was "definitely" or "probably" guilty. In the last-minute motion, the defense said questionnaires filled out by the prospective jurors only reinforced the earlier survey results. "They demonstrate widespread awareness of the case, extensive factual recall . . . and widespread opinions about Mr. Robinson's guilt . . . and the appropriate sentence," the defense argued.

While he ignored the defense request to throw out the panel, Judge Anderson granted them permission the next day to send Robinson for medical testing at the University of Kansas Medical Center, as long as it did not interfere with regular courtroom proceedings. In asking for the medical examination, the defense said that New York psychiatrist Dorothy Lewis had talked to Robinson and members of his family and suspected that he suffered from a bipolar mood disorder. "History obtained independently of Mr. Robinson reflects that as many as four generations of family members may have suffered from such psychiatric illness similar to his," the defense wrote in a brief.

Lewis, a professor of psychiatry at New York University School of Medicine, was quoted by the defense as saying that Robinson also "has a history of severe physical and emotional abuse throughout childhood." Noting that a 1990 magnetic resonance image (MRI) had found "potentially significant brain abnormalities," Lewis was recommending further testing.

A more detailed explanation of her findings was provided to the judge under seal but would never be discussed in open court. Lewis did not return repeated phone calls from this author to discuss the case.

In a separate decision on September 12, the Kansas Supreme Court reversed Anderson's decision to close the jury selection process. The court noted that it had ruled in 1981 that all court proceedings must be open "except where extraordinary reasons for closure are present."

It was a small but important victory for the media. Tony Rizzo of *The Kansas City Star*, Gerald Hay of the *Olathe Daily News* and John Milburn of the Associated Press would be in the courtroom daily to report on the jury selection process. A few authors and Kansas City's top broadcast reporters would join them, including Peggy Breit of *KMBC 9 News,* whose station had broken the story. "The John Robinson case gripped this city like maybe none other," Breit recalled. "He looked like the man next door yet was accused of incredibly hideous crimes and living a juggling act of a life that had the people closest to him completely fooled."

As the case unfolded, Breit added, it was as if one right hook followed another—a pummeling of information and accused atrocities. "The decision at our station was to cover it gavel to gavel," she said, "even though the judge made it very difficult for TV: no cameras allowed, only a courtroom sketch artist, and the catch-as-catch-can glimpses of witnesses as they came and went from the courthouse. In the end, though, I think we all agreed it was the right thing to do. Every day brought something new to the story."

Chapter 23

It was a crisp, clear Monday in mid-September when the first of twelve hundred potential jurors—the largest number the county had ever called in a single case—began reporting for duty at the redbrick courthouse in downtown Olathe. Court officials handed each potential juror a tag with a number and instructions not to discuss the proceedings with anyone. Shuffling them in large groups upstairs to a windowless fourth-floor courtroom, they began the painstaking process of selecting the twelve jurors and five alternates who would ultimately decide Robinson's fate.

Judge John Anderson III welcomed each group to his wood-paneled courtroom and introduced them to the cast of characters who would occupy center stage throughout the high-profile trial, including prosecutors Morrison and Welch and Robinson's defense team—Pat Berrigan, Sean O'Brien, Joseph Luby and Jason Billam. Even the fifty-eight-year-old defendant, looking thin and pale but sharply dressed in a suit and tie, stood and bowed slightly, offering a brief smile and a pleasant "good morning." Security was tight, with as many as six uniformed deputies standing guard outside the door.

Anderson began proceedings much like a teacher on the first day of school—asking jurors with hardship requests to stand or raise their hands. Those who did were brought back in small groups of six, starting that afternoon, to explain why they should be excused. Most of the requests came from those who said they would suffer financially because they were self-employed or had employers who would not pay them for jury duty. One gutsy mom even went so far as to demonstrate her conflict by bringing her two small children before the judge, who scarcely contained his displeasure. "With great chagrin, I excuse this juror," he said, leading Morrison to joke: "Her strategy appears to have worked, Your Honor."

One man in his seventies was discharged because he and his wife were planning their fiftieth wedding anniversary celebration. A woman whose father had died unexpectedly was released from duty after she tearfully claimed she wasn't emotionally stable enough to serve. In all, about half of the 560 prospective jurors who reported for jury service in the first two days claimed some kind of hardship, and roughly half of those, in turn, were excused. Apologizing for the time-consuming process, the judge said, "This is not the sort of thing that can be rushed."

By Wednesday morning, September 18, 2002, however, attorneys had begun quizzing potential jurors who had been passed to the second phase about their exposure to pretrial publicity and their attitudes toward the death penalty. Once again, they called upon them six at a time, spending an average of ninety minutes before moving on to the next group. "There has been a lot of pretrial publicity that arguably has not been favorable to Mr. Robinson," said Berrigan, patting his client on the shoulder. "I want to caution you: There are no right or wrong answers here. It's kind of like the Billy Joel song. We just want honesty."

Because Robinson's crimes had generated so much media attention, the prosecution and defense spent a lot of time asking potential jurors what they already knew and whether the coverage had caused them to form an opinion about his guilt or innocence. "You'd almost have to be living under a rock to not have heard of this case, if you live in these parts," said Morrison, who repeatedly asked if those he was interviewing could check their opinions at the door.

Indeed, virtually everyone said they had heard about

Robinson from watching the nightly news or reading *The Kansas City Star.* A large number who were subsequently dismissed had already made up their minds. "He's guilty as charged," insisted a woman, No. 17. "I can't imagine anything that would change my mind," agreed a man, No. 328. "He's guilty. He's sick. He's playing the court," said No. 357. "I might not be the most impartial juror, but at this point, who could be?" asked No. 327.

Berrigan took to using a chart he had devised to illustrate the two phases of a capital murder case. The state, he explained, was alleging that Robinson had committed two counts of capital murder by killing Suzette Trouten and Izabela Lewicka and one count of first-degree murder in the death of Lisa Stasi. For a defendant to be found guilty of capital murder, he went on, the state must prove beyond a reasonable doubt that the crimes were intentional, premeditated and met one of seven special circumstances outlined by Kansas law. In Robinson's case, the state was alleging the special circumstance was that the murders were "part of a common scheme or plan" involving the six women in Kansas and Missouri.

Only if Robinson was unanimously convicted of capital murder would the jury enter the penalty phase, where they would be required to consider aggravating and mitigating factors. Under Kansas law, there was a list of eight possible aggravating factors and nine possible mitigating factors. There was also a broader category of mitigating factors that the defense could choose to present. "They could include, for example, any evidence about a person's background and how they were raised, or if they were subjected to a horrific abusive childhood," said Berrigan, who was believed to be hinting at defense strategy. "The Supreme Court has also recognized mercy as a mitigating circumstance."

Mitigating factors would not have to be proven beyond a reasonable doubt, Berrigan said, and the jury would not assess them as a group. They would consider them individually and could also assign to them different values. "It's much like Lady Justice and her scales," he told them. "The jurors individually conduct their own weighing process and determine what weight to give aggravating and mitigating circumstances. The determination is up to each juror."

If any of the twelve jurors decided that mitigating factors outweighed aggravating factors, or that they were tied, the sentence for Robinson would be life without parole for twenty-five or fifty years. Even if all but one juror decided that aggravating factors outweighed mitigating factors, the sentence would still be life without parole for twenty-five or fifty years. "It's only if each juror, in conducting this weighing process, is convinced beyond a reasonable doubt that aggravating factors outweigh mitigating factors that the death penalty would be the punishment," he concluded.

Prospective jurors ultimately approved for the third and final phase claimed to have formed no opinion about his guilt or could at least set aside what they had been told and make a decision based solely on the evidence. "I will not listen to the media. I will not form an opinion," vowed a woman, No. 366. "Reports don't look too good for John Robinson, but they don't give the whole story," said another woman, No. 87. "I don't think anybody should be tried in the media," insisted a man, No. 140.

In addition, those who were passed on to the third phase agreed to consider aggravating and mitigating factors in the event Robinson was convicted of capital murder, ruling out anyone who said they would vote automatically to execute him. The comment from No. 129, released from duty, was typical of many: "The punishment should fit the crime." It also ruled out a smaller number of prospective jurors who were firmly opposed to the death penalty regardless of the circumstances. "I can't imagine a situation where I could vote for death," said No. 108, who was one of those excused.

The death penalty, in fact, elicited an enormous range of opinions. "I've thought about it a lot more in the last six weeks than I ever have before," said one man, No. 14, who hadn't made up his mind. Another man said he believed in capital punishment in theory but was "not very comfortable" with the idea of actually sentencing someone to death. "I never thought I would be a part of it," said No. 5. "It would be something that I'd think about every day until the day I die." One woman, No. 244, actually thought death was too easy. "Life," she said, "would be a harsher penalty."

No. 152 was easily the most radical proponent. He said he firmly believed that Robinson was guilty and should die for his crimes, but he also thought capital punishment in the United States was too benign. He recalled a case in Pakistan where an accused serial murderer of children was convicted and executed by hanging. Afterward, his body was chopped into a hundred pieces in front of young witnesses, he said. After suggesting that Robinson deserved the same treatment, he was excused.

Court officials had originally estimated that jury selection would take only a week. Within the first few days, however, Anderson had delayed the start of testimony to Monday, September 30, noting that the court would need more time for the thorough questioning necessary to selecting jurors in a capital murder case. "We have never been through a process of this magnitude," he said. At the end of the second week, Anderson again delayed testimony—this time to Monday, October 7. In a sign that they were approaching the finish line, however, he announced that the court would not need to summons the remaining six hundred potential jurors who had been on standby.

By Wednesday, October 2, after approving 83 of the more than 250 potential jurors they had interviewed, the court was ready to begin the third phase of the selection process. Calling in the first forty, Anderson explained that the attorneys would now be asking another round of questions. They would do the same with the forty-three remaining jurors the next day, he said, and then pick the panel at 1:30 P.M. on Friday. For the first time, too, Anderson solemnly read aloud the amended criminal complaint that included charges of capital murder, first-degree murder, interference with parental custody, aggravated kidnapping, aggravated sexual battery and felony theft. As he listened, Robinson removed his glasses and nervously rubbed his nose.

Morrison then took the floor and read the list of witnesses the state expected to call in the case, about one hundred in all, including family and friends of several of the victims, women who had met Robinson for sadomasochistic sex, police officers and detectives, FBI agents and coroners. He asked whether anyone had a personal relationship with any of the witnesses or attorneys on the case and, if so, to detail those relationships. Morrison also asked how many of the potential jurors were teachers or had a background in nursing, medicine or dentistry; how many had a specialized knowledge of DNA, genetics or computers. In a hint at the seamy nature of the case, he then asked if they had trouble with gory pictures and with listening to evidence about BDSM. "There will be a lot of talk about this stuff," he said. "Does anyone find this so disturbing that it will be difficult to listen?"

Then it was O'Brien's turn, who also warned potential jurors that there would be graphic evidence presented at trial, including all the sordid details of Robinson's relationships with women. He specifically mentioned that they would be shown a videotape of the defendant engaging in sadomasochistic sex with Suzette Trouten. "I see some of you grinning," he said, noting the uncomfortable smiles on the faces of some jurors. "It's kind of hard to talk about. But these are practices that happen between consenting adults. What I want to know is if there's anyone here who would have a hard time listening to that evidence and rendering a fair and impartial verdict?"

O'Brien also said jurors could expect to hear evidence that on numerous occasions Robinson had been unfaithful to his wife. He asked if anyone in the room had difficulty with the fact that Robinson might not take the stand in his own defense. He also worried aloud that too much of the earlier questioning had centered on the death penalty and not enough on presumption of innocence. "For the last two and a half weeks, we've spent a lot of time talking about punishment and it's sort of like putting the cart before the horse," he said. "I'm concerned that some of you might think that's all this case is about. Are there any people here who think Robinson is guilty [but haven't spoken up] because we've spent all this time talking about the death penalty?"

After several hours of questioning, the court eliminated just seven of the forty prospective jurors. They included a Secret Service agent who knew several detectives who worked the case, a woman who was squeamish at the thought of gory pictures, another woman who said she would hold it against Robinson if he didn't testify and a man who had trouble with Robinson's sadomasochistic practices. The court also dismissed a woman who listed Morrison as one of her personal heroes, right along with George Bush and Oprah Winfrey. "Your Honor, I think he came after Oprah," O'Brien joked, proving that he might be defending a serial killer, but he still had a sense of humor. Even Robinson smiled.

The next day brought an interesting story, latched onto by media hungry for a human interest angle. When Berrigan asked if any of the forty-three prospective jurors knew each other, No. 316 stood and said he knew No. 454. "And how do you know Miss 454?" asked Berrigan. "She's been my spouse for thirty-eight years," No. 316 answered. There were peals of laughter in the courtroom and those present marveled at the odds of two married jurors surviving several rounds of the winnowing process.

Berrigan chuckled, too, but in the end he protested the ability of the couple to be independent thinkers and told the judge he was particularly worried they wouldn't be able to weigh aggravating and mitigating factors individually. "Mr. Robinson is entitled to twelve people making their own decisions," he said. "We don't need to put them to the test."

Morrison disagreed, saying that both had indicated they could be fair and impartial and had presented no hardships. "That's what the peremptory challenge is for," he argued.

To Berrigan's disappointment, the judge sided with Morrison. The couple made it through the final round, along with thirty others.

Before final selections were made on Friday afternoon, October 4, the judge listened to the defense as they renewed arguments to dismiss the entire panel and move the trial out of Johnson County because of excessive pretrial publicity. O'Brien said that a majority of the jurors already thought he was guilty, that he should be sentenced to death—or both. He also said the defense found "no comfort whatsoever" in the fact that they promised to set aside preconceived notions. "We're on trial for Mr. Robinson's life," he said. "We shouldn't be trying this case with this panel in this county at this time."

O'Brien also brought up the fact that the defense had been denied repeated requests for more time to prepare an adequate defense. "Frankly, Your Honor, we're not ready to go," he said.

Morrison, however, argued that he thought the court had allowed plenty of time and had gone to extraordinary lengths to ensure a fair trial. "I'm very comfortable we have a fair jury," he said. After hearing from both sides, Anderson denied the defense's requests, saying he thought the fifteen days of "very careful attention" to picking a jury had produced a fair and impartial panel. "Impartiality does not equal ignorance," he concluded. "It is the belief of the court that the panel that we have is fair and impartial and that we can have a fair trial."

Tension filled the air as the first thirty-six of the sixty-five finalists were summoned to the courtroom and took their seats in the gallery. To many of those watching, it felt like the final moments of a beauty pageant when, after scrutinizing and rating each contestant, the time had come to pick the winners. Only in this case, the opposing sides would be allowed twelve strikes each to arrive at the finalists. There was complete silence as Morrison and Berrigan took turns jotting down their strikes on white pieces of paper, handing their ballots to bailiff Pam Langenfeld, who solemnly carried them to Anderson and to court reporter Annette Pascarelli.

When they were done, Anderson read off the numbers one at a time. As he did so, those who had been called left their seats in the gallery and stepped to the bench to make sure their numbers matched the names on the judge's list. Within fifteen minutes, seven women and five men of varying ages had taken their seats in the jury box. Calling upon fifteen more finalists, the court repeated the process to select four men and a woman as alternates. The married couple, however, didn't make the final cut. The husband had been struck as an alternate; his wife was among fifteen not even considered. Most who were dismissed showed little emotion, but at least one woman broke into tears of joy as she left the courtroom.

While the seventeen-member panel remained seated in the jury box, Anderson stressed the importance of court orders that prohibited them from talking about the case or letting anyone discuss it in their presence. Though they would not be sequestered, he said, they would be closely supervised. Instead of coming to the courthouse individually each morning, they would meet at a central location and take a bus. They would be kept together for lunch and bused back to their cars in the evening. To ensure anonymity, they would continue to be known only by their numbers. Issuing his "simple but very important" admonishments, the judge released his new charges until Monday morning.

Chapter 24

As his wife watched proudly from the courtroom gallery, prosecutor Paul Morrison opened his remarks in the long-anticipated capital murder trial with the snowy day in January 1985 when Lisa Stasi and her baby vanished after Robinson collected them from her sister-in-law's house. "He knocked on the door," said the prosecutor, rapping on the podium for emphasis. "And with urgency in his voice, he said, 'We gotta go. We gotta go right now.'" Robinson's brother and sister-in-law flew to Kansas City the next day, he said. After hearing from the defendant that the baby's mother had committed suicide, Morrison summarized, "they returned to Chicago and they raised that baby as their own."

That was only the beginning of the murderous crimes Robinson committed, the prosecutor charged on October 7, 2002. Beverly Bonner, forty-eight, of Missouri, Sheila Faith, forty-five, and her fifteen-year-old daughter, Debbie, both of Colorado, and Izabela Lewicka, twenty-one, of Indiana, had also disappeared in the 1990s after meeting up with Robinson. But when Suzette Trouten vanished in March 2000, Morrison said, her family reported her disappearance to police and touched off a massive investigation that culminated in the defendant's arrest on June 2, 2000.

Police subsequently found two of the bodies in barrels on Robinson's farm and three more in his storage locker, Morrison said. Though Stasi's body had never been found, he added, they soon learned that the defendant had arranged for his unsuspecting brother to adopt her baby.

"This investigation culminated in the execution of many search warrants," Morrison carefully explained to the court. "Discovered were many, many personal items belonging to each woman found at the Olathe storage locker rented by the defendant as well as the Linn County farm. A lot of what these women owned were jewelry, Social Security cards, identification documents, high school diplomas, birth certificates.

"Also found at the Olathe storage locker was a briefcase," he continued. "There were stacks of preaddressed letters and cards to relatives of Suzette Trouten ready to be mailed for birthdays and whatnot. The investigation uncovered that those alimony checks that Dr. Bonner was sending to his [ex-] wife, Beverly, they went into the defendant's account. Those Social Security checks [for Sheila and Debbie Faith] that kept coming for years to that P.O. Box in Olathe, they, too, were cashed by the defendant and went into his bank accounts. Evidence will show . . . that the defendant went to elaborate means to have all these letters sent from all over to make it appear as though these ladies were still alive. The evidence will show that when Tiffany Stasi disappeared, in fact, a baby was given to the defendant's brother to raise as their own by the defendant.

"During the course of this case we'll expose many elaborate scams by the defendant. Scams to steal their money, scams to exploit them sexually, scams to kill them, scams to cover up their deaths." By the time the state finished constructing the last days of each of the women's lives, Morrison concluded, "the evidence will be crystal clear that the defendant has been killing women for over 17 years."

But one of Robinson's four attorneys insisted that, although his client may have known or been sexually involved with the women, he didn't kill them. He also stressed that the defense had come into the case late and was unprepared for trial—an argument they would make several times in the next several weeks. "This is a very humbling experience because . . . we don't know what we need to know to effectively defend our client," said defense lawyer Sean O'Brien. In fact, he added, "the only thing we know for certain is that we don't know the things that we should."

Noting that Robinson's "life and liberty are at stake here," O'Brien nevertheless maintained that his client was unfairly targeted as the only suspect. "This was not a murder investigation," he argued, motioning to his client, who was sitting impassively before him in a navy pinstripe suit. "This was a John Robinson investigation. His phones were tapped. His trash was collected. They focused exclusively on him until they built a case completely on circumstantial evidence."

Some of that evidence didn't add up, O'Brien continued. First, he cited a mysterious fingerprint and blood smear on a roll of duct tape found in Robinson's Linn County trailer. DNA results showed that the smear belonged to Izabela Lewicka, he said, but the fingerprint did not belong to Robinson. Secondly, he also claimed that the barrels containing the bodies of Lewicka and Trouten required as many as seven police officers to lift them, and several people besides Robinson had access to the farm where they were discovered. And lastly, he mentioned a man who had been interviewed by police who had gotten rid of the Faiths' van, electric lift and wheelchair. The same man, he said, moved Beverly Bonner's belongings into a storage unit and sold other items of hers at a garage sale.

O'Brien also warned jurors that the trial would open a window into the secret and disturbing world of BDSM. They would hear terms like "master" and "slave" and "dom" and "submissive." They would learn that practitioners of BDSM looked for willing partners in alternative papers like Kansas City's *Pitch Weekly* and Web sites like ALT.com, that they often used pseudonyms to mask their real identities and signed elaborate sexual contracts that were emotionally but not legally binding. "Social scientists have different views about BDSM," O'Brien explained. "Some consider it kind of a harmless erotic fantasy play. Others say that people who derive sexual arousal from pain probably have been sexually or physically abused as children or had unusually cold parents. You're going to hear a lot of evidence about this culture. We're not saying that [Lewicka and Trouten] deserved anything bad to happen to them because they were involved in BDSM—it's just an important aspect of this case. We will try to handle this subject as sensitively and tastefully as we can."

In order to convict Robinson of capital murder, O'Brien argued that the state had to prove he murdered all six women as part of a common scheme or plan. Yet the circumstances surrounding their deaths were so different from one another and occurred so far apart in time, he said, that prosecutors could not possibly prevail.

"The evidence in this case isn't there," O'Brien told the jury. "Not just because of the questions we have surrounding the case but because of the circumstances of each of these women and their relationship to John, if any, is completely different and they span more than 15 years. We don't know anything that indicates the disappearance of Lisa Stasi in 1985 had anything to do with Izabela Lewicka or Suzette Trouten. This is important because if you don't find beyond a reasonable doubt that there's a common scheme or course of conduct, then you have to acquit Mr. Robinson of capital murder."

O'Brien spoke in a rambling manner about each of Robinson's alleged victims. "Lisa [Stasi] and [her husband] Carl, you'll find, had a relationship that was very turbulent," he said. "They had problems with drugs and alcohol abuse and addiction. They fought frequently and often those fights were physical. And to make matters worse, they lived with Carl's family who strongly disapproved of Lisa living there. They didn't like her. In late December Carl told Lisa the marriage was over and that he was re-enlisting in the Navy. He left Lisa alone with the baby and didn't make any provisions for their care. Carl's family thought Lisa partied too much. When Carl left town, they pretty much rejected her and she ended up in a battered women's shelter temporarily. She would stop by

Carl's relatives and leave Tiffany with them while she would go out to party."

O'Brien continued, "In January of 1985, as Mr. Morrison said, John Robinson brought Tiffany Stasi to his home and called his brother Don Robinson in Chicago and said, 'We can arrange this private adoption we've been discussing.' One of the reasons that Don had turned to John for help was he looked to John for advice and he trusted John completely. Don Robinson will testify that he did send John Robinson several checks . . . one of the things we don't know in this case is whether Lisa Stasi received any of that money. We do know that she had bus tickets to leave town for Chicago. . . . Unlike Izabela Lewicka and Suzette Trouten, there was no relationship, romantic or sexual or otherwise between John Robinson and Lisa Stasi. Unlike the other allegations surrounding Lisa Stasi, no one gained anything financial or otherwise from the deaths of Suzette Trouten or Izabela Lewicka. These cases are as different as night and day."

O'Brien turned his attention to Beverly Bonner. "After leaving her husband, Beverly moved to the Kansas City area and eventually divorced Mr. Bonner," he stated. "Beverly Bonner and John Robinson were friends. They did a lot of things together and they went into business together. She was somewhat older than he was and on occasion would affectionately refer to him as her son. Her father had been a TWA pilot and you'll hear evidence that she told an acquaintance that she had tickets that will allow her to fly anywhere in the world that she wanted for free, all she had to do was pay taxes on the ticket. She told this person, who was not John Robinson, about her travel plans and that person helped her move her things into the storage locker in Raymore, Missouri. And it was in that storage locker that Beverly Bonner's body was later found along with the bodies of Sheila Faith and Debbie Faith."

"You know the State has told me they think the motive for Beverly Bonner's homicide was financial, but we don't know that to be true," O'Brien asserted. "It may or may not be. We don't really know why Beverly Bonner was killed. We do know that at least one person other than John Robinson gained financially from Beverly Bonner's death."

(Several sources familiar with the case later said they believed O'Brien was referring to a man who was an acquaintance of Robinson's and whose name had appeared in his red address book. Interviewed by police not long after Robinson's June 2000 arrest, this individual reported that he had met the defendant in the early 1990s but didn't know him well. He said Robinson approached him in 1994, saying that his "aunt," whom he did not name, had fallen in love and was planning to move overseas. She was apparently tired of storing her personal property in a storage facility and had asked Robinson to get rid of it. Robinson asked this individual to help him remove the items from a storage locker in Raymore, Missouri, presumably Stor-Mor For Less, and to hold a garage sale, which he did at the home of a friend. Over the course of about two weeks, Robinson's acquaintance said he sold many of the items—couches, beds, dressers and a lot of women's clothing—and netted about $2,000. Robinson allowed him to keep 25 percent of the proceeds but took the rest for himself, he said.)

O'Brien moved on to the Faiths. "Debbie and Sheila Faith came to Kansas City in 1994 with a van that was outfitted for Debbie, who was in a wheelchair," he stated. "We know the van they drove was sold, but not by John Robinson. We know that the electric lift in the van that was to accommodate Debbie's wheelchair was also sold, but not by John Robinson. We know the wheelchair was sold, but not by John Robinson. The person who sold them was interviewed twice by police and apparently withheld that information. This was the same person who moved Beverly Bonner's belongings into that storage facility. Other items belonging to the Faiths ended up in a garage sale in the south part of Kansas City. That garage sale was being held by a man who says he has never met John Robinson."

"The State has told you that Sheila and Debbie Faith were killed for their Social Security benefits, but again, we don't [really] know why they were killed. We do know [that] at least three people gained financially from their deaths. And remember, nobody gained financially from the deaths of Izabela Lewicka and Suzette Trouten."

(When O'Brien mentioned that at least three people gained financially from the Faiths' deaths, he didn't specify whether he was referring to Robinson, his acquaintance and the man who held the garage sale. He also didn't elaborate on whether he knew something more about the acquaintance's alleged involvement in selling their items than prosecutors and investigators. To the knowledge of sources familiar with the case, however, the acquaintance and his friend had nothing to do with selling the Faith's property. In talking about the disappearance of Bonner and the Faiths and the disposal of their property, O'Brien is believed to have confused some of the facts. The defense attorney declined to comment for the book, making it difficult to know for certain what he meant.)

O'Brien then moved on to discussing Robinson's most recent alleged victims, Izabela Lewicka and Suzette Trouten. "It's a fact that Mr. Robinson's relationship with Izabela Lewicka and Suzette Trouten involved BDSM," he stated. "They're unique from all the other allegations of homicide because they involved consensual bondage and absolutely no doubt Izabela and Suzette were very deeply involved with that culture. As with other witnesses you may hear from during the trial . . . John Robinson was involved in that culture as well.

"In West Lafayette, Indiana, [Izabela Lewicka] was very active in the bondage and discipline lifestyle," O'Brien asserted. "She had a regular master and her best friend Jennifer Hayes was told by Izabela that she had 'a disaster with my master.' Those were Izabela's words, and that she was leaving town to seek a new life because of a relationship with her parents, a relationship with her slave master falling apart. She lied to her parents about why she was coming to Kansas City. She told them she was coming here to the Art Institute and in reality she was coming here for a BDSM relationship. . . . We also know that John Robinson paid her rent and gave her money to live on. . . . She also enrolled in classes in the Junior College. She took lessons in martial arts and fencing and art classes and John Robinson paid for those courses. . . . It's also true that she worked on a magazine that was produced and published by John Robinson called *Manufactured Modular Home Living*. It's a magazine that's . . . directed specifically to people who live in mobile home communities. John did business through a bank account for the publication, which he called Specialty Publications, and many of Izabela's activities were funded through that account. In fact, she did design some of the artwork on the covers of various issues and helped to lay out the magazine. So . . . in addition to their personal and sexual relationship, there was also that business relationship. . . . Although her first contact with John Robinson was over the Internet for bondage and discipline purposes, their relationship became much, much more serious . . . John Robinson's relationship with Izabela Lewicka lasted over two years."

The disappearance of Suzette Trouten caused police to focus on John Robinson, O'Brien said. But the prosecution's charge that Suzette had been lured to Kansas under false pretenses was inaccurate. "John met her through an ad that she herself placed on the Internet," O'Brien stated. "She placed the ad and John responded to it. It was not an ad for a job. She was not looking for employment. It was an ad for a dominant bondage and discipline partner. . . . She was obviously a troubled young woman. She had a self-inflicted gunshot wound in the abdomen. . . . She appeared to have a good relationship with her mother and the rest of her family. But . . . she frequently and regularly deceived her mother about where she was going and what she was doing and who she was with and why she was going there because she didn't want her mother to know that she was involved in the BDSM lifestyle. She told her mother she was coming here to accept a job as a nurse's aid for an elderly person for a salary that is an absolutely ridiculous salary for that kind of work. You'll also hear evidence that Suzette told many, many different stories about why she was coming to Kansas City. She owed money to her landlord [John Stapleton], over $1,300 in back rent. . . . So she told her landlord that she had cancer [and] she was coming to Kansas City because her cancer had returned. The welfare benefits were better and she could immediately be considered for oncology treatment at KU Medical Center. She told her Aunt Marshella Chidester that her boss in Michigan had found her a placement as a home healthcare worker here in Kansas City. And essentially after several rounds of half-truths with people, she told Lore Remington the truth. The reason she was coming to Kansas City was for a BDSM relationship because she had found a new master."

O'Brien reached his conclusion after speaking more than an hour. "There's just no plausible relationship between the deaths of Suzette Trouten and Izabela Lewicka and the women who died five to fifteen years before," he said in summary. "Whatever the State's evidence might be, it will not show that this is a capital crime. At the end of the case, we're going to come back and are just going to ask you to do one thing and that is to consider all of the evidence and return a verdict that, in your consideration, is truly just."

Chapter 25

Suzette's mother was the first witness for the prosecution to take the stand on the sunny afternoon of October 7, describing the close relationship she had shared with her youngest daughter, a nurse's aide who dreamed of completing her education. Wearing a pale flowery pantsuit with a pink blouse, the petite blond-haired woman nervously clasped and unclasped her hands as she testified before a crowded courtroom. "We talked on the phone almost every day," Carolyn stated. "I thought we talked about everything."

But Trouten told Morrison that she didn't know her daughter was involved in the BDSM lifestyle. "Would you have approved?" Morrison asked. "Oh no!" she replied. She said her daughter had told her about meeting a man on the Internet named John Robinson, but he was a wealthy businessman with international connections, who purportedly offered a $65,000 salary if Suzette would move to Kansas and care for his elderly father. The job would entail a lot of travel, Carolyn said.

After taking two trips to Kansas City in the fall of 1999, she said Suzette decided to take Robinson up on his offer, packing up her belongings and driving out in mid-February 2000. For a few weeks, she stayed in close touch via e-mail and telephone. At 1:00 A.M. (EST) on March 1, she called for the last time, her mother said. "I said, 'What are you doing up at this hour?' " testified Carolyn, who added that she was getting ready to close the restaurant for the night. "She said she wasn't tired and she wanted to let me know they'd be leaving in the morning. They were driving to California to pick up a yacht and then they would be sailing to Hawaii."

When two days passed, she grew worried that she hadn't heard from Suzette. Then she received two letters. The first one was handwritten just before she left town. But the second letter, Carolyn testified, was different: it was typewritten and contained only Suzette's signature. "I knew immediately that it was not from my daughter," she stated. "This was nothing like Suzette would write or talk."

Part of the way through Carolyn's testimony, Morrison announced that the state needed to put another witness on the stand. Lidia Ponce, a Mexican businesswoman who had a plane to catch later that day, briefly testified through an interpreter that she had visited her son in Olathe in the spring of 2000 and had mailed some pastel-colored letters for a friend of his upon her return to Vera Cruz. Before she stepped down, she explained that her son, Carlos Ibarra, was a maintenance man at Santa Barbara Estates.

Ponce was followed by Lore Remington, Suzette's best friend, from Nova Scotia. A thirty-six-year-old heavyset woman with shoulder-length brown hair and bangs, she explained to Assistant District Attorney Sara Welch that she had sought contact with Robinson "to get as much information as I could about Suzette."

Her voice cracked with emotion as she talked about her murdered friend. "I felt there was something very wrong," she stated, "and he was the only link I had to her."

To Remington's apparent surprise, prosecutors played a tape of a phone conversation she had with Robinson a few months after her friend had disappeared. On the tape, the two could be heard discussing sadomasochistic sex and Suzette's possible whereabouts. They also talked about whether Suzette was sexually involved with other men. "I'm getting a profile of a psychotic bitch out fucking people for money," said a voice that Remington subsequently identified as Robinson's.

He added, "Any master . . . doesn't want the slave to fucking be touched by anyone else."

The Canadian woman was heard steering the subject toward Trouten's disappearance. "I haven't heard squat from anyone as far as Suzette is concerned," she told him. "I've got a PI (private investigator) working on it," he replied. "From what he tells me, she went to Mexico and is sailing around. All he can do is trace the credit cards and gas receipts. . . . I just wish she'd do the right thing and get ahold of people and let them know what's going on."

Remington testified that she had forwarded any and all information she received from Robinson to the Lenexa Police Department, which had launched a full-scale investigation into Robinson.

"Were you playing him?" Welch asked Remington.

"Yes," she said. "If I was cold and aloof, he would have stopped all communication."

As 5:00 P.M. approached on the first day of testimony, Judge Anderson dismissed the jury. The court, however, wasn't done with Remington and he asked if she could be counted on to show up the next day.

"No," she answered firmly, to the surprise of many sitting in the courtroom.

Upon hearing her response, the judge slapped her with a $25,000 material-witness bond and placed her under arrest. She would be spending the night in the Johnson County Jail.

Remington returned to the stand the next morning, October 8, wearing a plaid flannel shirt, faded blue jeans and a defiant demeanor. Before the jury was called in, defense attorneys argued that some of the e-mails she had received were tainted because of questions about the time they had been sent. After listening to Remington's explanation, however, the judge disagreed. "Technology creates evidentiary problems quicker than we can create solutions," he said, ruling to admit the e-mails into evidence.

The reluctant witness admitted to the court that she had

been intimately involved with Suzette and said they had been in constant communication after she moved to Kansas City in mid-February. At some point while Suzette was staying at the Guesthouse Suites, Lore said, she was dismayed to learn that her friend was not only working for John Robinson but was also sexually involved with him. She testified to telling Suzette she didn't think it was good to mix business with pleasure.

On the morning of March 2, 2000, she received two e-mails from her friend, she said, that she immediately suspected were fakes. Remington said that the first March e-mail indicated that Trouten was off "on the adventure of a lifetime" with an unnamed master and contained the signature, "Sees ya, Suz [*sic*]."

"Was there anything about [the e-mail] that was not like Suzette?" asked Assistant District Attorney Sara Welch.

"It was not normal," Remington replied, adding that Trouten usually signed her e-mails with "Love you, babe."

About an hour later, Remington received a second e-mail that really raised her suspicions. "Caught you [*sic*] response just before I unplugged," the message read. "If you're interested in a master who is really great, write him."

Included was the master's e-mail address: eruditemaster@email.com. Remington said Trouten would never send such an e-mail. "She wouldn't find me a master or imply 'Here's a master for you,'" she stated.

Remington testified that she began an e-mail and phone relationship with Eruditemaster—who called himself JT, Jim or JR Turner—and that he sent her pictures of himself. Asked if the man in the pictures was in the courtroom, Remington identified the defendant. Sitting behind him as she did so was Robinson's twin daughter, Christy Shipps. She was the first family member to make an appearance in the courtroom.

Tami Taylor, from Ontario, Canada, took the stand later that day, testifying that she had become a friend of Remington's and Trouten's after meeting them in a BDSM chat room a few years earlier. Taylor added that she had met Trouten several times in Michigan and engaged in sadomasochistic sex with her on one occasion. Shortly after her friend disappeared, Remington told her she was communicating with a master who somehow knew Trouten, she said. "I thought it sounded suspicious," Taylor testified. "I said, 'Ask the gentleman if he knows another gentleman who would be interested in me.'"

A short time later, Remington e-mailed Taylor with the name and address of another man named Tom. Taylor wrote to him and soon heard back. "He was seeking a full-time slave," she said, noting in one e-mail that he wanted her to move to Kansas City. "He wanted somebody to serve his every whim." At one point, Taylor said she asked Tom for a reference. "I wanted to confirm that he was a genuine master and basically a nice guy," she said. Tom put her in communication with someone she knew only as Slavedancer, who vouched for him via e-mail.

Taylor said Tom also called her and left two voice mail messages. Morrison played one of the messages left on her machine, giving her a new e-mail address and checking on her well-being. The voice heard on the machine said he was "getting anxious" about meeting Taylor and wanted to hear from her soon. "I worry and I don't like to be kept in the dark," he said, sounding identical to the man who called himself JT and had been heard talking the day before to Remington.

All the while, Taylor and Remington were conferring with one another about Tom and JT. "We felt that the same man that was e-mailing me was e-mailing her," Taylor said. Both women were forwarding their correspondence to Detective Jake Boyer of the Lenexa Police Department, they said. Like Remington, Taylor said she only continued to stay in touch with Tom in order to find out more about Trouten. "I wanted to build his trust," she said. "I wanted to find out about Suzette."

"Did the e-mails continue?" asked prosecutor Paul Morrison.

"Until John Robinson was arrested," Taylor replied.

* * *

Outside the Johnson County Courthouse on Wednesday morning, October 9, a young man working for a local shock jock almost found himself in trouble with Judge Anderson when he began handing out T-shirts printed with: ROLL OUT THE BARRELS. JOHN E. ROBINSON TRIAL 2002." Defense attorney Sean O'Brien held up one of the T-shirts in court, offering it as evidence for a renewed defense motion for a change of venue. The judge, while denying the motion, voiced his displeasure with the publicity stunt. "If I said what I really felt, it would probably not be a good thing," he said.

Prosecutors quickly got down to business, calling to the stand the mysterious California woman who had struck up an e-mail and phone relationship with Robinson.

Jean Glines said she had met him years before when she once worked for his wife at another trailer park in Missouri. She had bumped into him again after splitting from her husband. She said Robinson told her he, too, had divorced his wife. The two began corresponding after her move to California in 1997. "He wanted to know if he could call me if he was feeling down because we were both in the same situation," she explained. Not long after that, Robinson asked her to have phone sex, she told the court. "I told him it wasn't my bag," Glines said, adding that Robinson seemed much more interested in her than she was in him.

In March 2000, Robinson asked her if she would send some letters from her home in San Jose, she testified. He wanted to help out a woman who worked for him who was in an abusive relationship and wanted her husband to think she was living in California. Robinson told Glines he would overnight the letters and asked if she would mail them for him immediately. She agreed to do him the favor.

Because of a mix-up at her post office, however, Glines didn't immediately receive the letters and called to tell him. It was then that she saw Robinson's ugly side. "He went totally ballistic," she testified. "He was cursing up one side and down the other. It kind of shook me up. He got so upset so fast."

Glines said that three pastel-colored letters ultimately came a few days later and were addressed to either Minnesota or Michigan. She also remembered that there was no return address but only the name Suzette or the initials ST.

Shortly after she mailed the letters on March 27, 2000, her relationship with Robinson ended, she said.

Marshella Chidester, Suzette's aunt and godmother, followed Glines to the stand and identified several of her niece's personal belongings, including a desk lamp and a yellow legal pad containing the names, birthdays and addresses of various family members. She also identified cards and letters signed by Suzette that the family received after her disappearance, including the letters that Glines had just testified about mailing for Robinson from California. "We hadn't heard from her over the telephone for a couple of weeks," she said sadly, "I couldn't understand why she hadn't called."

Contents of the letters piqued their suspicions even further, Marshella said, including odd references in a typewritten letter sent from Mexico to her and her husband shortly before Suzette's body was discovered. Chidester confirmed that the signature was that of her niece, but she found the way it was written to be most unusual. She said it was as if the person who wrote the letter wanted to convince the family that it was authentic by mentioning the brand of cigarettes she smoked. "She said she quit smoking Marlboros," she stated. "I thought that was odd. If you quit smoking, you just say, 'I quit smoking.'"

Carlos Ibarra, who worked in the trailer park where Robinson lived, testified after Chidester that the defendant had asked him if his visiting mother, Lidia Ponce, could mail four or five pastel-colored letters upon her return home to Mexico in May 2000. In broken English, he explained that Robinson had told him he had a friend who was in hiding because she owed money to a bank and police were looking for her.

Robinson said the letters were to be sent from Mexico to her family so they wouldn't worry about her.

Ibarra also told the court that Robinson had often talked about girlfriends and shown him pictures of one woman with dark hair who was tied naked to a table. "He told me he had girlfriends," he said. "He always talked about them. He wanted me to find a Mexican woman for him. He would pay rent, take care of her legal situation if she would be ready sexually for him."

Robinson had asked for another favor in 1999, Ibarra testified. He wanted his help in finding two barrels to make a fishing dock at his pond. But two or three days later, when Ibarra told him he knew where to get some, Robinson told him he had found the barrels on his own.

"Did he ever make a dock?" Morrison asked.

"No," Ibarra replied.

Carolyn Trouten returned to the stand on Wednesday and spent an emotional afternoon identifying boxes of personal articles, including jewelry and knickknacks owned by her daughter. Morrison took out the thirty-one pages of pastel stationery and forty-two preaddressed envelopes and a bag of cards, all addressed and signed by Suzette, which had been found in Robinson's Needmor Storage locker. Her mother identified the dates written where stamps would be placed as birthdays of Suzette's friends and relatives. The stationery was blank except for her signature—"Love Ya, Suz" or "Suzette"—already written at the bottom of the page.

Carolyn also described how she had tried to call Robinson several times in an effort to find out more about her daughter's disappearance. She said she had first called his cell phone in a panic shortly after her daughter disappeared, but a message said the phone was turned off. When she finally reached him several days later, he told her Suzette had decided not to take the job and had run off with a man named Jim Turner. "I knew it was a lie," she testified. "She might have met somebody else, but she never would have gone off without calling home. I thought, 'Something is radically wrong here.'"

After she contacted police a short time later, they suggested she tape a call to Robinson, which she did on April 21, 2000, she said.

On the tape, which Morrison then played for the court, Robinson could be heard telling Carolyn that he had recently received a postcard from Suzette and Jim Turner saying they were off on an adventure. "I wouldn't get nervous," he told her. "From what I understand, they were on a boat somewhere. I thought they were going to Hawaii."

When Trouten told Robinson she was thinking of calling the police, he told her that her daughter "was a big girl." He also said that Jim Turner was a lawyer who was so rich he didn't need to work. "I really wouldn't worry," he reiterated.

Carolyn then lied and told Robinson she had received a doll from her daughter.

"You did?" he asked, sounding surprised.

"Yeah, but it was sent from Kansas City," she replied.

"Well, she mighta done that before she left here," he said. "When did you get this doll?

"Yesterday," Carolyn answered.

"When was it sent?"

"I didn't really pay any attention."

"What kind of doll are we talking about here?"

"Well, she's a Hawaiian doll. That's why I thought maybe that she had gotten back."

"Oh, no, no, no. From what I understand, they're not comin' back for . . . they're, they're going to sail around the world."

"You don't think I should notify someone?" Trouten asked him.

"Why?" he replied sharply, noting that he often didn't hear from his daughters for months when they traveled in Europe. "You know how young people are today."

The next morning, October 10, jurors watched the hotel

security tape that showed the defendant returning the key to Suzette's room on the day she disappeared. The tape, presented by the prosecution, showed Robinson, looking heavier than he did at trial, entering the hotel office and tossing the key on the front desk. He sat down, leaned over, perhaps tying his shoe, stood up and adjusted his trousers, then strolled out.

Several witnesses who worked at the Guesthouse Suites testified that they never saw Trouten that day—March 1, 2000—and that Robinson appeared to be alone. Tim Herrman, assistant manager at the hotel, said he was in the office when Robinson came in to check out. He testified that the time was about 3:20 P.M.

One former housekeeper said sometime that afternoon she saw a male matching Robinson's description checking out of room 216. Isabel Clark, the housekeeper, said she got just a glimpse of the man and described him as "white, bald-headed, medium to heavy [build]," but admitted she wouldn't be able to identify his face. "I saw a male checking out of the room," she said. "He was loading stuff in his truck. It was totally full."

Clark, who had gotten married and changed her name since the investigation, also told the jury that she and her coworkers had noticed an unusual amount of blood on Trouten's linen and towels several times since the Michigan woman checked in on February 14. They first thought it was related to her menstrual cycle, but they weren't so sure when it continued for more than a week.

Morrison and Welch continued to focus on Robinson's activities on March 1, calling the manager of a rural telephone company who testified that someone had placed a call at 11:43 A.M. from Robinson's rural property to Santa Barbara Estates, where his wife, Nancy, was the front-office manager.

Janile Cosby, a former veterinarian assistant at Ridgeview Animal Hospital in Olathe, testified that Robinson brought Trouten's dogs to be boarded on February 16, 2000, and told her he was the employer of the dogs' owner. They stayed, she said, until March 1, when the defendant picked them up by himself shortly after 2:00 P.M. and put them in a small carrier. "He was in a hurry," stated Cosby. "He seemed aggravated. He was angry that the bill was as much as it was. He said he had to get to the airport and he was rushing me."

As the court broke for lunch recess, ACO Rodney McClain was on the stand, testifying that he had been called to Santa Barbara Estates that same afternoon to pick up two strays. When he arrived about 2:35 P.M., he found two Pekingese dogs in a carrier in the front office, he said. They were later identified as Suzette's dogs.

Even Robinson's wife acknowledged that she remembered the dogs when the widely anticipated witness took the stand after lunch. Under initial questioning from Morrison, Nancy Robinson said that the clerk in her office, Alberta, had received a phone call from John about the stray Pekingese. "She turned around and said, 'Your husband is playing dog-catcher,'" testified Nancy, who was under subpoena to appear as a prosecution witness. "'He wants me to call the animal control officer.'"

Robinson, wearing a white pantsuit and blue top, also testified about the baby that her husband had brought home in January 1985. "She was dirty," his wife remembered, sighing heavily and trembling as she spoke. "She smelled. You just didn't hardly find dirt under a baby's fingernails."

Nancy stated that she bathed the baby, and her brother-in-law and his wife came to pick it up the next day. Morrison showed the court a family portrait that was taken at the reunion. In the photo, relatives surrounded a grinning Robinson, who had the baby seated on his lap.

"What was the baby's name?" asked Morrison.

"I think it was Tiffany," Nancy replied cautiously.

Asked by the prosecutor how she knew, Nancy said, "Because I was told."

"By who?" he asked.

"By John."

Nancy told the court that her husband had owned a business for several years called Specialty Publications, which produced a magazine, *Manufactured Modular Home Living*. In June 2000, when he was arrested, he was in the process of turning it into an online magazine. She admitted to knowing that her husband used the alias James Turner, but she insisted he only did it "for research to get statistics for the magazine. The manufactured housing community is a very small community," she explained. "Everybody knows everybody else. If you want to find out anything, you have to kind of be somebody different."

She had also stated that on several occasions in the spring of 2000 she had visited her husband's rural property—and even mowed the lawn near the barrels where the bodies of Touten and Lewicka were later discovered. She said she also had visited the storage locker in Missouri where the bodies of the three other women were found, but she acknowledged that it had been several years earlier. In both cases, she noticed nothing out of the ordinary.

Nancy grew emotional when Morrison asked her if the name Izabela meant anything to her. "I knew she was working on the magazine," she said.

"Did you ever meet her?" Morrison asked.

"No," she answered. "But I wasn't real happy with her because my husband was having an affair with her."

"Did you protest to your husband?" he followed up.

"I'm sure I did," she said evasively.

Morrison then asked Robinson's wife if she knew what BDSM meant. More or less, she answered, but then insisted it wasn't something she was interested in. When Morrison asked if she was aware of her husband's interest in BDSM, she nodded her head yes but didn't elaborate.

Morrison said he had no further questions.

"Would you like a glass of water or to take a break?" defense attorney O'Brien asked Nancy as he began his cross-examination.

"I would sure appreciate a glass of water," she replied sweetly. "Thank you."

With O'Brien's gentle guidance, she began to tell the court about her husband's obviously troubled relationships with most of his siblings and parents, by then both deceased. She described his oldest brother, Henry junior as a "very cruel person" who "walked off and left a wife with cancer and three children." John, she said, didn't have a relationship with him. He continued to be close to his sister, Joann, and had once been tight with his brother Donald. His sister Mary Ellen, she said distastefully, "was not very clean, weighs about three hundred pounds and never goes outside her house." His father, Henry senior, "worked the same place his whole life—Western Electric." His mother, she said, "was a very cold person" and the relationship had been strained for a long time before she passed away. "There really wasn't . . . [a relationship] after our first child," she stated. "I'd kind of force him to go up [to Chicago]. I finally quit doing that."

During O'Brien's cross-examination, Nancy said she knew her husband had had numerous affairs during their thirty-eight-year marriage. She was much more cooperative with the defense lawyer than she had been with the district attorney. She told the court she had asked her husband twice to move out. But both times she had taken him back. The second time was in late 1997 when she discovered he was having an affair with Izabela Lewicka, who was working for him on the magazine. "Probably in his briefcase, I saw a bank statement and a canceled check, where he was paying her rent," she stated, crying and dabbing at her eyes with Kleenex when asked how she knew. "Usually when I found out about [one of his affairs], it was over. This one wasn't. I truly thought he would probably leave me for her."

Robinson said she even visited an attorney about a divorce but didn't go through with it, largely because of her granddaughter, who visited their house several times a week. "This was a way of life for her," she said. "We were like a second home. I didn't want to hurt her."

On the day her husband was arrested, she left for work early, she said. She had been angry with her husband over Barbara Sandre. "She had been in and out of our marriage over some thirty years," she said. "I tried to tell her [we were married]. I wrote her a letter. And she moved here."

When two detectives came into her office on June 2, 2000, she asked them: "Who are you after today?" When they told her they were arresting her husband for aggravated sexual battery, felony theft and blackmail, she said, "I thought I was going to pass out."

Robinson, crying again, also testified how she had lost her job at the mobile-home community shortly thereafter because of all the publicity about the case. Even so, she said, she still loved her husband and continued to visit him regularly at the Johnson County Jail. "I've always loved him," she said. "I don't understand all this."

O'Brien asked her if she could recall the events of March 1, 2000, the day Robinson had allegedly murdered Suzette. In testimony that both shocked and angered the prosecutors, she then informed the court that her husband had been baby-sitting his grandkids that morning because his daughter Christy had a meeting she needed to attend. Nancy said she left early for work. It was the first of the month, and as the manager of the mobile-home community where they lived, she had a lot of work to do taking in tenants' rent.

O'Brien asked when she next saw her husband that day. "Probably as he went by to pick up [his granddaughter]," she said, noting that the child needed to be fetched at school at 11:20 A.M. "My grandson, Jason, would have been with him."

When she went home for a late lunch, John was there with the kids and Christy had come to pick them up. Nancy said she stayed with them about an hour, then returned to the office. She didn't come home again until dinner.

"Probably about six P.M.," she said when asked what time

that would have been. "John would usually have dinner ready. I'm sure we had dinner."

"Why do you remember this day of all days?" asked O'Brien.

"Because of the dogcatcher thing," she replied, alluding to the animal control officer who had come to the mobile-home community that afternoon.

O'Brien gave the floor back to Morrison.

On redirect, the prosecutor asked Nancy why she had failed to mention the events of March 1, 2000, on two previous occasions when she had spoken to authorities and even during her testimony at the 2001 preliminary hearing. Authorities were alleging that Robinson had called her from the farm at 11:43 A.M. that morning, yet Nancy had just said she saw him about the same time with his grandkids in Olathe, roughly an hour away. He couldn't have been in both places at once.

Privately livid, Morrison believed she was lying on the stand in an attempt to offer an alibi for her husband on the very morning he murdered Suzette. State law, moreover, required defense attorneys to inform the prosecution in advance of any testimony that provided an alibi for the defendant. They hadn't done so.

"You said *nothing* about seeing your husband that morning!" Morrison thundered, apparently struggling to keep his anger in check.

"I guess, but I don't remember," replied the flustered witness before stepping down.

Detectives Lowther, Layman and Owsley spent what was left of Thursday afternoon and Friday, October 11, 2002, testifying about the treasure trove of items they found in Robinson's home and his Olathe storage locker, including sex toys, slave contracts, paperwork and personal effects connecting him to all six of his victims.

Their testimony laid the foundation for the disturbing evidence presented on Monday morning, October 14. The unlabeled videotape of Robinson engaging in sadomasochistic sex with Suzette, discovered by Layman in a brown briefcase in the locker, was admitted into evidence after a lengthy discussion between prosecutors and the defense.

Morrison said he wanted to show a nine-minute edited version of the tape to be sensitive to the jury, adding that he would be glad to make the full tape available to them if they wanted to watch it during deliberations. O'Brien objected, saying the edited version put Robinson's conduct in the worst possible light. He noted that the edited version showed Robinson using a medical device to administer electrical shocks to Trouten, but it didn't include the portion where she was teaching him how to use it. "The full tape shows bizarre sexual practices between two consenting adults," he said. "The edited tape doesn't do that. We believe the jury should see the entire tape or nothing at all."

On this point, Judge Anderson sided with the defense. "There's no question the content is relevant," he said. "If the defense wants the entire tape played, the entire tape will be played. This is the fair thing to do."

After hearing so much about Robinson's fondness for trysts, jurors were about to see if for themselves—whether they wanted to or not.

The lights dimmed in the courtroom as the 39-minute tape began to play on a large television screen placed in front of the jury box. It showed Suzette, in a black teddy, stretching out on her hotel-room bed in the Guesthouse Suites, the radio playing in the background as she began to masturbate. "These are your breasts, your cunt, your lips, your ass, everything is yours," she intoned softly, showing JR's initials on her right thigh.

Moments later the tape cut away to show her returning to the bed with nothing on but a collar around her neck and black hosiery. Her nipples were pierced and from them hung a chain with a dangling butterfly pendant.

"Who are you?" a voice, off-camera, was heard asking.

"Your slut," she answered.

"My what?"

"Your slut."

"Are you my slave?

"Yes, your slave."

"What does that mean, slave?"

"It means that I'm owned by you."

About this time, Robinson, naked, joined her. "Kiss your cock, bitch," he said.

She complied.

"What do you want your master to do to you, slut?" he asked.

"Anything he wants to," she replied.

"Do you know what it means to be a slave?" he asked. "You have no will of your own. You're totally owned by your master. Your body belongs to me, as evidenced by initials right there on my cheek. You're going to serve your master every morning . . . and every night."

He continued. "Your cock is your main concern. You will always please your cock. Do you understand?"

"Yes, master."

"Now I want you to get the Tens Unit set up. I want to see how this thing works while I drink my coffee."

As she obeyed him, Robinson used a whip to slap her several times on her backside. Suzette visibly cringed. "I just have a face thing," she explained.

"If I hit your face, it'll be with my hand, not with this," he told her sternly.

He sipped his coffee as she began to show him how to use the medical device to administer electrical shocks to her genitalia, jerking and jumping as he adjusted the pulse and frequency. "You've got to be an electrical engineer to use this thing," he said, seeming to grow bored.

He stretched out on his back. "Why don't you suck your cock, slut? Lick your balls, too. Do you like your balls, cunt?"

"Yes, master."

"Do you like the taste of your cock, the size of your cock? Do you like your master to face-fuck you often?"

"Yes, master," she answered.

"Take all of your cock, bitch, all of your cock."

But he switched positions after a few minutes, having her climb on top of him. "That's what you wanted," he said as she began moaning. "Do you feel your cock inside?"

"It feels so good," she gushed.

"Oh, my pussy is nice and wet," he murmured. "Don't you ever take your cock out of my pussy without my permission."

Robinson took her from behind, doggie-style. "Every bit of pleasure you get . . . is given to you by your master," he said.

"Yes, master," she moaned.

"You're just my whore, my slut, my cunt, my bitch, my slave. Who owns you?"

"You do, master."

"How do you know I own you? Did you sign a contract, bitch?

"Yes, master."

"Did you give your body to your master?"

"Yes, master."

"Did you give your life to your master?"

"Yes, master."

"Your master owns you totally and completely. You own nothing. You're just my slut. I allow you to service me because you are my slut, is that right?"

"Yes, master."

"Don't you dare let my cock come out!"

He slapped her backside several times with both of his hands. "Do you have those golf balls?" He asked. "I'm going to make you put them in my pussy and wear them. From now on you're going to be given a daily assignment, just like you were before. You do what your master tells you, when your master tells you. Do you want to come, slut? I want to feel you come, bitch. I want to feel you come, bitch. I want to feel you come . . ."

"Oh yes, please. Oh yes."

Seconds later, Robinson was finished. "Now your master feels better," he said.

In the final scene, Suzette removed the three golf balls that Robinson had alluded to only moments before. Then the tape surreally cut away once again to Willy Wonka and the Chocolate Factory. Robinson had apparently recorded his sadomasochistic encounter over one of his grandkid's movies.

Some of the jurors were clearly uncomfortable, shifting in their seats as they watched the extremely graphic images flash before them on the screen. One middle-aged woman held her hand over her mouth throughout and briefly covered her eyes. Robinson sat with his chin in his right palm, nervously stroking his cheek with his index finger. But, as many in the courtroom noted, he watched every minute of the video, from beginning to end.

Chapter 26

Retia Grant provided some welcome comic relief as prosecutors shifted the focus away from sadomasochistic sex and called several witnesses on Monday afternoon to testify about Robinson's rural property in Linn County. The simple countrywoman explained to the court she had moved next door to the defendant in August 1999. She didn't actually meet Robinson until one of her sixteen cats, Explorer, heard a loud banging and clanging coming from his pole barn in early November and ran to investigate.

"Explorer, I assume, is named Explorer for obvious reasons?" asked ADA Welch as Grant nodded her head yes.

The witness described how she stumbled and banged her knee on a wheelbarrow as she followed her cat inside the dark barn, which was located near her property line.

"Here, kitty, kitty—Oh sweet Jesus, that hurts," she recalled saying.

As her eyes adjusted, Grant realized she wasn't alone in the barn. She was startled to see a man holding a shovel and standing in front of a knee-deep ditch. A second ditch was next to it.

"How wide were the holes?" Welch asked.

"I'm a seamstress," Grant replied, "and so I know they were about a yard wide and five to seven feet long—longer than I am but not a lot."

Welch asked what happened next.

"I introduced myself and said, 'You must be Mr. Robinson,'" she recalled.

"Did he respond?" Welch asked.

"He had a very bad day, evidently," she replied. "He started cursing at me and told me I wasn't supposed to be in his blankety-blank barn and he would take care of my blankety-blank animals."

Welch asked the self-described devout woman if she could quote Robinson precisely.

"You want me to say curse words?" Grant asked.

Welch told Grant she thought this was one of those times when it would be okay to curse, causing several in the courtroom to chuckle.

"I believe he started off with 'goddamn fucking neighbors' and 'fucking animals,'" Grant stated matter-of-factly. "Those were his best words."

Welch asked her if the man she saw that day was sitting in the courtroom. "Yes, ma'am," she replied, indicating the defendant. There was more laughter when she noted: "He's the one sitting there smiling."

"After the defendant yelled at you, what did you do?" Welch asked.

"I got down on my hands and my knees and went after my cat," she said. "I figured I was having a bad day, too."

Just then, one of her eight dogs, Montana, rushed into the barn and threw its body against her, Grant said. She started to scold the dog, she said, but then realized that Robinson was following her. "I just saw the shovel and the bottom of his boots," she said.

Managing to grab the cat, she headed outside as Montana continued to stay between her and Robinson. "I could hear him breathing really loud," she said. "I felt really bad I made him so mad. I kept apologizing all the way out of the barn."

Asked by defense attorney Sean O'Brien on cross-examination if she recalled telling a detective that she had seen anguish in Robinson's eyes, Grant corrected him: "I didn't have a problem looking in his eyes and seeing great anger. There was no anguish."

Before jurors had been called in that morning, O'Brien tried to suggest to the judge that any testimony about the holes in Robinson's barn floor was irrelevant and immaterial, Morrison disagreed. "I think it's highly relevant," Morrison said. Lewicka had recently disappeared at the time of Grant's run-in with the defendant, the DA argued, and prosecutors were arguing that there were three other bodies in his storage locker in need of disposal. There was also a layer of bedrock about two feet beneath his 16.5-acre farm. "Our theory is that Mr. Robinson was attempting to find places to bury bodies," Morrison noted, "but because of the bedrock could not."

Convinced of the testimony's relevance, the judge denied the defense's motion.

Chapter 27

Dan Rundle, a forensic chemist with the Johnson County Crime Lab, followed Grant and other Linn County witnesses to the stand on Monday afternoon, October 14, 2002, to talk about the search for blood. The deputy said he and another crime lab analyst, Sally Lane, had been sent on March 29, 2000, to process the Guesthouse Suites hotel room where Suzette had stayed a month earlier. They detected several small reddish brown stains in the bathroom, on the curtains, on the bed and the mattress in the bedroom and in the living-room sofa bed. They also found a "fist-size" bloodstain on one of the sofa's seat cushions.

But while all that sounded promising—at least to some of those observing the testimony—Rundle said they could find no evidence of spatter patterns or drag marks and none of the stains they did discover were of evidentiary significance. "There were a lot of the typical stains you'd expect to find in a typical guestroom," he testified. "Nothing gave us any indication that anything really happened there."

Rundle, who returned to continue his testimony on Tuesday, October 15, said he and several other investigators from his crime lab were also assigned to look for blood, hair and skin in the three-bedroom trailer on Robinson's rural property. Beginning on June 3, 2000, and over the course of the next week, he said they found several items that tested positive for the presumptive presence of blood, including a wad of stained paper towels in the kitchen sink of Robinson's trailer. "It gave us a nice, good positive reaction," he testified, adding that the towels were packaged and sent to the Kansas City, Missouri, Crime Lab for further analysis.

The forensics expert also confirmed that a window and windshield of Robinson's yellow pickup, which was parked in the driveway of the Linn County property, and two 4' x 8' sheets of particleboard found in his pole barn tested positive for the presumptive presence of blood. In addition, he said they recovered nine knives, two chisels and a pick on the property. Though none of these tested positive, they, too, were turned over to the Kansas City Crime Lab, he said, which focused on analyzing blood and biological material that was recovered during the investigation, while the Johnson County Crime Lab concentrated on fingerprints.

That was the extent to which Rundle was asked about the prosecution's exhaustive search for a murder weapon, which never would be found.

Chapter 28

Izabela Lewicka's father took the stand on Tuesday and described his daughter as an independent and artistic young woman who insisted upon moving to Kansas in 1997 for what she called a summer "internship." Andrew Lewicki, who worked at Purdue University in West Lafayette, Indiana, said he couldn't get many details from his daughter. "She was very vague," admitted Lewicki, speaking with the thick accent of his native Poland. "All she told us was it was advertising for a small publisher. If she could find a good job after that, she might stay even longer."

Lewicki said Izabela had been born in Poland in April 1978 and was the older of his two daughters. Lewicki said he had moved to West Lafayette in 1988; his wife and daughters followed the next year. Graduating from Harrison High School in 1996, Izabela enrolled in Purdue's fine-arts program, taking drawing and painting courses, but continued to live at home.

Under cross-examination from O'Brien, Lewicki admitted that his daughter didn't appear to be happy in school and preferred to troll the Internet on their family computer at night. He said he didn't have access to her e-mail account and couldn't tell what Web sites she was visiting. "Izabela tended to keep to herself," he said. The art student was just finishing her freshman year, he added, when she suddenly announced her summer plans.

Lewicki and his wife both testified that they attempted to talk their daughter out of going, but they felt there wasn't a whole lot they could do. "She was past eighteen," explained her mother, Danuta Marona-Lewicka, who took the stand right after her husband. "She's protected by law. We cannot stop her."

She said her daughter had packed up her 1987 Pontiac Bonneville with books, clothes and several of her paintings and had driven to Kansas City in early June.

Izabela had left her parents an address in Overland Park, Kansas, as well as an e-mail address where they could write to her. When they did, however, they received no reply.

In August, when it was time for school to start and they still hadn't heard from her, they drove to Kansas City and discovered the address was that of a mailbox company, Lewicki testified. The manager refused to give them Lewicka's real address or telephone number and they drove home after a day without contacting police.

Andrew Lewicki testified that shortly after that he received an e-mail, purportedly from his daughter. "What the hell do you want?" began the note. "I will not tolerate your harassment." But the e-mail also instructed him to contact her in the future at another address, izabela..@usa.net. After that, "we exchanged e-mail messages every couple of weeks," Lewicki testified. "In most cases, it was her responding to my e-mail messages."

Around Thanksgiving, 1997, he e-mailed his daughter in Polish. "'I write in Polish because I'm not one hundred percent positive that your letters are coming from you,'" he said, translating his note as he read it aloud for the court. "'As you know, anyone could create an e-mail account and sign it as you. If you would telephone, I would feel much, much better.'"

But Lewicka purportedly replied only by e-mail, insisting that all further contact be in English. "I have told you I'm happy," the e-mail said. "I'm well. I have a wonderful job and a wonderful man in my life who loves me. I want to be left alone. I don't know how I can make it any clearer."

The family continued to receive e-mails purportedly from their daughter up until Robinson's arrest. At one point, she told her family she had gotten married. They invited her home several times, but she always refused, saying she was too busy. In the final months, she and her husband were always traveling in some exotic land, Lewicki said. Writing one of her last e-mails in the spring of 2000, she claimed to have just returned from a trip to China, he said.

Much like Carolyn Trouten had done, Izabela's mother also identified a number of items belonging to her daughter that had been found in Barbara Sandix's apartment—including a fiery Impressionistic painting, several pieces of clothing, the bedding she brought with her when she left Indiana, as well as a number of family heirlooms and books. "She used to read a lot of books," she testified.

On cross-examination, Marona-Lewicka acknowledged that they didn't know much about their daughter's move.

"Did she ever tell you the real reason she went to Kansas City?" O'Brien asked her gently.

"No," she said, her voice tinged with sadness. She stepped down.

But a friend from Lafayette, Indiana, acknowledged knowing much more. Jennifer Hayes said Izabela had confided that she was going to do secretarial work for an international publishing agent, who was also going to train her to become a BDSM dominatrix. However, Hayes said, she was going to start her education as his slave. "She wouldn't tell me anything other than he wanted her to call him master," testified Hayes, who said she had met Lewicka through friends at Purdue University. "She did call him John once."

Hayes said that Lewicka told her she was working on artwork for some BDSM manuscripts John had commissioned. She identified four photographs of her friend in different BDSM poses, which had been found in the defendant's Needmor Storage locker. She also identified two of the pencil drawings, which had been found in Barbara Sandre's duplex on Grant Avenue. She explained that Lewicka hadn't completed them when Hayes last saw her in spring 1997.

At that meeting, she said, they got into an argument when she tried to discourage Lewicka from going to Kansas City. "I was concerned," stated Hayes, adding that she couldn't understand why an older man was so interested in a nineteen-year-old girl. "But she told me she had checked him out."

On cross-examination, Hayes told O'Brien that Lewicka was a "quintessential hippie chick" who was also into exploring witchcraft, paganism, vampirism and gothic lifestyles. "Things that are dark and spooky," she said in explaining her friend's interests. Hayes also admitted that Izabela had taken a few trips to Chicago to visit a dungeon called the Black Rose and that it was common in the BDSM lifestyle for masters to assign tasks that their submissives must carry out.

"Is it common that a submissive is not allowed to talk about the assignments?" O'Brien asked Hayes.

"That's part of the game," she replied.

"Would it be fair to say that a [slave] contract is standard operating procedure?" he continued.

"More often than not," she answered, concluding her testimony.

Chapter 29

Jurors were shown gruesome autopsy photographs of both Trouten and Lewicka as Donald Pojman, the deputy coroner, followed Hayes to the stand on Tuesday, October 15, to describe in detail how the two women had died. Pojman told the court that they arrived at the morgue still inside the eighty-five-gallon barrels that were discovered in the brush near a shed on Robinson's rural property. When he opened the barrels, they were curled up in the fetal position with their heads toward the bottom of the barrels, he said.

As color images were displayed on a screen in the courtroom, Pojman noted that Trouten was nude and wearing a blindfold tied around her head with a piece of soft nylon rope. Her nipples were pierced with rings that were connected by a chain, from which hung a butterfly pendant, he testified. She also had a number of other piercings in her ears and labia. The first injury on her "mildly" decomposed body, a small tear in the skin on the left side of her chest, was not serious enough to be lethal and was probably caused after her death, he said. Above her ear on the left side, however, a single blow had punched a circular hole in her skull more than an inch in diameter. "The young lady died shortly after receiving [this] injury," he testified.

Lewicka was nude except for a short-sleeved nightshirt. Her "moderately" decomposed body was partially covered by a greenish blue pillow, Pojman stated. He said he found a number of items, including several fingernails, three pieces of gray duct tape and two kitchen-size garbage bags, among the body fluids. Pojman said he believed Lewicka died from two blows to the left side of the head. "The two defects were overlapping," he told the court. "It wasn't an immediate death. [But] I don't believe she would have been conscious."

Judging by the state of decomposition, Pojman estimated that Trouten had been dead a few months to a year while Lewicka had been dead as long as two years. Not knowing their identities at the time of the autopsy, performed on June 4, 2000, he explained that he referred to her and Lewicka as Unknown No. 1 and Unknown No. 2, respectively. A forensics dentist identified them by their dental records a short time later, he testified.

Under questioning from Patrick Berrigan, he also said it was difficult to know if Trouten's and Lewicka's head wounds would have produced large quantities of blood. "Any type of scalp wound usually produces quite a bit of blood," Pojman acknowledged, though he added that the amount would depend on the elevation of the head at the time of the blow.

The next morning, Wednesday, October 16, Judge Anderson announced that one of the jurors—No. 214, a redheaded nurse—had been excused for an "extra compelling hardship" due to a family emergency. They were down to six women and five men. "One of our five alternates is part of the main jury," the judge said, adding, "Who that person is [they] will find out when they go in to deliberate."

Resuming testimony, Morrison called Johnson County forensic chemist Andrew Guzman, who testified that he had found a roll of gray duct tape in a green bucket in one of the trailer bedrooms on Robinson's property. "I noticed on the smooth surface there were some reddish brown stains or smears," he stated.

Guzman also said that fingerprint examiner Lyla Thompson asked several days later for his assistance in examining the severed hands of Suzette Trouten. During the course of extracting her fingerprints, they removed several strands of hair from between her fingers, which were carefully packaged in a plastic bag, along with the duct tape, and sent over to the Kansas City Crime Lab, he said.

Allen Hamm, who was promoted to assistant director of the Johnson County Crime Lab not long after the investigation, told the court he noticed several reddish brown stains on pieces of loose wallboard and molding when he was examining the south wall of the trailer's living room. Strands of hair mixed with what looked like human tissue were stuck to one of the boards. All of the spots, he testified before stepping down, tested positive for the presumptive presence of blood.

The months surrounding the trial had been a trying time for Roth and Welch. "Sara was in war mode for several months," the sergeant recalled. "There were all the motions filed by the defense and constant worry that something would go amiss. Flaws or oversights began to pop up here and there [and] was causing me quite a bit of anxiety. It seemed that all we talked about was the upcoming trial."

Once the trial started, the couple couldn't talk to each other about testimony because Roth was scheduled to testify. Of course, that was standard stuff at trials. The detectives couldn't talk to each other, either. But Welch and Roth were both concerned that the defense might try to make an issue out of the fact that they were dating. So, once the trial began, they kept their conversations very vague—when they saw each other at all. "I was constantly at work," Welch said. "When I wasn't at work, I was sleeping. Rick had to start taking care of my dry cleaning because I got to the office before the dry cleaners opened and I left the office after it was closed! I have never worked so hard in my life. I digress."

For Welch, not talking about the trial was less of a problem than she anticipated. What was difficult was if one of Roth's detectives did well or poorly on the stand, that's all she could say. Or if a witness said something funny, she could not tell him. "I never had a clue what she was talking about," Roth said. "I had to get my news like everyone else the next day. Then I could usually piece together who so-and-so was and why they did or didn't do well. It was awkward—drove me nuts—but we were determined that it would not be a matter that the defense could make an issue [of]."

As a precaution, therefore, it was decided that Morrison would be the one to question Roth when the time came. So when the jury came back from its midmorning recess on Wednesday, October 16, and two yellow metal barrels stood in the middle of the courtroom, it was the district attorney who called the police sergeant as his next witness.

Taking the stand, Roth explained how the metal barrels had originally been found among some plastic barrels and lawn equipment in undergrowth next to the shed. When a dog from search and rescue showed an interest in them, he had tilted one of the barrels and edged it away from the shed, he testified.

"Was it just you or were you being helped?" asked Morrison.

"It was just me," Roth replied, countering the defense suggestion in opening arguments that the barrels were so heavy that at one point it took seven police officers to move them.

Using the actual barrels as props, Morrison had Roth demonstrate to the court how he had moved the barrels. Laying one on its side, he rolled it before propping it back upright.

"Why did you do it like that?" Morrison asked.

"Because of the congestion in the area," Roth replied.

When the barrel was once again upright, he noticed a small bead of reddish liquid running down the side, he testified. That's when he called for Johnson County detective Harold Hughes and proceeded to roll out the second barrel.

On cross-examination, defense attorney Pat Berrigan asked Roth if he had detected an odor. "No, I did not," the sergeant stated.

Berrigan noted that Roth had rolled the barrels but had not lifted them. "Did you see anybody on June third lifting those barrels?" he asked.

"No," Roth stated.

"When did you notice the smell?" Morrison asked his witness on redirect.

"When they popped the lid on the first barrel," Roth replied. "It was horrendous."

"You saw [the reddish] liquid and did not smell a thing?" Berrigan, on recross, asked incredulously.

"I did not smell a thing," Roth insisted.

Morrison next called Johnson County detective Harold Hughes to the stand, who testified that he had been examining the trailer on Robinson's rural property when another investigator informed him that a cadaver dog had focused on some barrels out by the toolshed. He went to investigate and found one of the yellow metal barrels standing upright near a shed on the property, he stated.

Hughes told how he used pliers to loosen the bolt on the seal of the first yellow barrel and popped the lid to look inside. He said he repeated the same procedure with the second yellow barrel. "I opened the barrels and determined there was a body in each barrel," he testified.

At this point, Morrison asked him to identify the two yellow barrels that had been rolled into the courtroom. Hughes confirmed that they were the same yellow barrels from that fateful day, but he added that they looked considerably different since they had been cleaned. Morrison, who had also set up a VCR in the courtroom, played a clip that showed Hughes opening the second yellow drum and a glimpse at what was inside: a bluish-green pillow partially covering the back of a body that was curled up in a fetal position.

"Did you smell anything?" asked Morrison.

"I could smell it as I walked up to it," replied Hughes.

Opening the lid to the first barrel, the clip showed another body slumped over in a similar manner.

The jury, which by now had viewed graphic autopsy photos and a sex tape, did not visibly react to the tape of the crime scene. Robinson appeared to be watching, tilting his head in the direction of the screen.

Chapter 30

After the Linn County sheriff and Captain Keith O'Neal briefly testified about the crime scene at the farm, testimony on Wednesday, October 16, 2002, shifted back to the young woman from Indiana who had moved to Kansas City to be with Robinson.

The assistant property manager of the Deerfield apartment complex in Olathe took the stand that afternoon and testified that Robinson had rented an apartment for a young woman named Izabela Lewicka Robinson from March 1, 1998, until February 28, 1999. Jennifer Boniedot said Robinson had introduced her to the young woman as his adopted daughter. "He said he met her at a graphic-arts trade show and she had been abused by her parents, so he had adopted her," she testified.

Izabela had paid for the rent only one time, Boniedot noted. Otherwise, Robinson took care of it using a check from Specialty Publications. After the first year, he decided not to renew the lease, she said.

"Did anyone else besides Izabela Lewicka live in that apartment?" asked Welch.

"To my knowledge, no," she replied.

On cross-examination, defense attorney O'Brien asked Boniedot if it appeared that Robinson and Lewicka were, indeed, in a father/daughter relationship. She replied that, to her, it did.

Marilyn Wilkinson, the former manager of the Mail Boxes Etc., testified that Robinson had once rented a private drop box at the Overland Park business. Lewicka's name was on the agreement, she noted, along with that of another woman. When it was updated in 1999, the paperwork indicated that John Robinson had added his name to the list of those persons eligible to receive mail, she said.

A second friend of Lewicka's took the stand to talk about what she knew of her decision to move to Kansas City. Dawn Carter of Columbus, Ohio, who met Lewicka in a dance class at Purdue University in August 1996, said her friend had a key to her apartment and often stayed with her or came over during the day just to hang out or use her computer.

ADA Welch asked Carter, a thirty-one-year-old graduate student with cropped blond hair, if she was aware of other interests that Lewicka had. "She loved art," she said. "She took sketchbooks with her everywhere she went. She also liked purple ink. If she was writing a note to say she'd be home at seven-thirty, she would write it out in ink and decorate it."

In the spring of 1997, Lewicka told her she was going to move to Kansas City and get a job, Carter said. She also had plans of hopefully traveling, she testified. "She talked about John, a guy she met on the Internet," she said. "She said that John was helping her to get set up and helping her to get an apartment."

Carter said they had a little argument because she didn't think Lewicka should go, and so Lewicka put her on the phone to talk with John.

"What did you talk about?" asked Welch.

"Silly things," she replied. "I think she told him I collected fountain pens. He said he had a big collection. He had a dragon pen. He said he cared about her. He said she had a lot of talent. He said he wanted to help her."

But when Carter told him she didn't trust him, he appeared threatened by that, she said. "Izabela took the phone," she testified.

Lewicka also showed her an e-mail that John had sent. "We were having a conversation about her sex life and things she liked," she said. "[The e-mail] described what he was going to do to her—take her into a downstairs room, tie her up and put metal things to spread out her legs. . . . It involved pain."

Carter, who said she was familiar with BDSM but was not a practitioner, described her friend as being fairly open about the subject. "That was the reason she was going to Kansas City," she stated. "She'd have a job, an apartment and a master."

"Did she use that term?" Welch asked.

"Yes," she replied.

When Welch asked her if she knew when Lewicka left for Kansas City, Carter responded that the date was June 8, 1997. "She marked it on the calendar for me," she said, her voice cracking as she began to cry. "I spent that evening with her and walked her to her car."

At first, Lewicka kept in touch with Carter and their circle of friends at Purdue. But then the phone calls and e-mails came less often. Around August 1999, Lewicka called her for the last time, Carter testified. "She was pretty excited," she said. "She was going to Europe. She was going to get to travel."

Carter didn't know if anybody was going with her. "She just said she was going to be gone for quite a while and not to worry. It would take her a while to get set up" and then she'd be in touch again.

On cross-examination, Carter admitted to Sean O'Brien that Lewicka wasn't doing well in school and didn't get along with her parents. "She felt they didn't understand her. [Andrew Lewicki] pushed her hard in school," she said. "[It was] typical late-teen stuff: I want my own apartment. I want my own life."

Chapter 31

Barbara Sandre followed Carter to the stand that Wednesday afternoon, testifying that she was a German translator who had met the defendant nearly thirty years earlier when he had come to Toronto to see the Boy Scout production she was involved in. They struck up a pen pal relationship but eventually lost touch, the heavyset woman with short blond hair and glasses recalled.

They were back in touch again around 1971, when their friendship turned romantic. But after he paid her a brief visit, she didn't hear from him again until 1993. Out of the blue, Sandre said, her parents received a letter purportedly from John Robinson's "adopted son." They forwarded it to her in England, where she was then residing.

At this point in Sandre's testimony, the prosecution attempted to submit the letter as evidence, but O'Brien called for a bench conference and, within seconds, the jury was ushered out. Welch explained that they wanted to submit the letter to show a pattern of conduct in Robinson's regular use of forged letters. She also pointed out that Nancy Robinson had found the letter and it was what prompted her to write Sandre, as she had mentioned in her testimony. But O'Brien said the letter was immaterial and didn't make any difference why or how Robinson rekindled his relationship with Sandre. Without explaining his rationale, the judge sided with the defense, refusing to allow the letter.

With the jury reseated, Sandre testified that she had responded to the note, sending her reply to one of Robinson's known mailbox drops on East Blue Ridge Boulevard. "We always had a certain friendship and so it wasn't that hard to pick up," Sandre said. "We started writing and talking and went back to where we had been."

In March 1994, not long after Beverly Bonner had disappeared, Robinson wrote Sandre, asking if she would be willing to mail some letters from England and other cities for his daughter Kim. Sandre told him she would and recalled mailing two sets of letters from France and Switzerland. She couldn't remember the names or addresses on the envelopes, she said.

"Had you been asked to do that previously?" asked Sara Welch.

"No," she answered.

Shortly thereafter, she and Robinson began e-mailing every other day and talking on the phone about once a week, Sandre said. Asked his e-mail address, she said it was posseder@hotmail.com. She said it was from the infinitive of the French word that meant "to own" or "to possess."

Sandre moved back to Canada in 1998 and came to Kansas City for a three-day visit in early July 1999. During that time, she found and rented a furnished apartment in the Hunters Point complex in Overland Park, Kansas, she testified. When she came back down a week later, she brought only her computer, a dictionary and her clothes.

She told the jury she hoped that Robinson, who told her he was single, would move in with her. On the very few occasions that they were intimate, their relations never involved BDSM, she testified. "As far as I was concerned, he didn't have a wife," she stated. "He was never married. He was never divorced. He was most of the time out of town."

Sandre said Robinson told her he traveled a lot because he had a government job—as an assistant director of the CIA. He often called her, she stated, claiming he was in Washington, Denver or Houston.

He also told her he had four adopted children.

"What were their names?" asked Welch.

"John junior, Chris, Chrissy and Kimberly," Sandre replied.

"Did you meet any of these children?" Welch asked.

"No," she replied.

"Go to their homes?" she continued.

"No," she repeated.

In late August 1999, Sandre moved to an unfurnished apartment on Grant Avenue in Overland Park, signing a lease with John Robinson. "He said he had furniture in storage that I could use," Sandre testified, adding that Robinson paid for her move with a Specialty Publications check and soon arrived with another moving truck full of furniture.

Upon further questioning, she recalled that the name of the moving company was something like Two Men and a Truck.

By the end of the month, he had also arrived with a host of other items, she said, including artwork, bedding, towels, dishes, pots and pans and cutlery. "He told me he had bought the older things from estate sales and that some things were his grandmother's," Sandre said.

The Canadian woman then identified several items as among those that Robinson had brought over. They included a fiery Impressionistic painting that was hung in her living room and was signed "John 1992." Two pencil drawings also had his signature and initials with the year 2000. Only the day before, her mother and friend had identified the paintings and drawings as having been done by Izabela Lewicka.

Sandre, moreover, identified the bluish green Aztec-printed sheets that she said had come from Robinson, which matched the pillowcase found in the barrel with Lewicka's body. "I had an almost brand new and large garbage can that I packed all my bedding in so they wouldn't get damp and musty and dirty," Sandre stated. "These things were all standing in the dining room in readiness to go to storage or be packed away or whatever . . . I don't believe there were any pillowcases, to my recollection."

"When the defendant brought [the Aztec-printed sheets]

over to the house, did they appear to be clean to you?" asked Welch.

"They appeared to be clean, but I washed everything," Sandre replied.

"But there were no big, obvious stains on them?"

"No."

Sandre said she also got a new computer and e-mail address from Robinson. She said he told her to delete all the personal information before using the computer, which she did. Then he phoned one day, she stated, and said there had been a security leak and "the powers that be" at the CIA had insisted that she change her e-mail address. "He said my old one no longer existed and I was to use a new one: barbara robinson@hotmail.com," she testified.

Welch, wanting to show that Robinson had given Sandre his old girlfriend's computer, asked her for the password. Sandre said she couldn't pronounce it, but Robinson had told her it stood for "rat" in Polish. Lewicka, others had testified, used the same password.

Robinson had told Sandre about his farm in rural Kansas and she told the court she had even helped him to purchase it in 1994. But then he insisted that they couldn't go down there because it wasn't secure. Cell phones didn't work there, Sandre said he told her, which could be a problem in an emergency. "The powers that be [at the CIA] didn't want him there," she stated.

Even though his name was on the lease at the Grant Street apartment, Sandre noted that Robinson didn't live with her and almost always visited during the day. She could recall only one occasion when they went out, to breakfast.

In the late spring of 2000, Robinson asked Sandre to provide him with a list of names and addresses of all the people she knew, Sandre testified.

"Did he tell you why?" Welch asked.

"I asked him," she replied, "and he just said, 'I *need* it.'"

When Robinson wanted something, he didn't take no for an answer, she added.

Resuming her testimony the next morning, on Thursday, October 17, Sandre relayed several more incidents in which Robinson misled her about his marital status.

She was living in England in 1998 when she received a letter signed by a woman named Nancy Robinson, who claimed she was Robinson's wife.

"Were you aware of her existence prior to receiving this letter?" asked Welch.

"No," she replied.

"Had you heard the name Nancy Robinson before?"

"Never."

Sandre testified that she immediately sent John Robinson an e-mail, saying she had just received a letter from his wife. "He e-mailed me back and said, 'What wife?'" she said.

After Sandre faxed John Robinson the letter, she received an explanation that apparently satisfied her.

"He said that she was someone he had hired when his kids were little when he was working and she was now working for his daughter baby-sitting her children, and that he, after I had given him the letter, had been to a lawyer and had gotten a court order so that she couldn't harass anybody in his family anymore."

In October 1999, Sandre went to Sam's Club with a friend who had a store membership. "We're pushing the trolley around on one particular row," said Sandre. "I'm going down the row and I think to myself, 'That looks like J.R. coming towards me. So I got a little bit closer and I think I actually almost rolled over his toe. He looked right through me like he had never seen me before in his life."

Robinson was with a woman who looked older, Sandre said. The woman had grayish hair and wore glasses. When Sandre got home that evening, she e-mailed Robinson to say she had seen him at the store with another woman.

"That's impossible," she said he wrote in a return e-mail. "I'm in Russia. How can I be at Sam's Club?"

Sometime after that, Sandre finally decided to drive by the address in Olathe that Robinson's "wife" had included in her letter, she said. When she drove by the Monterey Lane mobile home, she recognized Robinson's white Dodge Ram parked in front. To explain that, she said the defendant told her that his daughter used his truck when he was out of town and often parked it there because she had relatives who lived in the doublewide.

Sandre also testified that she had been in Canada during the first few weeks of May 2000 to stay with her elderly father while her mother traveled to Europe. While she was there, she rented an apartment for herself and Robinson. Upon her return to Kansas City on Sunday, May 21, Robinson instructed her to "pack up everything." She was to leave as soon as she could, she told the court, and he was planning to follow her by the end of June. They had already informed the apartment manager of their plans to vacate the duplex, and she packed many of the household items—including the linens—into boxes in preparation for the move.

She said the move would have eased difficulties she had in receiving payment for her overseas work. Most of her clients paid her in German and English currency with rates that often varied in the United States. The cost of living also was less in Canada than in the United States, she said. "We decided jointly that that was the way to go," she testified.

Welch didn't question her about the supposed threat on Robinson's life and Sandre didn't mention it in her testimony. Instead, the assistant district attorney asked how long Sandre thought Robinson was planning to stay with her in Canada.

"Permanently," she replied.

Chapter 32

That Thursday afternoon, October 17, prosecutors paraded several more witnesses through the courtroom to testify about Lewicka's relationship with Robinson. Robert Meyers, owner of A. Friendly's Bookstore, in Overland Park, said Lewicka was a regular customer from 1997 to 1999. Her main interests were books about the occult, vampires, sorcery, witchcraft and historic events, such as the Salem witch trials. She spoke with an Eastern European accent and often dressed in dark clothing, Meyers said. "She would come in maybe once a month for two years or more," he said.

Most of the time, Lewicka came in alone, Meyers said. But on one of her last visits, around August 1999, an older man who looked about fifty-three years of age and was "somewhat corpulent" accompanied her into the store. Meyers said the visit stood out because Lewicka was wearing a black dog collar with silver studs and announced to him that she was moving. In the future, the man with her would be shopping for her books, she told Meyers. "He seemed to be disinterested," Meyers said in describing the man's reaction to Izabela's comments, adding that he never saw the man again. "I believe very possibly he's the defendant."

Karen Scott, a print broker for Robinson's magazine, *Manufactured Modular Home Living,* testified that the defendant told her Lewicka was his adopted daughter. Izabela worked with Robinson as a graphic designer in 1998 and for most of 1999, she said. But that had changed in September 1999 when Robinson called Scott, seeking names of people to design an Internet Web site for him. When she asked about Lewicka, Robinson told her his "adopted daughter" had been deported "back to Czechoslovakia" after police caught her smoking marijuana with her boyfriend, she said.

Eric Collins testified he had met Lewicka in two capacities. One was with a group of people, outside the Ranch Mart Shopping Center in the Kansas City suburb of Leawood, who participated in a role-playing game involving vampires. Collins said Lewicka told players she originally came from the place in Europe where Count Dracula once roamed. She often dressed like a goth, wearing dark clothing and white facial makeup. "Her character name was Special," he said.

Collins ran into her again when he was working in Overland Park at a company called Express Signs. Lewicka ordered the design of an 8' x 2' banner and picked it up a few days later with Robinson. While waiting for Collins to finish the banner, the defendant noticed a vampire role-playing book lying out on his desk. " 'My wife here plays that game, too,' " Collins quoted Robinson as saying.

Pam Sadewhite, who operated a Lenexa graphic-arts company that put together one edition of Robinson's magazine, said Lewicka told her in 1998 that the defendant was her uncle and that she was an immigrant from Denmark. She noted that their relationship seemed far closer, however. "They were very affectionate," Sadewhite testified, "and very handsy in inappropriate places."

Margaret Davis, a drafting instructor at Johnson County Community College, testified that Lewicka was one of her students in fall 1998. Lewicka identified herself as Izabela Lewicka-Robinson, Davis testified, and said she was married. "All I knew was that he was an older man," the witness stated, adding that Lewicka wore a ruby ring on the ring finger of her left hand. "She told me it was her wedding ring," she said.

Testimony then turned to the incriminating evidence investigators had discovered in Lewicka's last apartment on Edgebrook in Olathe.

Julie Brown, an employee with the property management company, testified that Robinson had rented the apartment for Lewicka in January 1999 but broke the one-year lease early in September. Inspecting the apartment after it had been vacated, Brown found that the kitchen and front room were not terribly clean, while the two bedrooms were immaculate and looked as though they'd recently been repainted. "It looked like someone . . . sucked all the dirt out of the area, it was so clean," she testified.

Brian Palmeter, vice president of daily operations at Two Men and a Truck, followed Brown to the stand. He told the court that on August 23, 1999, Robinson called them to move a few belongings from Izabela's Edgebrook apartment to Sandre's duplex on Grant Avenue.

Welch asked Palmeter to examine and explain the company's "move sheet."

"Just looking at this information, I would have to guess the contact person was probably the one that called it in," Palmeter stated.

"That's John Robinson?" Welch asked.

"Yes," he replied.

"This would be the move to Grant Avenue?"

"That's the information that was given to us at the time of the scheduling."

"The date would be 8/23/99?"

"Yes, ma'am."

Welch said she had no further questions for Palmeter and moved to her next witness: Johnson County crime scene analyst Sally Lane.

Obtaining a search warrant for the apartment more than a year after Lewicka vacated, Lane said she focused on the doors, flooring, carpeting and walls because other tenants had since occupied the apartment. In the southwest bedroom, she hit pay dirt: discovering what appeared to be hundreds of pin-size blood specks sprayed on two walls and a set of window blinds. "The majority of them were from waist to chest high," said Lane, who swabbed about 10 spots on the walls and delivered them along with the blinds to her crime lab.

The suspense was almost unbearable by the time Frank Booth, a senior criminalist and DNA analyst with the Kansas City, Missouri, Crime Lab, took the stand at the end of the day, Thursday, October 17. He carefully explained how he had created DNA profiles for Suzette and Izabela using pieces of ribs removed during their autopsies and saliva samples from their parents. He then compared the profiles with several pieces of evidence his lab had received from Robinson's Linn County property and Izabela's apartment. He said the size of the blood sample didn't matter to him. "If you can see it, you can definitely profile it," declared the confident analyst.

Morrison first asked Booth about the results of his DNA tests on several evidence samples from the trailer on Robinson's Linn County farm. Two sheets of paper towels from the kitchen sink contained five bloodstains—the largest about the size of a quarter—and eight strands of human hair, he said. "It was exactly the same," he said of the DNA match. "It came from Suzette Trouten."

He echoed that opinion when asked about the blood swabs taken from the pieces of wallboard and molding in the trailer's main living area, saying they, too, contained droplets of Trouten's blood.

Booth told the court he had also performed DNA testing on the roll of gray duct tape recovered in the trailer bedroom and determined that the reddish brown stains were, in fact, blood. Morrison then asked if he knew who was the source of the blood.

"Izabela Lewicka," Booth replied.

Hair samples taken from Trouten's hands, Booth said, could be a match to hair that was found on the paper towel and on the wallboard taken from the mobile home. He explained that hair comparisons were not "a positive identification" of a person but provided general characteristics that helped to group people with similar hair while eliminating others. Asked if the hairs from either the paper towel or wallboard could have belonged to Robinson, Booth said his tests were conclusive. "It's not his hair," he testified.

Booth also said the swabs taken from a yellow pickup truck and from inside a pole barn on the property did not contain blood. Neither did the nine hammers, two picks and a chisel seized in the mobile home. The mystery of the missing murder weapon would remain unsolved.

Finally Morrison shifted his questioning to Izabela's apartment, where crime lab technicians had taken the swabs of stains from two walls in the south bedroom and one swab from window blinds. The blinds quickly were ruled out as having stains of significance. "It was definitely not blood," Booth said. "It was like a soft drink had exploded."

But all six swabs taken from bedroom walls tested positive as being human blood, Booth said.

Morrison asked whose blood it was.

There was a pregnant pause in the courtroom as observers strained their ears to hear Booth's answer. They needn't have bothered.

"Izabela Lewicka," he crowed triumphantly.

The blood evidence supported the prosecution's theory that the twenty-one-year-old Indiana art student had been killed in her apartment and her body somehow transported to the farm.

Chapter 33

Shortly after nine o'clock the next morning, Friday, October 18, an attractive and smartly dressed African American woman strode into the courtroom, taking the witness stand.

Morrison asked her to state her name. "Alesia Cox," she replied.

"Do you know John Robinson?"

She said she did and pointed him out in the courtroom.

Cox told the jury that she had met Robinson in 1997 through an ad she had placed in *Pitch Weekly*. At the time, she lived in South Kansas City and was working as a receptionist for a temp agency, she said. Her ad stated she was looking for a generous white male, she testified.

"Was sex involved?" Morrison asked.

"I didn't say that [in the ad], but it was implied," she replied.

Robinson answered the ad, saying he was a wealthy businessman who would be willing to take care of her financially if she would become his mistress. He was in the process of getting a divorce, he said. "I know he wanted me naked all the time," she said. "If he was interested in having sexual relations, I should be there for him."

They agreed that he would pay Cox $2,000 a month, plus give her an allowance for her housing and a wardrobe. He did pay her rent a time or two, she said, but that was about it.

Morrison asked if the relationship was peaceful or stormy. "On his part, he was domineering, cavalier—come when you want, leave when you want," she testified. "He wanted things done when he wanted them done."

"How did you treat him?" Morrison asked.

"As best I could," she replied.

Robinson wanted sex often and he would usually come to her apartment to get it, she testified. Later on in the course of their two-year relationship, they would meet at other locations. Under further questioning, she insisted they had a normal sexual relationship, although from her descriptions it sounded as if he at least tried to introduce aspects of BDSM. He always wanted oral sex, she testified, and also had a leather collar with restraints for her hands, which he had tried on her one time. He took pictures of her getting undressed and later made a video, she said. "He would sometimes call me his personal slut and whore," she said. "Not really during sex but during foreplay—to try to put me in my place."

At one point during their relationship, she was working part-time at an athletic club and he took a black Magic Marker and wrote his initials on her hip. "He wanted to know if I got undressed in the locker room," she testified. "When I said yes, he said he wanted to me wear his initials so everybody could see."

In the fall of 1998, Robinson told Cox he needed to do some traveling for his business, she testified, and he wanted her to go with him to London, Paris and Australia. At his suggestion, she gave up her job and her apartment, moved her furniture and belongings into storage, and applied for a passport. Morrison asked her how long the trip was supposed to last. "About six weeks," she said. "I asked him [about that] several times because my family was curious and I didn't get a straight answer until I pushed and then he was still vague."

Before they left, he had her prepare several letters in advance to her mother and young daughter, pretending she was in places such as London and Paris, she said.

"Did he say why he wanted you to write these letters?" Morrison asked.

"I asked [him] because I thought it was rather odd," she replied. "He said we wouldn't have enough time to write. I asked him what I should write. I didn't have much to go on and I had to improvise. I asked if I should date them all. He gave me dates."

Morrison showed her four letters that Detective Dan Owsley had previously identified as coming from the black hardcover case found in Robinson's Needmor Storage locker. She confirmed that they were the letters she had written to her mother and daughter at the defendant's request. She had never mailed them, she said, and didn't know what had happened to them.

The night they were supposed to leave, he had checked her into the Best Western just off I-135 in Olathe, she said. For the first time in their relationship, Robinson spent the night with her. The next morning, she woke up very early, around 5:00 A.M., she testified. "He was still asleep," she said. "He woke up and he acted like he was irritated and asked me why I was awake so early."

Robinson then jumped in the shower and told her he had errands to run. He asked her to meet him at the Country Kitchen restaurant in Olathe a little later that morning. From there, they'd drop her car at his farm and head to the airport, he said. When she showed up at the restaurant at the appointed time, however, Robinson was nowhere to be found. She called him about one hundred times and began to look for somewhere to spend the night, she testified. Eventually she moved in with a relative.

Cox said she didn't talk to Robinson again until early 1999, when she placed another ad in *Pitch Weekly* and he again responded. He offered a lame excuse as to why he never showed up at the restaurant that day. "He told me he was embarrassed [because he couldn't trust me] and had to make the trip alone," she stated.

"Did the relationship continue?" Morrison asked.

"Yes, it did," she replied.

Morrison then asked her if she'd signed a slave contract and she admitted that she had. "It was done at his insistence," she said, emphasizing that they never had a master/slave relationship.

"Did you take this thing seriously or not?" Morrison asked, referring to the slave contract. "No," she answered.

Sometime later that year, she recalled Robinson showing her an apartment he said he owned on Edgebrook. She remembered seeing boxes, clothing, a computer and miscellaneous items. She said Robinson asked her if she wanted to live in the apartment, but she declined. He also asked her if she wanted any of the clothing and she accepted a few garments. She identified the garments—including a green velour dress, a black velour sweater and a white silk camisole—in court that afternoon. They were the same items of clothing that Izabela's mother had identified only three days before as belonging to her daughter.

Cox also said she paid a visit to an apartment on Grant Avenue. Robinson told her that a woman he knew from London was using it and would be back soon. In the meantime, he said, she could stay there since she was living out of her car. She stayed two or three nights, she said.

The witness also admitted to Morrison that she had signed paperwork giving power of attorney to Robinson on July 13, 1999. "It was his idea," she said. Morrison asked her to identify another item that had been found in Robinson's black hardcover case in the Needmor Storage locker. It was the title to her car, a 1986 Chevy Cavalier. She didn't know why he had it.

Finally Morrison asked her if she'd ever been to the defendant's farm. He had talked about it, she said, but they never visited. "He said we'd have sex and lots of it," she testified. "He said he would like to tie me up in the barn and have sex with me and leave and come back whenever he chose and fuck me some more."

On cross-examination, Berrigan asked Cox if Robinson had ever hurt or threatened her. "He did hurt me once when he tried to put nipple clips on me," she said, though she admitted that the relationship was consensual.

"Is it true that Mr. Robinson wanted you to tell him that you loved him?" Berrigan asked.

"He did ask quite often," she replied.

"Did he propose to you?" he continued.

"Yes," she said, but added that she didn't take the offer of marriage seriously.

Berrigan asked her why not.

"I guess you have to know the source," she replied.

Chapter 34

Prosecutors had spent nearly two weeks calling more than sixty witnesses to take the stand to testify about Trouten and Lewicka. Returning from morning recess on Friday, October 18, however, they finally moved fifteen years back in time to focus on Robinson's third alleged murder victim in the Kansas trial: Lisa Stasi.

Karen Gaddis, the former ob-gyn social worker at Truman Medical Center in Independence, Missouri, a hospital well known for its care of the indigent, kicked off testimony about Stasi by describing the1980s as lean years for social-service agencies, forcing them to think outside the box to solve problems. She said it was in this context that Robinson called her in December 1984 and purported to be a businessman who wanted to give back to the community. He told her he had formed an organization to help needy young mothers. But Robinson never produced any paperwork regarding his purported venture. "It made us feel somewhat uneasy," she testified.

Robinson specifically said he was looking for white women in their late teens or early twenties who were pregnant or had newborn babies, Gaddis said. He also said he was looking for women who did not have strong family ties in the area because they would be most in need of his help.

"Did that raise a red flag?" asked Morrison.

"It did," she said.

Contradicting what she had told Overland Park detectives and probation officer Stephen Haymes more than fifteen years earlier, Gaddis insisted to the court during cross-examination that she never referred any women to Robinson. Instead, she testified that she had spoken to Robinson in January 1985 and that he had already come into contact with Stasi at Hope House, telling her he was putting her up in a hotel until an apartment was ready. Neither prosecutors nor defense attorneys pressed the matter.

Her brief testimony was followed by Carl Stasi, who said he had met his young wife through a friend and that in August 1984 they had gotten married in Huntsville, Alabama, where Lisa had grown up. She was eight months pregnant at the time. They had planned to stay but, without insurance, they were forced to return to Kansas City.

Their daughter, Tiffany Lynn, was born a few weeks later at Truman Medical. Broke and without jobs or a home, the Stasis' marriage quickly went downhill. "It was shaky," Carl stated. He and Lisa separated in mid-December, he said, and Carl reenlisted in the U.S. Navy, just outside of Chicago, a few days after Christmas.

Morrison showed Carl Stasi a picture of an infant and asked if he could identify her. "That's my daughter," he answered softly, barely keeping his emotions in check.

Upon learning from his mother that Lisa and Tiffany had disappeared, Stasi said he had twice requested emergency leave from the navy to return to Kansas City to look for them. His requests were denied, he said, because there was no proof of foul play and his new stint in the military had barely started.

Asked by Morrison if he ever saw or heard from his wife again, Carl Stasi answered no. Asked the same question about his daughter, the answer was no different. "No," he said, almost in a whisper.

Kathy Klinginsmith followed her brother to the witness stand and described in subdued tones how Lisa had stopped by her house on January 8, 1985, to drop off Tiffany. Lisa told her sister-in-law that a group of Johnson County businessmen were going to help her find a job and earn her GED and that a man named John Osborne was spearheading the effort.

While Lisa went out that evening to a local bar called The Log Cabin, Klinginsmith said she looked after four-month-old Tiffany. "I fed her; she slept a long time; she took a bubble bath," stated Klinginsmith, who testified that she became a little upset when it grew late and Lisa hadn't returned. Klinginsmith called her brother, John Stasi, and he fetched Lisa from the bar and brought her to his parents' house to spend the night.

Returning to Klinginsmith's home the next morning, Lisa told her sister-in-law that Osborne was putting her up in room 131 at the Rodeway Inn in Overland Park and that they had tickets to go to Chicago.

"Did you give her any advice?" asked Morrison.

"Yes, I did," Klinginsmith replied. "I told her she ought to be cautious because, for one, she didn't know him that well. She didn't know what his intentions were."

But Lisa Stasi replied that Osborne was looking for her and that she had left a message with the Rodeway Inn for him to call. The phone rang a few minutes later and Klinginsmith wound up giving Osborne directions to her house. "He came to the door about twenty-five minutes later, rang the doorbell," said Klinginsmith, who noted that he'd traveled through a bad snowstorm to get there. "I went to the door with my son, who was five, and Lisa put on her coat."

He seemed like he was in a hurry and didn't waste any time on pleasantries. "He didn't say anything to me," Klinginsmith stated. "He just stood there and looked at me."

Morrison asked her if she recognized the man in court who had called himself John Osborne. "Yes," she replied.

She indicated the defendant.

Lisa carried Tiffany to Osborne's car, which was parked down the street, leaving her own yellow Toyota Corolla and many of her belongings behind, Klinginsmith continued. The young mother called about an hour later to let her sister-in-law know she'd arrived safely back at the Rodeway. "She sounded normal to me," she stated.

The next morning, January 10, Klinginsmith phoned the Rodeway Inn, only to discover that Lisa and Tiffany had already checked out of room 131 and that the bill had been settled not by John Osborne but by John Robinson. Alarmed, she testified to driving halfway across the city to file a missing persons report with the Overland Park Police Department.

During cross-examination, Klinginsmith admitted she didn't know very much about her sister-in-law. O'Brien asked her if she recalled explaining to the police in 1985 that Carl and Lisa were having marital problems.

"Yes," she said.

"They argued and fought and occasionally hit each other, would that be correct?" O'Brien asked.

"Yes," she replied, then stepped down.

Betty Stasi, Lisa's mother-in-law, followed her daughter to the stand, describing the disturbing phone call she had received from Lisa late on January 9. "I took it for granted she was at her motel," she said. "She was crying real hard, hysterical. She was telling me that 'they' said I was going to take her baby from her, that she was an unfit mom."

"Did she say who 'they' were?" asked Welch.

"No," she replied.

In the same conversation, Lisa also told her "they" wanted her to sign four blank sheets of paper, Betty Stasi said. "I said, 'Don't sign nothing, Lisa,' " she testified. " 'Don't put your name on anything.' She calmed down."

"Did you have plans to take Lisa's baby?" asked Welch.

"No!" the petite, white-haired woman replied emphatically. Welch asked what happened next.

"[Lisa] said, 'Here they come,' and she hung up," she testified.

"Again, did she say who 'they' was?" Welch asked.

"No!"

That was the last time she spoke to Lisa, Betty Stasi testified. Within a few weeks, however, she received a typed letter with Lisa's signature at the bottom.

Welch asked her about the contents of the letter. "She said she was going out of town somewhere and she was going to start a new life for her and Tiffany," she stated.

Also testifying on that Friday, October 18, was Cindy Scott, the former Overland Park detective who had originally investigated Lisa and Tiffany's disappearance. She told the court that part of her job was to determine whether the individuals in question had met foul play or simply wanted to be left alone. She said she was aware right from the beginning that Lisa's family was suspicious about John Robinson. "Some of Lisa Stasi's family had concerns," she stated. "They knew she left with Mr. Robinson."

Scott said she had questioned Robinson almost immediately, along with numerous members of Lisa and Tiffany's family. He told her that he was trying to help Stasi as part of his program for young mothers, but she had changed her mind, Scott testified. She said Robinson told her that Stasi came to his office to thank him and left with her baby and a young man. "He hadn't heard from her since then," she stated, adding that he also told her he didn't ask Lisa to sign any papers.

Stephen Haymes, called to the stand next, had to be careful not to make any mention of Robinson's criminal record, lest prosecutors risk a mistrial. He testified that he, too, had questioned the defendant about his connection to Stasi, though the jury was never told that Haymes was Robinson's old probation supervisor. Again Robinson said he had put Stasi up at the Overland Park motel, but she had changed her mind about the program, Haymes testified. Robinson said Lisa Stasi was with a man named Bill and was going to Colorado.

In March, however, Haymes said Robinson told him another story. "He told me that Lisa and the baby had been found in the Kansas City area," Haymes stated. Lisa, with Tiffany in tow, had apparently done some recent baby-sitting for a young woman and she was trying to locate her in order to pay her for her work. He told Haymes he referred her call to his attorney, who relayed the information to Overland Park police.

Monday morning's testimony began with Sergeant Ron Whistle, who briefly described taking the initial missing persons report on Lisa and Tiffany Stasi. But it quickly moved to Cora K. Holmes—previously known as Cora Kristine Pebley—who admitted under oath that she had made up the story about Lisa baby-sitting for her in 1985. She stated that she had been in an abusive relationship and needed to move out of her apartment. Robinson, whom she had met through a friend, offered to lend her $800 if she would tell the Overland Park police that a girl named Lisa Stasi spent the night at her house and left with a man named Bill Summers to go to Arkansas, she testified.

"Did you tell his story?" Morrison asked.

"Yes, I did."

"And did you end up telling the truth?" Morrison continued.

"Yes," said Holmes, acknowledging that she had confessed to investigators when they returned to her home a second time to confront her about her fabricated story.

A hush fell over the courtroom as Don Robinson walked down the center aisle and took his seat in the witness stand after a midmorning break, Monday, October 21. The defendant's brother told the court how he and his wife had tried for several years to get pregnant on their own. Because of health problems, he stated, they began to look into adoption around 1980. They signed up with Catholic Charities and the Lutheran Church but were told they faced a long wait. Other agencies were too expensive or looking for parents of a different race.

Then Robinson's wife, Frieda, read an article in a parenting magazine that suggested they ask friends and relatives if they knew any attorneys who handled private adoptions. He said they raised the subject with the defendant at a 1983 family reunion. "He told us he knew of an attorney who handled adoptions and he'd get in touch with him for us," said Don Robinson.

In early 1984, the defendant called to let the couple know that an attorney by the name of Doug Wood was willing to work with them and that a baby should be ready in October. But, Don Robinson said, his brother also explained that he would serve as the go-between for them and the attorney because "Doug wasn't very easy to get along with."

At that point, the Robinsons borrowed $2,500 and wrote out a cashier's check to Equi-II, Robinson's business, to start the adoption process. The couple also fixed up a room in their house for the baby and put a crib on layaway. In September, Frieda quit her job at Ace Hardware in anticipation of the baby's arrival.

Don Robinson said he never met Wood but that the attorney had called him once. "I did talk to somebody one time who said he was Doug Wood," he stated. But October came and went with no news about a baby. "I don't remember the exact reasons, but it fell through," stated Frieda, who took the stand immediately after her husband.

Then, in early January 1985, his older brother called, Don said. He said a baby girl was available and they should come quickly to Kansas City to pick her up. The baby's mother had wanted to give her up for adoption when she was born, the defendant said, but a social worker had talked her out of it. Disowned by her family, the young mother left her baby in a shelter, checked into a hotel and killed herself.

Don Robinson said he and his wife flew from Chicago to Kansas City to pick up their baby daughter on January 10, 1985. His brother met them at the airport and drove them to the offices of Equi-II, where they signed what they thought were official adoption papers and gave him a second $3,000 check made out to Wood. In return, Don Robinson said his brother handed them a wallet-size photo of their new baby daughter. In court, Don Robinson identified a photo of his adopted daughter. It was the same photo that Stasi's relatives had previously said was Tiffany Stasi.

From there, they drove to the Robinson home, then in Stanley, Kansas, where Robinson's wife, Nancy, and the rest of the family were waiting. That night, they held a joyous family reunion, he said, even taking photos that depicted the smiling defendant holding the baby on his lap. Also in the picture were Robinson's wife, Nancy, his two daughters, Kim and Christy, and his son Chris. Don and Frieda flew back to Chicago the next day with their new daughter.

John Robinson had also told his brother and sister-in-law that the baby's name was Tiffany, Don said. "We named her Heather Tiffany Robinson," he testified. "[Tiffany] was the name her mother had given her, so we wanted to keep that in some way."

Don Robinson said he received copies of the adoption papers in the mail that summer. He identified the papers in court and confirmed that he and his wife had signed them.

During a break in testimony, the defendant grinned as he was led by his brother in the witness stand. Don Robinson smiled faintly in return and shook his extended hand. On cross-examination by the defense a few minutes later, he admitted he had once been "fairly close" to his brother and had looked up to him.

Upon learning fifteen years later that his brother had been charged with capital murder, he said he was in "total shock. There's no way I would have expected that."

His family would soon become even more intimately involved in the case than they ever imagined. "My daughter looked it up on the Internet" at the time of Robinson's arrest, Frieda testified. "She showed me the missing persons report related to herself and Lisa Stasi."

Frieda Robinson said she didn't believe at first that the Web site pictures of Tiffany Stasi were actually of Heather. But the next morning, when Heather was asleep, she and her husband went through their daughter's baby album and made a heart-wrenching discovery. She was wearing the same outfit as the missing baby, Frieda said, and both pictures appeared to be a part of the same series.

A fingerprint examiner followed the Robinsons to the stand on Monday to confirm briefly that prints taken from Tiffany Stasi at the time of her birth in September 1984 matched those of Heather Robinson. Three other witnesses—including a district judge, Ron Wood, (Robinson's old attorney) and another attorney, Doug Wood—also testified that their signatures on Heather Robinson's adoption papers had been forged.

While Doug Wood, who at the time of the trial was up for reelection as Johnson County commissioner, had briefly rented office space to Robinson, he stressed that he had never helped him with any adoptions or accepted any money.

A fourth witness told the court that she had been Robinson's BDSM mistress in the mid-1980s and signed blank sheets of paper at his request. Even though a notary public stamp and her signature, Evi Gresham, appeared on the adoption papers, the woman insisted that she had never been a notary public and had never seen the papers until authorities showed them to her after Robinson's arrest.

The testimony about Lisa Stasi and her four-month-old baby prompted lively discussion on Court TV's Web site, which was covering the case. One young woman, writing under the moniker of 'LoveConquersAll,' first chimed in on Oct. 12, complaining about the media coverage. "I won't lie and say it isn't interesting because it is," she wrote on a message board devoted to the Robinson trial. "But these people have suffered enough. How much more must they suffer because of our curiosity? And it is sad that the victims are labeled "The Missing Baby" and "The Brother" and so forth. I am sure the poor child does not need to hear that. [She] must have been traumatically affected from this. The loving family that took good care of her was betrayed as well. I believe they had no part in it. The man who is the brother: someone he loved betrayed him. [That] is the worst feeling in the world."

On Oct. 22, the day after Don and Frieda Robinson had taken the stand, prompting several readers to write in with sympathetic comments, "LoveConquersAll" began a shocking new thread: "I'm Heather Tiffany. I have been reading the posts about all this and reading your comments," she wrote. "Thank you for caring so much. It is nice of you. I am 18 now and a senior. I contact my grandma all the time. And I refuse to have anything to do with the 'Stasi Family' for reasons I'm sure you can assume. And because of my lack of respect towards them and the way they treated my Mom and Dad (The Victims). And yes, I found my picture online. And I am the one who keeps up with the trial. I read news articles everyday. And so on . . ."

Of course, this prompted a flurry of responses and questions. Heather Tiffany wrote again on October 23, explaining that the handshake between her father and the defendant had been portrayed inaccurately by the media. "While the judge and jury left for a break, John was led past the witness stand, where 'Don,' my Dad, was staying. John put his hand out. My dad just simply shook his hand. He used proper behavior. He was in a courtroom and he was not going to become over dramatic and make a scene."

In another post a few days later, Heather Tiffany explained that her father had, indeed, looked up to Robinson when he was growing up. "My dad is ten years younger than John," she wrote. "He never grew up with him hardly. And they were in two different worlds. John was the golden child. He accomplished a lot. A kiss from Judy Garland, met the Queen, etc. . . . If I was in my dad's place, I would look up to him as well. But my dad never had that much contact with him."

Heather Tiffany, assuming she was who she said she was, would post on only a few more occasions. But she would wait to deliver her final remarks until after the jury had spoken.

Chapter 35

Nearing the homestretch of the prosecution's case, DA Morrison called several witnesses on Tuesday, October 22, 2002, to testify about the two women and teenage girl discovered in Robinson's Missouri storage locker.

Dr. Thomas Young, the Jackson County coroner, who testified that the murderer had wielded a blunt object, like a hammer to kill the three females with several powerful blows to the head. One of the women, he said, forty-five-year-old Sheila Faith, also had a fracture on her right forearm that was consistent with a defensive injury. Judging by the advanced state of decomposition, Young said, all three could have been dead five or six years.

Next up was Beverly Bonner's younger brother, Larry Heath, who described a series of letters he had received from his dead sister beginning in January 1994. In the first one, a recently divorced Bonner wrote in her own hand, he said, that she had taken a new job in the human resources department of a large international corporation and would be training in Chicago and then traveling extensively throughout Europe. She told him to write her at a mailbox facility in Olathe, Kansas, which would forward her correspondence to wherever she was stationed. Her next letter, which arrived in April 1994, and all subsequent letters were typewritten, he said, and in them she described working closely with new boss "Jim Redmond" as they circled the globe.

Heath, a bald and bearded truck driver from Florida, identified thirteen letters that his sister had sent to him from countries in Europe and Australia. He stated that he had always kept in touch with his sister through letters and didn't grow overly concerned about her until they stopped coming in January 1997. When Welch asked what he did at that point, the tough-looking guy broke down.

"Can I have some water?" he asked.

Regaining his composure, he said: "We contacted the State Department and the FBI. I wrote to my congressman. My mother also wrote to her congressman."

"Were you able to find her?" asked ADA Welch.

"No," he replied.

Lowell Heath, Beverly's older brother, told the jury that he had last seen his sister when he retired from the U.S. Navy in 1992. She had come to a retirement party for him in Mississippi with her then-husband, William Bonner, and two sons by her first husband, Ryan and Randy Lake.

"Were you aware that she might be having marital problems [with Bonner]?" Welch asked.

"Yes," said Lowell.

Prior to her disappearance, he and his sister stayed in touch sporadically by letters and phone, Lowell Heath said. The last time he had spoken with her was in early 1993. In October 1994, he moved to Kuwait for three years. While he was living over there, he got married.

"Was she invited to the wedding?" Welch asked.

"Absolutely," he answered, adding that she never showed up.

About the same time, Beverly's eldest son had died, he said. She didn't attend her son's funeral, either. According to a letter she wrote later, Heath said, she was changing her mailing service and didn't get the news in time.

On cross-examination, defense lawyer Berrigan asked Lowell Heath the same question he had posed moments earlier to his younger brother, Larry: "Your sister was never involved in sadomasochistic sexual activities, was she?"

"As far as I know, no," Lowell Heath replied.

Colleen Davis, co-owner of the Mailroom, located in

Olathe, followed Beverly's brothers to the stand, testifying that the defendant, using the name James Turner, had rented a mailbox for Beverly Jean Bonner in 1994. "He told me she was working for him and was going to be going to Australia and he was going to take care of her mail," she testified, explaining that Robinson had provided copies of Bonner's identification to open the mailbox.

Robinson rented a second mailbox in June 1994 for Sheila and Debbie Faith, Davis said. "Mr. Turner picked up mail at least once a month," she said, still referring to him by his alias. "He received two government checks monthly in the names of Sheila Faith and Debbie Faith."

Davis testified that she never saw anyone collect the checks except Robinson.

"How long did he receive them?" Welch asked.

"It would have been June [2000] because they were still sitting here when Mr. Turner was arrested," she replied.

On cross-examination, Pat Berrigan questioned Davis's ability to remember just who had rented the mailboxes, since it was so many years ago and she had many patrons. But she stuck to her story. "In my business, we try to remember our customers and to speak to them on a regular basis," she said firmly.

Two of Sheila Faith's sisters then took the stand, saying they had begun to receive typewritten letters from their sister and niece not long after they disappeared in the summer of 1994. "She always handwrote her letters," said her sister Kathy Norman, who received letters postmarked from Canada and the Netherlands. "This isn't Sheila," testified her other sister, Michelle Fox, referring to a letter she received from her sister in 1995. "It was happy. Sheila wasn't a happy person."

Perhaps the most compelling testimony about the Faiths, however, came from a close friend from Pueblo, Colorado, who described how the lonely widow left Colorado with her teenage daughter, never to return. "Sheila and I were as close as sisters could be," said Nancy Guerrero, who met her friend in Santa Ana, California, when both of their daughters entered in the 1980s a school for the physically challenged. Debbie was wheelchair-bound with cerebral palsy, she testified. Not long after Sheila's husband, John, died of cancer, she and Debbie followed the Guerreros to Pueblo. The Faiths were very poor, surviving on Social Security checks, Guerrero testified. "That's all they had to live on," Nancy said. "We helped them as much as we could."

Guerrero also admitted to knowing that her friend was interested in BDSM and used newspaper personal ads to meet men. "She would start to talk about [BDSM] and I said, 'I don't want to hear it. It's not my thing.' " In 1994, Sheila told her friend that she had met a Missouri man named John, Nancy testified. "She told me he was an executive in a big firm and that he was very wealthy," Guerrero said. "He promised to take her on a cruise and to put Debbie in a very good private school."

About two weeks later, the Faiths made plans to drive their beat-up white van to visit relatives in Texas but stop in Missouri on their way and see John, Guerrero testified. They packed clothing but left their furniture, bedding, dishes and silverware behind.

Under questioning from Morrison, Nancy identified a cross-stitch of an angel in a gold frame as belonging to Faith and said she had last seen it hanging on her friend's living-room wall. Her friend had taught her how to cross-stitch, she said, and they planned to enter their work in the Colorado State Fair. They had even bought tickets for the September 1994 event. "It was just supposed to be a short trip and she was supposed to be coming back," said Guerrero.

With tears in her eyes, the Colorado woman said she never saw the Faiths again.

The prosecution's next witness was a young woman named Sondra Shields, who testified that she had met Robinson in February 1995 after responding to his personal ad in *Pitch Weekly* for a submissive. Before she could get very far, however, the defense interrupted her testimony and suggested they break for the day because prosecutors had failed to include her on their witness list and O'Brien and Berrigan were in the dark as to who she was. "Neither Mr. O'Brien nor I have ever heard of this woman in our lives," Berrigan stated. "I just wrote him a note, 'Who is this woman?'"

Returning to the stand on Wednesday morning, October 23, Shields explained that Robinson—using the alias "BJ Bonner"—had hired her as a researcher for his company, Specialty Publications, but that their relationship primarily consisted of BDSM sex sessions at her apartment. At one point, he told her that his sister had died and brought over several items that he said came from her storage locker. Among the items he gave her, Shields said, was an angel cross-stitch encased in a gold frame. She said it was hanging on her wall when the news broke about Robinson's arrest.

Beverly Brewington, senior vice president of the Community Bank of Raymore, then testified that a James Turner and Beverly Bonner had opened up a business account at her bank under the name of Hydro-Gro, in February 1994. She also said that the account holders had cashed Social Security checks made out to the Faiths and deposited them into the business account from July 1994 to September 1995. In the fall of 1995, Brewington's bank sent a notice to Turner and Bonner, saying that they could no longer deposit personal checks into a business account, she said. There was no further activity on the account, she noted. But Bret Manz, a Bank of America supervisor, testified that Social Security checks made out to the Faiths had also been deposited more recently into a business account at his bank. The account was for Specialty Publications of America, Inc., d.b.a. Manufactured Modular Home Living.

Beverly Bonner's ex-husband also took the stand on Wednesday, testifying that he last saw her in court when their divorce was finalized around February 1994. At that time, their house had been sold and she was in the process of moving to Raymore, Missouri, Dr. William Bonner said. She told him she was taking a job with a company out of Chicago that involved world travel and sales, he said. "Selling what, I don't know," he added. "I'd inquire, but she'd never give me an answer."

Welch asked Bonner if his ex-wife ever mentioned John Robinson. "Yes, she did," he replied. "She mentioned that she was helping him find some land for a prospective hydroponics business."

"Did she ever mention taking a job with this hydroponics outfit?" Welch continued.

"Not to my knowledge," he said.

After the divorce was finalized, he sent his ex-wife $1,000 checks for eighteen months to a post office box in Olathe to repay her for an old tax loan, the doctor said. Bonner identified fifteen of the checks he sent in court. He noted that all of them had been cashed and acknowledged that the signature on the back appeared to be that of his wife.

On cross-examination, Bonner said he had been married to his ex-wife from 1989 until 1994.

"Is it fair to say your wife was not into sadomasochistic sex?" defense lawyer Patrick Berrigan asked.

"True," Bonner replied.

"She was not into whips or chains or restraints?"

"Not to my knowledge."

Under further questioning from Berrigan, Bonner also acknowledged that he had been a physician at the same prison where Robinson had been incarcerated and had treated him for high blood pressure on a number of occasions. "I got along with him fine," Bonner testified.

"Your wife, Beverly, worked as a librarian at that same institution?" Berrigan asked.

"Yes."

ADA Sara Welch, on recross, queried: "Was your wife employed as a prison librarian at the same time that John Robinson was there?"

"Yes," he replied.

"Were you aware why Robinson was there—that he had violated his probation?" asked Berrigan, on recross.

"No, sir."

"If I told you that Mr. Robinson was incarcerated because he violated probation for stealing out of Clay County, would you have a quarrel with that?" Berrigan followed.

"The only thing we ever had access to was medical records," Bonner replied. "I had no information to the contrary."

The brief exchange marked the first and only time that jurors would hear testimony about Robinson's prior criminal record.

R.E. Holtz, a special agent for the Social Security Administration, told the court that in 1993 his agency had been sending monthly survivor benefit checks to Faith and her daughter in Colorado after her husband died of cancer. But in June 1994, they began sending them to a post office box in Olathe, he said.

"How does one go about changing one's address?" Morrison asked the witness.

"By telephone or by letter," replied Holtz, who identified about 150 Social Security checks worth more than $80,000 that had been cashed between June 1994 and June 2000, when Robinson was arrested.

Latent-print examiner Lyla Thompson took the stand that Wednesday afternoon, October 23, testifying that she found Robinson's fingerprints on several glass items that belonged to Suzette Trouten packed in a box in his rural trailer. Thompson also noted that a fingerprint on a bloodstained roll of duct tape did not match Robinson's prints or those of the law officers who had handled it. Earlier DNA testimony matched the blood on the tape to Lewicka, but Thompson said she could not compare the fingerprint on the tape with Lewicka's because the young woman's body had been too decomposed to obtain "known" prints.

Returning to the stand on Thursday morning, October 24, Thompson revealed a couple of surprises. Robinson's fingerprints, she testified, were all over several of the Faiths' Social Security checks—further proof that the defendant had picked up the checks at the Mailroom and cashed them in two local banks. "Those prints could not have been made by any other person," she stated.

His prints were also found on three $1,000 checks for loan repayment that Dr. William Bonner had sent to his ex-wife and on a piece of plastic covering two of the barrels found in his Missouri storage locker, Thompson stated. Inside those barrels were the bodies of Sheila and Debbie Faith.

In cross-examining Thompson, however, Berrigan noted that sixteen fingerprints on the Faiths' checks did not belong to Robinson. Thompson acknowledged that he was right and also that an unidentified palm print on the plastic covering the barrels did not match those of the defendant.

Berrigan also questioned Thompson about a fingerprint found on a roll of duct tape that, according to previous testimony, also contained a spot of Lewicka's blood. The fingerprint did not match Robinson's, and Berrigan suggested that the print's placement on the outer surface of the roll indicated that whoever left it was likely the last person to have touched the tape.

But Welch, on redirect, again noted that the unknown print could not be compared to Lewicka's because she left no prints for comparison.

Frank Booth, the DNA analyst, returned to the stand a second time that Thursday for the prosecution's final presentation of physical evidence, testifying that he had randomly tested nine envelopes purportedly sent from Bonner to her brother Larry Heath, and he found that eight of them contained the defendant's DNA. In one of the trial's most compelling moments, Booth enthusiastically exclaimed: "The person who licked all eight of those envelopes is John Robinson!"

Chapter 36

Vickie Neufeld was the prosecution's last witness, taking the stand for more than an hour on Thursday afternoon, October 24. The psychologist broke down as she described her sexual encounters with Robinson. " 'This is how we find out if we have chemistry,' " she quoted the defendant as saying as he took off his clothes, stretched out on the bed and demanded oral sex. When she complied, he pulled out a camera and started taking pictures of her, she said. "I didn't want him to do that," she testified, softly crying. He then moved to a chair, took her by the hair and pulled her to her knees in front of him. Still gripping her hair, she said, "he thrust himself in [my mouth] and thrust my head back and forth until he ejaculated."

As Neufeld testified, Robinson's daughter Christy Shipps sat in the front row of the courtroom gallery, her hand covering her mouth. At one point, John Robinson glanced back at his daughter, gave her a little smile and shook his head, as if to say he couldn't believe what the witness was telling the court about him. With tears in her eyes, she managed to smile back.

Robinson, Vickie continued, returned to her hotel room the next day. This time, she testified that he grew angry when she didn't take off her clothes quickly enough. He yanked her sweater off and demanded she take off the rest, she said. He then put around her neck a leather collar that was attached to handcuffs he fastened to her wrists. She told him the collar was too tight, she said. "I was afraid," she testified. "In BDSM, you have role-playing. But you also have negotiation."

The woman said she stayed for another day and one more sexual encounter with Robinson, in which he slapped her twice, harder than she'd ever been slapped before. "I was afraid," she stated again. Afterward, he told her he had to fly to Israel and would send a moving truck to get her things and bring her to Kansas. He also told her to leave her bag of sex toys with him because, as she said he put it, "'this is one way to get you back.'"

She drove home and waited, but the moving truck never came. When she told him she had done some checking and there were no flights from Kansas City that connected to Israel, Robinson had an explanation, she said. "He said he was a colonel in the air force and he owned a private jet," she told the jury. Though she wasn't sure whether or not she believed him, Vickie told the court she was so financially desperate she didn't want to give up on the possibility that he might be able to help her with job interviews and obtaining a license.

Not long after, they broke off their relationship, but he refused to send her the sex toys, she said. "He said if I continued to harass him, he would take my slave contract and photos to the [psychology] licensure board," she testified. It was at that point she called the authorities, she said.

On cross-examination, defense attorney Jason Billam showed the witness several e-mails she had sent to Robinson, including one that quoted her as saying the trysts with him "were pure joy and more satisfying than anything I'd ever encountered."

Though humiliated and privately furious at Billam, particularly when he scattered her sex toys across the courtroom floor, Vickie steadfastly maintained that she hadn't consented to several of Robinson's advances. In trying to make this point to the judge, prosecutor Paul Morrison likened her experience to intimidation rape, where no words were spoken but consent was clearly violated.

The prosecution rested its case late on Thursday after calling more than one hundred witnesses, submitting some five hundred pieces of evidence and dozens of photos. Despite Neufeld's testimony that she did not consent, the judge ruled that there was not enough evidence to support a criminal charge of sexual battery. "Frankly, the evidence at the preliminary hearing was borderline," he said dismissing the charge. "If anything, it got thinner here."

However, he let stand the charge in which Neufeld claimed Robinson had stolen about $700 worth of her sex toys.

After only a short break, the defense called its first witness, Marsha Keylon, another housekeeper at the Guesthouse Suites. Keylon briefly testified that she saw Suzette only three times during her evening shift at the Lenexa hotel. Twice she was alone. The third meeting was as Suzette entered her suite with a man in his thirties not fitting Robinson's description.

Suzette's former employer, Sharon LaPrad, was their second witness and she wasn't on the witness stand much longer than Keylon. Suzette had worked for her off and on for nine years in Monroe, Michigan, before leaving to take a job in Kansas she stated. LaPrad cautioned her about taking the job, presumably to care for Robinson's elderly father. The job was to involve world travel and a $60,000 salary. "I just thought it was too good to be true," LaPrad told the court.

Suzette's landlord and friend from Monroe, Michigan, testified that she had given him a different reason for moving to Kansas City. Trouten said she had cancer and was going to an oncology clinic, John Stapleton said. She was also going to apply for welfare assistance, Stapleton said, and she told him it was easier to obtain in Kansas. She would then send him the $1,200 she owed him for rent and telephone bills. Before stepping down, Stapleton said he later learned from Lore Remington and Carolyn Trouten that he had "been told an out-and-out lie."

After Stapleton's testimony, Berrigan told the court that the defense had no other witnesses for the day but would return with "somebody" the next morning, Friday, October 25.

However, when morning came—and after a couple of

hours behind closed doors—the defense announced that they, too, planned to rest, even though they had called only three witnesses who did nothing to bolster their case. They also never called Robinson or the key witness O'Brien had alluded to in opening statements, the one who allegedly had access to the defendant's Missouri storage locker. In the words of one courtroom observer, "the defense had no defense. But they didn't have anything to work with, either."

Before the jury was summoned, O'Brien once again moved for acquittal, saying that his team did not have enough time to prepare for trial. He also said that they had been unable to present evidence about what was at the heart of the case: Robinson's mental state. "The jury will never hear about how crazy this man is," O'Brien said, claiming that Robinson had been on suicide watch at the Johnson County Jail for the better part of the trial.

But Judge Anderson denied the request for acquittal, saying that "the case has been pending, not weeks or months, but literally for years and Mr. Robinson chose to change counsel well into the course of the case." He said that the current defense team had been working with Robinson for more than a year and yet again repeated his "belief that there has been adequate time to prepare."

Once the jurors were called back in and had taken their seats, Pat Berrigan officially rested his case and Paul Morrison said he did not wish to call any rebuttal witnesses. Noting that they were at a "critical stage of the proceedings," Judge Anderson then warned the panel: "You've now heard all the evidence you're going to hear and it's very, very important that you follow these admonishments. Don't let anybody talk with you or even try to talk with you about this case. Keep your thoughts on other things over the weekend."

He explained that on Monday they would receive instructions and listen to closing arguments by both sides. They had not been sequestered to this point, he noted, but that would change once they went into deliberations.

Chapter 37

In his closing remarks on Monday morning, October 28, Paul Morrison called the defendant a "sinister" man who for years had lured women to their deaths and gone to great lengths to conceal his crimes. "There is one common thread between all of these women and that one common thread is John Robinson," he told a courtroom filled to capacity, which once again included the relatives of several victims and Robinson's wife and daughter. "When we're done [with our closing arguments], we will prove this case not only beyond a reasonable doubt but beyond any doubt."

Morrison told jurors that Robinson had lured Suzette Trouten from Michigan not only to take part in a sex and bondage relationship but with the promise of a $60,000 job and world travel. "Do you think she would have willingly come down to Lenexa, Kansas, to be murdered?" he asked. "The defendant sold her a bill of goods, like he's sold so many others a bill of goods."

He described how, in one e-mail, Trouten had fantasized about being blindfolded and taken to some rural area to service her master. "Perhaps that's why she was blindfolded," the prosecutor said. "Perhaps that's why she was nude" when her body was found in the barrel.

Referring to the thirty-nine-minute videotape of the two having sadomasochistic sex, he said the words were almost as disturbing as the images on the screen. "He thought he owned her—but it got old," he argued. Trouten, he said, wanted a full-time relationship with Robinson and that was pretty hard when he had to play grandpa and loving husband in the evenings. "You can't do both at the same time," he said. "So what did the defendant do? He put her body in a barrel, like a piece of valueless trash."

On March 1, 2000, the day Trouten was allegedly murdered, Robinson was a very busy man, Morrison continued. At 11:43 A.M., someone placed a call from his trailer in the country to the front office of Santa Barbara Estates, the mobile-home community his wife managed. "I submit to you that that person who called was the defendant," Morrison said.

At 2:13 P.M., an agitated Robinson dropped by the Ridgeview Animal Hospital and picked up Trouten's Pekingese dogs, who had been boarding while their owner stayed at the Guesthouse Suites in Lenexa, Morrison said. Eleven minutes later, the defendant paid a visit to his storage locker in Olathe, the prosecutor said. "Was he getting a dog carrier?" Morrison asked. "Five minutes later, just up the road, these dogs are dropped off and an animal control officer is called."

Then shortly after 3:00 P.M., Robinson is caught on hotel videotape turning in Trouten's room key and loading up her belongings into his truck, Morrison said. "[Suzette Trouten] is not in that picture because she's dead," Morrison said. Robinson went to elaborate means to conceal Trouten's death, the prosecutor said, recruiting two different women—Jean Glines and Lidia Ponce—to mail letters to her relatives from Mexico and California. "People are on his back," he maintained. "The pressure is on. Those letters gotta go out."

Moving on to Lewicka, the prosecutor described how the Purdue University art student had moved to Kansas City not only because Robinson was training her to become a dominatrix but because he had offered her a job. "It was the same old story, the same old deception," Morrison said. "The girl comes down here and he strings her along for two years. She's telling people she's married to him. He's telling people he's married to her."

But in August 1999, an old lover of Robinson's comes to

town at the same time that Lewicka disappears, Morrison said. Robinson moves the woman, a Canadian named Barbara Sandre, into an apartment and brings over furniture, bedding, books and a fiery Impressionistic painting. "Lewicka died so his new girlfriend could have furniture," Morrison argued.

The prosecutor said he also believed that Robinson killed Lewicka in the apartment he had rented for her, noting that hundreds of pin-size spots of her blood were sprayed on the bedroom wall. Lewicka's body was clothed in a nightshirt and covered by a pillow in the barrel, Morrison said. "It was as if she were sleeping in the bedroom when she was killed," he stated.

Shifting back in time, he described how Robinson was under pressure in the mid-1980s to find a baby for his brother and sister-in-law to adopt. He said the defendant contacted social-service agencies looking for white girls with babies, preferably those who didn't have strong family ties. "Do you think it's because no one will be looking for them?" he asked.

Lisa Stasi and her baby met that description, Morrison said, noting that Kathy Klinginsmith, her sister-in-law, had testified that Robinson came to collect Stasi and her baby from her house on January 9, 1985. Because there was a snowstorm, he said, Stasi called Klinginsmith when she got back to her room at the Rodeway Inn to let her know she had arrived safely. She called her mother-in-law a little later and this time she was hysterical. Morrison quoted her as saying, " 'They want me to sign papers. They're coming to take my baby.' "

Morrison maintained, "That's the only evidence of anybody else being remotely involved in these crimes."

He said Robinson's brother and sister-in-law showed up the next day to adopt their baby. Morrison showed one of the photos they took that day to the jurors. "There he is, grinning like a Cheshire cat, within hours of Lisa Stasi having that baby ripped from her arms," Morrison said. "It's the same old story—just a different year."

Defense attorney Sean O'Brien, however, insisted that the

nature of Robinson's relationships with the women were so different and occurred so far apart in time that they couldn't be part of a common scheme or course of conduct. "I urge you to take the high road," O'Brien said, after quoting Robert Frost's famous poem "The Road Not Taken." "We ask only for a verdict that is true and just."

O'Brien talked about how Stasi and Trouten "were kind of like bookends—the first and last in a series of people who had died." He also noted that Stasi's body had never been found and that it was possible that she was still alive. "What if someday, in the future, we find Lisa Stasi or Lisa Stasi's remains, and what if the circumstances make us look at this in a whole new light?" he asked.

He noted that Robinson's relationship with Trouten and Lewicka involved bondage and sex, yet his relationship to Stasi involved nothing of the kind. He noted that there was alleged financial motive with Stasi and the three women found in the Missouri storage locker, but no such financial motive with Trouten and Lewicka. "[These cases] are separated by so much time and are so different, it's difficult to say that they were part of a common scheme or course of conduct," O'Brien said.

He also argued that Robinson had a much deeper, longer relationship with Lewicka than he had had with Trouten or Stasi. Unlike the other women, he added, the judge's instructions allowed for the jury to find Robinson guilty of second-degree murder for Lewicka. "There were no letters and no steps taken in advance with respect to her disappearance that reflect forethought," he argued.

The defense attorney also talked about how it was difficult to know the facts of the case because so many of the players had fantasy lives that involved bondage, sex and role-playing. As an example, he said, Robinson had a two-year affair with Lewicka and in her presence he told others she was his wife, his niece and his daughter. "She went along with each and every one of those [descriptions]," he said. "It was part of their fantasy."

O'Brien also said that Robinson's admitted relationship with all of these women did not mean he killed them. "He's directly connected to these women, but he's not connected to the violence," he argued. He added that Robinson's wife and brother, the two people who were closest to him, had expressed shock and disbelief upon learning that he'd been arrested. " 'I thought I was going to pass out,' " he quoted Nancy as testifying.

O'Brien also said that the physical evidence raised a lot of unanswered questions and suggested that more than one person committed the crimes. He argued that the barrels were too heavy to be lifted by one person. He cited the mysterious fingerprint on a roll of duct tape that contained a smudge of Lewicka's blood, which did not belong to Robinson. And he said that there was a palm print on the plastic wrapping two of the barrels in the Missouri locker that also did not belong to him. "Maybe in ten, fifteen years, we'll find out who [those prints] belong to and it will make us look at this case in a very different light," he said.

After the court heard from O'Brien, Paul Morrison came back to deliver his rebuttal. "Before we spend a lot of time talking about the fingerprint on the duct tape or why there were no letters from Izabela, let's think about the fact that those barrels with those bodies are on *his* farm," he thundered. "The defense is saying, 'Look at all the questions.' Over seventeen years, that's the best that they can come up with? I think you'll find that there are very few unanswered questions. The evidence in this case is overwhelming."

Morrison acknowledged that there was an unidentifiable fingerprint on the duct tape. However, he said, that didn't mean it wasn't Lewicka's and, in fact, he thought that it probably was. "We don't have Izabela's fingerprints because her body was too decomposed," he argued. "It's highly likely that that print was Izabela Lewicka's."

The prosecutor also attacked the defense's suggestion that Lisa Stasi might have abandoned her baby. "I think we all know she wouldn't just walk away from her baby," Morrison said. "O'Brien says, 'How do we know that in a couple of years that she's not going to walk in here?' Do you really think that's going to happen? Or do you think she's dead?"

Morrison began to talk about the similarities between the murders. All of these women, he said, were looking for something: jobs, travel, sexual relationships and security. Robinson took advantage of that, luring and exploiting them. From Stasi, Morrison said, he wanted her baby and his brother's money. From the three women in the Missouri storage locker, he wanted money. And from Trouten and Lewicka, he wanted sex.

All five of the women whose bodies were found in barrels, he said, died the same way, from powerful blows to the head. They were hidden the same way, in barrels. The fact that Stasi's body was never found, Morrison said, was the "ultimate concealment." And in all the cases, he said, the defendant sent letters and e-mails purportedly from the victims to allay the concerns of family and friends. "The victims are too numerous to mention," Morrison said in conclusion. "The ripple effects are far and wide. The misery is beyond human comprehension. Now it's up to you to decide if you want to hold the defendant accountable for all of his actions all of these years." He paused before delivering his final sentence. "I hope that you do."

Chapter 38

It was 2:55 P.M. Tuesday, October 29, 2002, when the jury foreman hit the buzzer to let the bailiff know they had reached a verdict. The six men and six women had deliberated for a total of eleven hours over two days, prompting speculation that they might be deadlocked on one of the counts or simply taking their time in considering the testimony of 110 witnesses and some five hundred pieces of evidence. Within twenty minutes, the prosecutors, defense lawyers and family members had reassembled in the courtroom for the long-anticipated moment of truth.

Linda Carter, the Victim Assistance Coordinator for the trial, caught Carolyn Trouten's eye as she and her ex-husband made their way down the aisle to the front row directly behind the prosecutor's table. "Are you okay?" Carter mouthed silently. Even with Harry by her side, Carolyn barely managed an unconvincing shrug in response to the question. She was so nervous. "Good luck," Carter mouthed again as Kathy Klinginsmith, Lisa Stasi's sister-in-law, and her mother-in-law, Betty Stasi, took seats next to the Troutens. Lisa's aunt Karen Moore was behind them.

Robinson's most ardent supporter throughout the trial, daughter Christy Shipps, sat on the opposite side of the crowded courtroom looking pale and apprehensive. She mouthed the words, "I love you" to her father as he was led in by two deputies, taking his customary place at the defense table between Billam and O'Brien. The deputies stood guard behind his chair and four more took up positions at the doors.

Judge Anderson entered a few minutes later. Asking everyone to be seated, he said he understood that many people had an emotional investment in the outcome of the case. He insisted that those who didn't think they could contain themselves leave immediately and warned the media against making a beeline for the exit until the jury had spoken and been ushered out. "This is a courtroom and I expect everyone to act accordingly," he admonished. "I don't mean to sound harsh, but I do mean to be firm."

Terri Issa, in the DA's office, had paged Lenexa and Overland Park police who worked the case to let them know the verdict was in. Rick Roth had dropped off Layman and the task force's police secretary Ginny Brandenburg and gone in search of a parking spot, literally running the three blocks back to the courthouse. Huffing and puffing, he and Dougan, who arrived separately, barely made it in time. As the judge was speaking, they slipped into seats behind Christy Shipps. Several of their colleagues were already in the room. Wilson and Reed, arriving just seconds later, were forced to wait for the verdicts outside the door.

Without further ado, Judge Anderson summoned the twelve jurors and four alternates, who looked weary as they filed in and took their places as usual in the jury box. The foreman, a blond-haired young man in a pale blue shirt who had been an alternate until deliberations, solemnly approached the bench and handed the verdicts to the judge.

"Will the defendant please stand," Anderson commanded.

John Robinson slowly rose to his feet, staring straight ahead and showing no emotion. Seconds later, it was all over: he was guilty as charged on all six counts. It was only as the judge read the verdict for the last and least serious of the charges—the felony theft of Vickie Neufeld's sex toys—that Robinson's demeanor suddenly changed. He shook his head and rolled his eyes, then looked down at the floor as if finally defeated. Though found guilty of capital murder, he seemed to those closely watching him that he was more upset about the sex toys conviction.

Unbelievable, Roth thought.

Several jurors would later confirm that they had never come close to being deadlocked on any of the charges. They were simply being careful, reviewing all the evidence for each of the six counts. "We spent a lot of time on each one," said Carl Macan, a retired pharmaceutical salesman who was known as Juror No. 184 for the duration of the trial. "We didn't rush through any of them. We decided we were not going to try and sell anybody if they didn't agree. But it was a slam dunk. Every vote we took in the guilt phase was twelve to nothing."

Back in the courtroom, O'Brien attempted to console Christy, who was quietly crying as she gathered her coat and purse. Across the aisle, tears of a different kind were streaming down the faces of Klinginsmith and Moore. Dave Brown went over and gave Carolyn a big hug. "At the risk of sounding sappy, I did get a little teary-eyed," the detective remembered. "I was so happy for Carolyn and her family and the families of the other victims."

Roth and Dougan exchanged looks of victory but kept it at that out of deference to Shipps, so distraught right in front of them. "It was the cap to the biggest case I would ever be involved with," Roth later said. "I was on cloud nine."

The sheriff's deputies standing just outside the courtroom door had been able to relay the verdicts to Reed and Wilson as soon as the judge read them aloud. "Finally justice was being served," said Reed, who felt vindicated.

"He had been such an arrogant jerk for so long," agreed Wilson. "I really believe he thought he would beat the charge [and] I found satisfaction in the fact that we finally got him!"

Members of the press corps gathered on the steps of the courthouse to await the families of the victims. Lisa Stasi's aunt Karen Moore was the first to emerge from the building. "It's just been a long time coming and we're very happy about the verdict," said the short, round woman with dark hair and red glasses. "I'm glad he's being held responsible for his actions."

Moore also said she had been in contact with Heather Tiffany Robinson, who had recently turned eighteen and would be graduating from high school in the spring. "She is a beautiful young woman," she said. "Her family is our family now and we love them." Moore added softly that she thought Heather would be "glad" that Robinson had been convicted.

Kathy Klinginsmith read a prepared statement on behalf of the Stasi family. It stated: "[We're] pleased with the jury's verdict, but deeply saddened by Lisa's death and missed opportunities with Heather Tiffany and in being part of her life."

Klinginsmith began to cry as she spoke of her brother's biological daughter: "It was real overwhelming for me. I knew back in 1985 he murdered my sister-in-law and kidnapped my niece."

Her mother, Betty Stasi, broke her silence. "We've been waiting all these years for this," she shyly told the group of reporters.

None of Stasi's relatives at the time said what kind of sentence they thought Robinson deserved to receive. "I believe in the death penalty, but I'm going to let God handle this one," said Moore. "It was hard to know that a man could do this, but you can't let the hatred eat you alive."

Betty Stasi said she hadn't yet made up her mind what she wanted to happen to him and Klinginsmith said she would leave that decision up to the jury.

Trouten's parents left the proceedings without speaking to reporters, explaining later that they had decided to wait until he was sentenced. Christy Shipps pulled her hooded jacket over her face and was escorted out of the building by O'Brien, who shielded her from several reporters clamoring for comment. None of Lewicka's family members had attended the proceedings. Neither the attorneys nor the detectives were able to comment because Anderson's judicial gag order had not been lifted. With their reporting done for the day, the media rushed to computers to write their stories or broadcast live from in front of the courthouse.

Back in Virginia, Vickie had been checking her e-mail and Web sites carrying Kansas City news by the hour since arriving home. It was hard for her to sleep or think about anything else. She was furious about the judge's decision to throw out the aggravated sexual battery charge and believed, erroneously, that the detectives had tape-recorded her encounter with Robinson. "I know you do not want to hear from me," Greg Wilson e-mailed her upon returning to the office that afternoon, "but the jury just returned a 'guilty' on ALL charges and I thought you'd like to know."

Within minutes, she received similar messages from Linda Carter and *The Kansas City Star*'s Tony Rizzo. "I was ecstatic . . . and somewhat stunned," Vickie later said. "For the jury to be so open and so unanimous gave me back a faith or confidence that I had lost at trial. Also, the jury had read parts of my testimony during deliberation . . . or so I was told and the judge allowed it. I hoped that something—anything—I said during my testimony had made an impact. The 'biggest' thought I had, however, was 'Well, you lost the battle, but you won the war.' I had spoken for the victims and now their justice had been served. The verdict began the closure process."

The same jury that had just convicted Robinson of capital murder would reconvene in two days to begin the death penalty phase. The judge had said he didn't expect testimony to last more than a few days, leading several reporters to speculate that Robinson's fate would likely be sealed by the weekend.

Chapter 39

The death penalty phase of Robinson's trial opened, appropriately enough, on a dreary and cold Halloween morning. Paul Morrison kept his comments brief as he asked jurors to consider the aggravating and mitigating factors surrounding the crimes. "No mitigating circumstances can ever come close to matching the weight of the aggravating circumstances," said the prosecutor, looking dapper in a navy suit and red tie. "At the close [of this phase], your path will be very, very clear."

But defense attorney Patrick Berrigan waxed poetic about how much Robinson loved his wife, his four children and seven grandchildren, and how he had raised an exceptional family. John junior was a district manager of Hollywood Video in Colorado and the proud father of three girls. His eldest daughter, Kim, had become an elementary schoolteacher in South Kansas City and was raising two toddlers. Christopher had recently gotten married and was a food and beverage manager for Hyatt Regency in the Florida Keys. Christy, a paramedic, was married to a Prairie Village police officer and the mother of two young kids. "If it can be said that the family is the inner sanctum of the soul," he said, "there's more to John Robinson than the horrible story you've heard so far."

Berrigan also told them that they should be allowed to hear more about his background and his mental state, but that would not be possible. "You're not going to hear how these two people—a killer of women and a man who loves his family—could live in the same body," he said. What they would hear, he continued, was testimony from two expert witnesses about how

Robinson would not pose a threat to anyone if given life in prison. "You don't have to kill John Robinson to incapacitate him," he said. "You can meet justice with compassion. One man or woman with courage can make a difference."

Nancy Robinson was the first witness called by the defense. For the first time in his four-week trial, Robinson showed his emotions as his wife, wearing a navy dress with a prim white collar, took the stand and testified about his eight-year-old granddaughter's visit to see him at the Johnson County Jail. The little girl was having some difficulties, Nancy said, and wanted very badly to see the grandfather who had taken care of her several times a week. "They have a bond that is unbelievable," she stated. "She is the apple of his eye."

Nancy explained that she and her daughter Christy Shipps waited in the lobby of the jail while a guard escorted her granddaughter to meet the defendant. Later, the little girl came back, Nancy said, and told how she had thrown her arms around her grandfather and, in reference to his prison garb, said: "Papa, orange is not your color."

Upon hearing her testimony, Robinson's shoulders shook and he took off his glasses and began wiping tears from his eyes with a handkerchief.

Nancy divulged several details in an effort to paint her husband as the devoted head of a tight-knit family: When Kim was about a year old, the little girl they called "Princess" had become very ill. They took her to the hospital, thinking she had a bad case of the flu. But doctors told them there was a problem with her brain and they wanted to perform exploratory surgery. "We talked about it and [my husband] said, 'We're not going to do that to her,'" she recalled, adding that they had to sign her out against medical advice. In the end, John had made the right decision. "In three days, she was acting like herself again."

She also described her husband as being very involved with their children as they were growing up. Kim and Christy played volleyball; John junior and Chris played soccer—and their proud father attended most if not all of their games. While John senior couldn't interest Chris in Scouting, John junior had latched onto it immediately, she said, and following in his father's footsteps, he eventually earned the rank of Eagle Scout. Robinson's relationship with all four of his children was "very close," she said. "That's part of the reason I was still married."

She explained that John junior was twenty-two, Kim was twenty and the twins were just sixteen when Robinson went to prison for five years in 1987. "They were very upset," she remembered. "They missed him." She took the twins about twice a month to see their father; the older ones couldn't go as often. "It wasn't my choice," she said of the regular visits. "I don't think I could have kept them from going."

She described how proud she was of her four children and the lives they were leading. She said John junior had married an "extremely nice person" named Lisa, and they had three little girls, the youngest having been born in April 2000 with a heart murmur, which only brought them closer together. "[Lisa] told both of us that we were the family she's never had," Nancy said.

Kim's husband, she continued, was the vice president of a publishing company and they had a little girl, who was just a year old, and a little boy, who was three. Christopher "is very laid-back and straight as an arrow," she said, adding that he had married in 1999 and didn't yet have children. "He's grown up to be an extremely nice man."

Nancy reserved perhaps her highest praise for Christy. "She's grown up to be one of the most compassionate people I've ever known," she stated. "Hopefully, [the compassion] comes from both of us. She received an award for what she feels was just doing her job." Christy and her father are "extremely close and always have been," she added. "Not a day goes by when we don't hear from her. After she had her little girl, she wouldn't leave her with anyone but us."

Robinson's wife also stated that she had spoken to her children about her decision to plead for her husband's life. "All four have asked that I do this," she said. "They've listened to

the facts as you have, but they grew up with somebody else."
Asked how they felt about the possibility of his execution, she
dabbed at her eyes with Kleenex. "It's devastating, absolutely
devastating," she said, sobbing. "He's their dad; he's their
grandfather. They love him."

On cross-examination, however, prosecutor Paul Morrison
poked several holes in Nancy's portrayal of John Robinson.
He noted that she had testified for her husband when he was
convicted of fraud in 1986. "That didn't break the marital
bond, did it?" he asked.

Calling Robinson the "infidel deluxe," Morrison questioned
how Nancy could stand by him despite numerous affairs over
the years. "In fact, you're still married to him today," he said.
"Is *murder* enough to break the marital bond for you?"

"I don't know," she mumbled nervously. "Not right now."

Morrison also asked her why she didn't tell the police that
her husband had brought home a baby when they were investigating the disappearance of Lisa and Tiffany Stasi in 1985.
"I was not asked," she replied. "If you don't know what
they're looking for, you can't volunteer anything."

Morrison continued to hammer away. "Would it affect your
opinion if you knew that your husband had taken [your grand-
daughter] along on BDSM liaisons?" Morrison asked.
"Would *that* change your opinion?"

"Mr. Morrison!" cried Nancy, visibly agitated, as the defense objected.

But Morrison insisted he had evidence that Robinson had
indeed brought his granddaughter along on sadomasochistic
sex encounters, and if necessary, he was ready to present the
proof.

"I know this is stressful for you; however, it is not an argument," said Judge Anderson as he instructed the witness to
answer the question.

"I don't know," she replied, flustered.

Morrison also presented her with the note she had written
to her husband in November 1999—the same note detectives

had found in the trash—complaining about other women and the fact that he hadn't found a job. "'You can only push a person so far and rub [my] face in shit so much,'" she read aloud at the prosecutor's request.

"That's hardly a description of a good family man, is it?" Morrison asked.

"It's not a description of a great husband, okay?" replied the witness, growing somewhat defiant.

Morrison persisted once more. "Do you believe your husband killed all of these women?"

"If that's what the jury said . . . yes," she admitted before stepping down for the second and final time.

Following Robinson's wife to the stand was Mark Cunningham, a forensic psychologist, who maintained that Robinson was not likely to pose a threat to anyone should he be sentenced to life in prison. He cited Robinson's age—fifty-eight—and the fact that he had been a model prisoner while serving five years in Kansas and Missouri correctional facilities and two years in the Johnson County Jail. "The likelihood that someone is going to be a disciplinary problem in prison falls steadily with age," said Cunningham, who said he had testified in seventy death penalty cases nationwide.

However, Cunningham acknowledged that Robinson had practiced deception and manipulation both inside and outside prison walls, including falsifying letters of recommendation to his parole board back in the 1980s. Based on that fact and examples of fraud brought out in the murder trial, Cunningham said he anticipated that Robinson would "continue to be deceptive and manipulative wherever he is."

Cunningham, who was paid $11,000 by the defense for forty-five hours of work, also admitted that he never checked with the Kansas Department of Corrections to find out whether Robinson would have access to a computer. He had, however, checked Robinson's visitor logs for the twenty-nine months he had been in the Johnson County Jail. Nancy and Christy, he said, were the only family members who visited with any regularity. His other three children—despite Nancy's testimony about how much they loved their father—had not been to the jail at all.

Standing before the yellow barrels that had served as coffins for Suzette and Izabela, Morrison began his closing remarks the next afternoon. In asking for the death penalty, he said the state was presenting only one aggravating circumstance—"and it's a big one," he added—the fact that Robinson had intentionally and with forethought killed five women and a teenage girl over a fifteen-year period.

He asked jurors to consider whether they had heard any facts or circumstances that reduced his moral culpability. "They're not there," he argued. "Words cannot describe the enormity of the crimes committed by the defendant [or] the enormity of the loss of the victims' families."

Citing testimony from the previous day, the prosecutor said Mark Cunningham had failed to find out if Robinson's bait of choice—a computer—would be available in prison. He said Robinson has always been a liar and con man and was unlikely to change his ways if allowed to live. "His way is manipulation. His way is deceit," he said. "And it often ends in tragic consequences."

Morrison also talked about Nancy Robinson, calling her a pathetic figure. "She takes the term 'stand by your man' to a whole new level," he said. "She is, in many ways, another victim of this man. Her life has probably been ruined because of what he has done to her and that family." And yet, as he noted, the family had begged the court to spare his life, claiming that his death would deprive them of his company. "It doesn't get any more audacious than that," he said. "Can you be a great dad when you're in prison? Can you be a great grandfather when you do the kinds of things he has done?"

Wrapping up the first half of his closing arguments by asking jurors to consider what's "fair and just," Morrison yielded the floor to Berrigan, who picked up on the same theme and spoke about how the jurors had been chosen for those very reasons. You must now grapple with a very big decision, he told them. "What punishment is going to be severe enough that it will reflect justice?" he asked as he raised several mitigating factors. "I'm not telling you that John Robinson is deserving of mercy. But you know in your heart of hearts we don't have to kill this man."

Referring to testimony about Robinson's numerous extramarital affairs, Berrigan said there was no dispute that "by day he was running around with all these women." But, he said, "at night this guy's home with his family. No, he's not been a good husband. But you know what? [Nancy] loves him. His family loves him."

Berrigan asked jurors to consider the testimony about Robinson's four children, described as productive and law-abiding members of society with families of their own. "That has to be some measure of the man," he said. "That's the fruit that has fallen from John Robinson's tree."

In fact, the monster described in testimony was not the same man he said the defense team had come to know—a polite, respectful and soft-spoken gentleman. "The person sitting here has been in jail for twenty-nine months," Berrigan said. "He's a different person than the one brutally killing women."

He brought up the testimony of two defense witnesses who said that Robinson would not pose a risk of physically harming anyone in prison.

"You know John Robinson is not going to be a threat to us," Berrigan said. "He's going to die in prison."

Concerns about him getting access to computers in prison, he argued, were nothing but another red herring. "Do you really think for a second any prison official is going to have John Robinson within a mile of a computer?" Berrigan asked. "Of course not."

As he had done previously, the defense lawyer also raised the possibility that someone else could have been involved in Robinson's crimes. He questioned the ability of one person to move barrels containing women's bodies and mentioned a palm print and a fingerprint found on key pieces of evidence that did not belong to him.

In establishing guilt, Berrigan said it didn't matter whether there was evidence of another person's involvement because all accomplices are equally guilty of a crime. But if someone else were involved in the crimes, Robinson would be less deserving of a death sentence. "These questions should be answered before anybody's put to death," he said.

Morrison, reclaiming the floor for his rebuttal, said he had been struck by Berrigan's description of his client as nonthreatening. "Look at him," he said as he pointed at Robinson. "Does he look like someone who would be into BDSM? Does he look like someone who would collect thousands and thousands of dollars in checks? Kill a nineteen-year-old woman for her baby? Stuff bodies into barrels? That's exactly why this man is so very, very dangerous."

Quoting from the Robert Duvall film, the district attorney said Robinson wanted the jury to grant him the "tender mercies" of life—small pleasures that included hearing rainfall on a roof or savoring a cup of fresh coffee in the morning. Yet, he said, Robinson had denied his six victims those same tender mercies. "They don't get to listen to the rain," he said. "They don't get to have a cup of coffee."

The defendant showed neither mercy nor remorse for his victims, Morrison continued. He didn't cry during testimony about the victims, he noted, but only when his wife talked about his granddaughter visiting him in jail. "He cried for himself," he thundered. "That says it all. He doesn't care about anybody but himself."

Concluding his remarks, Morrison said it was his belief that the death penalty should be reserved for only the most heinous of premeditated and intentional crimes. Rapping on the yellow barrels for emphasis, he paused and looked directly at the sixteen men and women sitting before him in the jury box. "If not him," he demanded, "who?"

Chapter 40

With the prosecutor's words reverberating in their heads, the panel of six men and six women began deliberating Robinson's sentence late on Friday afternoon, November 1, 2002. As they later revealed, jurors did not immediately agree upon the appropriate punishment. A vote taken not long into discussions found eight in favor of imposing the death penalty and four who were undecided. "Although I was one of the four undecided, I was leaning heavily toward the death penalty," said Juror No. 246, Debbie Mahan. "A couple jurors were having some personal struggles. But what Paul Morrison said really stuck in my mind. 'If not him, who?'"

The panel continued to deliberate until 8:00 P.M., when they agreed to retire to their rooms at the Holiday Inn, think things over alone and vote again in the morning. "I just wanted some quiet time to make sure the reasons for death far outweighed life in prison," said Mahan, who had been the one to suggest the idea. Carl Macan, Juror No. 184, had already made up his mind that Robinson deserved to die for his crimes and found even one night of sequestration difficult. A professional magician, he tried to pass the time by practicing some of his tricks. "I was going batty," he said. "There was no television, no radio, no nothing. I was working up some of my magic, but that got boring because I didn't have my mirror. I was like a prostitute in church."

The next morning at breakfast, a few of the jurors noticed that a red Gideon Bible was lying on the table next to one of the men on their panel. Mahan, a paralegal, wondered about the Bible for a fleeting instant but then forgot all about it as they returned to the jury room. Resuming their deliberations, they quickly took another vote. The tally this time was unanimous—12 to 0 for death. "We were getting ready to push the button, but the foreman asked if we would like to talk about our decision first," Mahan said.

They went around the table until they got to Juror No. 147—a big, burly man with dark hair and beard who had voted to impose the death penalty the night before. He picked up the Bible and cited several passages he had marked about mercy. "After I read this, I knew my decision was right," the juror allegedly said. No sooner had he done so than Judge Anderson strode into the jury room and asked, "Is there a Bible in here?"

When Juror No. 147 said he had one, "Judge Anderson's jaw about hit the floor," Macan recalled. The juror told the judge he had found the Bible in his hotel room. "It wasn't supposed to be there," the judge replied, escorting him from the room.

Over the next five hours, Judge Anderson and the lawyers individually questioned each juror privately about how or if the Bible was used. According to attorneys, during his night in sequestration, Juror No. 147 had read and jotted down several passages that stated that only God could grant mercy and only after a person had admitted wrongdoing and asked for forgiveness. He said the passages only confirmed that his decision to vote for death was correct.

At first, Mahan said she didn't think too much about the fact that the Bible had been brought into the jury room. "I figured it was like the newspapers or magazines we weren't supposed to have," she later said. "But as the day went on and the attorneys came and went from the judge's chambers, with my legal experience, I became extremely afraid of a mistrial. By the time the judge called us into the courtroom, I was physically sick to my stomach worrying about what was going to happen."

Rick Roth, who arrived at the courthouse that morning after hearing from Sara Welch that the jury had reached a verdict, realized there was something wrong when Sara walked into the

DA's office on the fifth floor. "She was totally pissed," he remembered. "It wasn't until she came in that I grasped what a major bag of worms it was." After venting, his girlfriend began researching case law, he said. "This was over my head, so I just spent the time watching the History Channel," he said. "My biggest contribution of the day was going out to buy pizza for everyone."

In fact, Robinson's lawyers were asking for a mistrial of the penalty phase or, at the very least, to remove Juror No. 147, arguing that it was inappropriate for anyone to consult a Bible during deliberations. But in the end, Anderson denied the requests. He decided it did not appear that the Bible or discussions about it had played a major role in the deliberations and he didn't think the juror had done anything so wrong that it merited his discharge. After all, as jurors insisted to the judge, the Bible had never been in the jury room before the last day. And they had already reached their verdicts before it had been introduced.

After his ruling, the jurors returned to their room to wrap up deliberations. As Macan described it, they quickly took a vote, signed the papers and "shot the bull" for about fifteen minutes. "We didn't want to look like we were too anxious," he said. As they filed back into the courtroom, many of the jurors looked directly at Robinson. No member of his family was in the courtroom as he stood and stared straight ahead, the yellow barrels that had held Suzette Trouten and Izabela Lewicka still in front of him. As the judge read the first "death" verdict, Robinson's knees buckled slightly, but otherwise he showed no emotion. The defense requested that the judge individually query each juror if that was his or her decision. "Yes, Your Honor" or "Yes, sir," they answered, one after the other.

From less than ten feet away, Dawn Trouten fixed her eyes on the man who had murdered her sister. "I wanted to be in the courtroom to see his face," she later said. "The man is so evil. He deserves to die. A death sentence is what we were hoping and praying for. If there had to be a purpose to my little sister's life, it's that she stopped this man from hurting another soul." Kathy Klinginsmith, Lisa Stasi's sister-in-law, was relieved. "I'm just glad it's over," she said.

Other family members who couldn't be in the courtroom that day also praised the jury's recommendation. "That's what we wanted because that's what he deserves," Lisa Stasi's mother, Pat Sylvester, later reached by phone in Alabama, told *The Kansas City Star*. "I'm happy knowing he will never hurt anybody else." Beverly Bonner's former husband, William Bonner, in Arizona, said he believed Robinson was a sociopath who would never show any remorse for his crimes. "I think [the death penalty] is appropriate," he reportedly said.

"The weasel got what he deserves," Sheila Faith's sister, Michelle Fox, in Texas, agreed. "I think it's too easy, though, to just put him on a gurney and shoot him up with toxins."

That night, after the trial was finally over, Morrison attended a charity board dinner with his wife. It wasn't until then, he noted, that the trial, the verdict and the death sentence really sank in. "I was in the rest room still sort of shell-shocked that this thing was finally over," said the prosecutor, chuckling as he recalled the moment. "I looked in the mirror and I had these big bags under my eyes. And I thought, 'Gosh, I look like hell.'"

The death penalty verdict prompted Heather Tiffany Robinson to post her final thoughts to CourtTV.com's message board November 11. "You people really amaze me," she said in response to several readers who had written that they were glad that Robinson had been sentenced to death. "You're happy he has the death penalty? So by supporting his death, you are supporting killing. You teach your children: "Two wrongs don't make a right." [Killing him] will not bring back the victims. Hell, it won't give me back part of my childhood I lost and it won't help his family, either. The worst punishment would be life in prison. If it were me, I'd say lock him up in solitary but since it's inhumane, that won't happen. But to wake up every day in a cold, dank cell for the remainder of his life is a lot worse than giving it to him easy and making it end."

Heather Tiffany also announced that she had just turned 18 and been adopted as an adult by her parents. "It was my idea and it got done," she wrote. "The blood may run through my veins but my heart and soul will never be a Stasi. I am a Robinson and proud of it. And I will defend my true Mother and Father and Lisa."

The teenage girl quickly posted another message, hotly defending her cousin, Christy Shipps, who had been lambasted by several members for standing by her father. "Christy is a wonderful, loving girl," Heather Tiffany wrote. "I don't think her father is innocent but I understand her defending the man she thought she knew. Ever think how you would feel if it was your father? No, probably not. Then you wouldn't have anything interesting to post."

She also skewered her biological aunt, Kathy Klinginsmith, and her biological father, Carl Stasi. "Kathy sent me letters the first few months," she wrote. "Then it stopped. Within the two years of this craziness, Carl sent me a letter. One letter in two years? To his darling missing girl?"

On the contrary, she said, Lisa Stasi's family contacted her all the time. "They supported my family—not attacked them," she said, seeming to direct her comments to one message board member who had said he was a Stasi relative. "And they never tried to publicize this like you guys like to . . . Everyone tells me to give you guys a chance. Betty [Stasi], I will. My parents, friends, Lisa's family tell me to be nice. But I am so not holding this in anymore. Even though my parents taught me to respect others. There is no respect for you and your family. Really where was your respect and love when Lisa got pushed around? Or respect to me and my family and our privacy? And now I come to this board and see you attacking an innocent family member of mine."

Heather Tiffany posted one final addendum, stressing that she was speaking only for herself. "My thoughts are my thoughts alone," she wrote. "They are spoken on my behalf and my behalf alone. Whatever I say comes from me, not my family or my friends."

A few weeks later, on December 9, 2002, the defense filed a massive 220-page challenge to their client's convictions, citing more than one hundred grounds for a new trial or an outright acquittal. The first issue on their list? The Bible brought into the courtroom on the last day of deliberations. They argued that Juror No. 147 had violated Robinson's right to a fair trial by using an outside source in making his decision. "As a general proposition, a defendant is entitled to a verdict based solely on the evidence and arguments presented in court and rendered in accordance with the court's instructions," the lawyers wrote.

The defense filing also attacked decisions and actions of the judge and prosecutors from the time detectives had begun investigating Robinson in March 2000 until final jury deliberations in early November 2002. Most of the issues had already been raised by the defense and ruled on by Judge Anderson before and during Robinson's trial.

Because the judge refused their request to move the trial, they argued that Robinson had been left with a jury biased by pretrial publicity. The defense also claimed that a lack of preparation time left them unable to effectively represent Robinson. "Counsel simply did not conduct an adequate investigation of Mr. Robinson's background, character and mental condition necessary for a constitutional trial on the issue of punishment," they wrote. They also objected to statements made by Morrison in closing arguments, saying he went beyond what was permissible under the law.

Prosecutors responded only to the new defense arguments. The juror who took his Bible with him into deliberations did not commit misconduct, they argued several weeks later. The jurors already had taken their final vote before there was any conversation about Bible passages. Kansas law prohibits "delving into the thought processes" of a jury to challenge its verdict, prosecutors wrote. They also defended Morrison's descriptions about the enormity of Robinson's crimes and the effect of those crimes on the victims in his closing remarks of the penalty phase. "Is the state not entitled to argue that the killing of six human beings made this capital murder case more egregious than most?" they asked.

These and other issues would later be the grounds for defense appeals to the Kansas Supreme Court. But in the meantime, the judge set January 21, 2003 as the date he would rule on their requests and decide whether or not he would follow the jury's death recommendation. He had the authority to modify the sentence, but nobody really expected that he would. If nothing else, history was against him. In the four instances since 1994 when Kansas juries had recommended the death penalty, the judges had carried out their wishes. "I would be very disappointed in him if he [modified the sentence] because the jury spoke," said juror Carl Macan, shortly before sentencing. "That would really destroy my faith in the legal system."

Chapter 41

Rejecting all defense motions for acquittal on Tuesday, January 21, 2003, Judge Anderson gave John Robinson one last opportunity to bare his soul, asking the convicted murderer if he had anything he wished to present before learning his fate. The defendant, however, rose briefly to his feet and declined. "I have nothing," replied Robinson, sharply dressed, as always, in a gray suit with a pale blue tie. While he chose silence, his daughter stood at a podium placed in front of the gallery and pleaded with the judge on behalf "of all the children and grandchildren" to spare her father's life. "Your Honor, you are in a position to both dispense justice and mercy at the same time," said Christy Shipps, who, with her mother, attended the final proceedings on the bitterly cold morning.

Robinson's most loyal supporter tearfully described her father's prosecution as an "emotional roller coaster" that had strained the familial bonds to their maximum limit. She said they had to accept things they would never understand, but she emphasized that the horrible things heard in court did not reflect the loving man who had taught them to put family first and to respect the law. "The John Robinson we know has always been a loving and supportive father and grandfather," said Christy, wearing a red turtleneck and black pants.

The paramedic described how her eight-year-old daughter had been deeply affected by being separated from the grandfather she used to see almost every day. "Every day she asks God for one little hug from her Papa," she said, sobbing. She asked the judge to think of Robinson's seven grandchildren.

"They have done nothing wrong," she said. "Your Honor, we beg you to spare his life because we do love him."

Pat Berrigan, too, argued for a life sentence, which he said would be lived out miserably in a maximum-security penitentiary. He asked Judge Anderson to emulate the courage of U.S. senator Edmund G. Ross (R-Kansas) when he cast the pivotal 1868 vote against the impeachment of President Andrew Johnson. "The right decision is often not the popular decision," Berrigan said. "There is much grief, anger and suffering attributable to this man, but it can stop here. We do not need to answer John's violence with violence ourselves."

However, Lisa Stasi's aunt Karen Moore eloquently urged the judge to do just the opposite. "Lisa," Moore began in her soft voice, "was the most beautiful little girl you've ever seen." She had lived with their family for a time, she recalled, and became very close to Angie, Karen's daughter. When Lisa and Carl split up around Christmas 1984, Lisa had slept on their couch for a night, her baby lying on her chest, she said. "I made some phone calls to see if I could find some help for Lisa, and talked to a woman at Hope House," she said. With obvious regret, she added, "I took Lisa to Hope House." She said Marty, Lisa's brother, later received a call from his sister but told her he couldn't talk just then and described the guilt he felt when he never spoke to her again.

When Lisa went missing, the lives of her family were shattered, Moore went on. They were filled with anxiety and dread every time police discovered an unidentified body. They'd get calls to check on her blood type or her dental X rays, but there never was a match. "Your Honor, I've lived for fifteen years with the guilt of taking Lisa to Hope House," Moore said. "Marty was never the same. Every girl he dated looked like Lisa. His wife looked like Lisa. He suffered from severe bouts of depression. Then one day [in 1995], he went into his garage and hung himself."

Heather Tiffany Robinson lives with a family that loves her and she loves in return, Moore continued, and she and her sister-in-law—Lisa's mother, Pat Sylvester—counted themselves fortunate to have gotten to know her in the 2.5 years since they learned she was alive. "But Heather had a right to be with her mother," Moore argued emotionally. "She had the right to know her uncle Marty and her grandmother, and her great grandmother, and her great, great grandmother, and all the rest of the family. My sister-in-law lost both of her children [Lisa and Marty] because of John Robinson, because when he killed Lisa, he killed Marty as well. And he put our family through hell on earth for eighteen years. John Robinson has shown no regard for human life, no regard for the highest laws of the land, and I have never seen one ounce of remorse on his face. He should receive that which he brought upon himself—the penalty of capital punishment."

Carolyn Trouten and Suzette's sister Kim Padilla, who had driven with several family members through a blinding snowstorm to get to Kansas for the judge's sentencing, also made passionate pleas. Carolyn said she didn't view death as a punishment for Robinson or revenge for her daughter's murder but merely as insurance that he would never be able to kill again. "He took my little girl and I am never going to quit missing her," she said, tears streaming down her face.

"John Robinson lured Suzette with promises of a better life and he took that life away," added an equally emotional Kim, who bore a strong resemblance to her murdered sister.

Mother and daughter both took issue with what Christy Shipps had told the judge. "[We] don't have the opportunity to beg for Suzette's life," Padilla said bitterly. Carolyn questioned why Robinson's family would even want their children to be around him. "Seems to me if they had any sense, they'd want him to be executed, too," she told the judge.

Paul Morrison followed the women to the podium and said he felt an obligation to speak for the family of Izabela Lewicka, who lived in Indiana and could not bear the thought of ever again setting foot in Kansas. He recalled the recent comments of Izabela's father, who described how the death of his daughter had left an "overhanging sadness" to their lives. In nearly twenty-three years of prosecuting criminals, Morrison noted, he had never encountered anyone who had caused so much misery for so many people. "I've seen people do unspeakable things to other people," he said. "I've seen a lot of reasons why people kill. But it is very, very rare indeed . . . when somebody kills just because they like killing, when somebody takes so many lives with such a cavalier attitude. I do believe Mr. Robinson is a sexual sadist."

The prosecutor reiterated his belief that capital punishment should only be reserved for the worst of the worst. "This is the first time—and I've had several opportunities—that I'm asking to impose the ultimate punishment," he said. In closing, he repeated the sentiment first uttered in his final remarks to the jury: "If not John Robinson, Judge, then who?"

For two hours, Robinson sat in silence, calmly listening to the proceedings but appearing indifferent to their content. Now Anderson asked him to stand. Having considered the jury's recommendation, the judge said simply, "The court . . . does find that the verdict is supported by the evidence in this matter." Then he soberly sentenced Robinson to death for murdering Suzette Trouten and Izabela Lewicka and to life in prison for killing Lisa Stasi. He also sentenced Robinson to 5 to 20 years in prison for interference with parental custody, to 20.5 years for kidnapping Trouten, and 7 months for the theft of Vickie Neufeld's sex toys.

With respect to the offenses of capital punishment, Judge Anderson ordered that "the defendant be punished by remanding [him] to the custody of the Secretary of Corrections who shall then, without unreasonable delay, cause the defendant to be put to death by lethal injection."

Just in case the death penalty did not withstand appellate review, he also ordered the sentences to run consecutively. "It is the intent of this court that the defendant be incarcerated for the maximum term provided by law," he said before lifting the judicial gag order that had been in place since Robinson's arrest.

There to witness the judge's sentence were several of the investigators who had worked so hard to bring Robinson to justice, including Rick Roth and Stephen Haymes, who had played such critical roles at the beginning and end of Robinson's decades-long murder career. Both men said they felt a measure of relief and closure that the defendant had at long last gotten what he deserved. Carl Macan and Debbie Mahan, who attended along with four of the other jurors, felt the same way.

Macan, mincing no words, said his reaction to the verdict was "Death cannot come fast enough for him—like give him the needle tomorrow morning." Mahan, more circumspect, agreed that he deserved to die, but she also noted that she could understand why Christy Shipps had pleaded for her father's life. However, she, too, questioned why she would want her daughter exposed to such a monster. "If he killed one woman instead of six, it might have made a difference," she said, "but his life certainly is not worth more than the six lives he took. What really sealed it was when he had a chance to speak and chose not to—maybe because he still [had] to stand trial in Missouri?"

Lisa Stasi's aunt and Suzette Trouten's mother, aunt, grandmother and two sisters gathered after the sentencing for an impromptu press conference in the district attorney's library on the fifth floor. It had been an emotional day and many of the women's eyes were red from crying as they squeezed around the rectangular table. Carolyn Trouten was still outwardly seething, not only at Christy for pleading with the judge to spare her father's life but also at Nancy for turning a blind eye to her husband's criminal behavior. "I am almost as mad at them [the Robinson family] as I am at him," she said. "I think his wife could have stopped all this. If she would have just done something, anything, when he brought that baby home in 1985, then all our girls wouldn't be dead now."

Carolyn and her daughters reiterated their belief—one that had been verbalized by many others—that Robinson finally got caught because he targeted the wrong victim. "Somehow he must have thought that Suzette wasn't close to her family," said Carolyn. "Suzette was really dramatic and she probably told him she raised herself. He evidently believed it—and that was John Robinson's mistake." Her daughter, Dawn Trouten noted. "We're so close, if anything happens in our family, within three minutes everyone knows about it." Chuckling, Kim Padilla added, "And is there—whether you want us to be or not."

When a reporter noted that the Troutens were smiling and laughing, Dawn admitted, "It is a relief. It is finally over. We have already cried as many tears as we can cry. The well is kind of dry."

Kim agreed: "Our lives have been put on hold for more than two years."

Suzette's aunt and godmother, Marshella Chidester, interjected. "There will never be a day that goes by that we won't think about Suzette," she said solemnly, "but at least we can put this behind us now. It is a terrible thing for someone to get death, but John Robinson deserves it and he is going to have to come before the Lord and make amends."

One reporter asked Carolyn if she was surprised that Robinson had never uttered a word in either his defense or in the way of an apology. "I wasn't a bit surprised," she replied. "I think he thinks he is innocent. I think he thinks these women were in his way and they were not any use to him and he had the right to get rid of them. I think he thinks we are all stupid to even suggest he didn't have the right."

Karen Moore, who had listened silently while the Trouten women spoke their minds, was singled out for her thoughts on the judge's sentence. "I'm not going to rejoice in this man's death," she answered softly, "but I am glad he received the death penalty. I don't know how old his grandchildren are, but at least he got to hold them. He got to see them grow up at least a little bit. Heather's grandmother didn't get to do any of that. She didn't even get to hold her grandbaby."

Paul Morrison and Sara Welch also spoke publicly to reporters about the case for the first time since the gag order had been imposed shortly after Robinson's arrest. The prosecutor told the group that one of the first things he tries to do when he meets the families of victims is to explain he can't make things the way they were. "We can't make their lives whole again," he said. "We can't reverse the clock. What we hope to be able to do for victims of crime is to let them walk away feeling like they got some measure of justice."

His office had put in thousands of hours on the case and Morrison joked that in recent months he had spent more time with Welch than he had with his wife. Even then, two people were barely enough to get their arms around and make sense of all the evidence, he said. They had taken off a few days in spring 2002 because they knew they'd be working long hours, seven days a week, all summer and during the trial. Often the seamy nature of Robinson's activities made the prosecutors feel like clerks in a sex shop, he noted, and they had only slowly become conditioned to the graphic nature of BDSM.

One of their biggest challenges, Morrison also said, was to make the enormously complicated case understandable to a jury. It was very gratifying when they talked to jurors after the verdict and were told that the trial was much like watching a movie. "They said they didn't have much trouble following it," he said. "They would come in each day and watch the next chapter unfold. Which is what we wanted."

There were hugs between Linda Carter, Terri Issa and Shirley Fessler from the DA's staff and the Trouten women as the press conference came to an end and everyone got up to leave.

Karen Moore quietly asked Linda if she could use her phone to call her sister-in-law and tell her the good news. Pat Sylvester, she confided, had suffered two heart attacks since Robinson's arrest and had not been well enough to attend. She was at home in Alabama, though, hoping and praying for the death penalty. "We are both very strong Christians and a lot of people don't understand, but there are consequences to the choices you make," she said. "We hope he is very distressed and suffers for the rest of his life. We have been suffering for such a long time."

Epilogue

On January 24, 2003, three days after Judge Anderson sentenced him to death, Robinson was quietly transferred from the Johnson County Jail, where he'd lived since his arrest, to a small solitary cell at the El Dorado Correctional Facility outside Wichita, the destination for men facing capital punishment in Kansas. There he joined six others waiting to die—including the notorious Carr brothers, recently convicted of raping and robbing four young adults before executing them in a snow-covered soccer field—and received the first taste of the maximum-security prison that will more than likely serve as his final home.

For two months, Robinson lived in the Administrative Segregation Unit, separated from other inmates, and was allowed outside for a maximum of one hour a day, five days a week, but only to shower or exercise. If he exercised at all, he did it alone in an enclosed area, where he could shoot baskets, walk around and stretch, but not lift weights. He received three meals a day, passed through a slot in a solid metal door. Through the "Bean Hole," too, he could talk to his death row inmates, though technically the prison does not allow such conversations. His cell, measuring 8' x 10', was comprised of concrete floors and walls, a metal combination toilet and sink, a bed mounted to a wall, a writing table and narrow windows with hardened glass. In order to earn the privilege of having a radio or television, he would have to follow every prison rule for 120 days. He also would have to demonstrate good behavior before he could receive visitors, and even then he would remain behind glass and tightly shackled.

But Robinson didn't stay that long. His brief introduction to El Dorado was interrupted on April 1, 2003, after he willingly signed extradition orders transferring him to a similarly austere cell in Cass County, Missouri, to face capital murder charges in the deaths of Beverly Bonner and Sheila and Debbie Faith. He was quickly taken to a Cass County courtroom, where he sat silently as a judge entered "not guilty" pleas on his behalf and scheduled a preliminary hearing for May 14. It was too early to tell if his first appearance in the Missouri court would lead to another death sentence or a deal with prosecutors to break his silence and take them to the bodies of the three women missing since the 1980s.

Cass County prosecutor Chris Koster said after the April hearing that he could not talk about any plea negotiations that were under way. But he did say he would prefer that Robinson's prosecution conclude with one death penalty and the recovery of eight bodies rather than two death penalties and three unresolved cases. Though Robinson had just received a sentence of life without parole in Kansas for the murder of Lisa Stasi, her body had never been found. Investigators had also never found the bodies of Paula Godfrey and Catherine Clampitt, who had disappeared in Kansas after they had begun working for the defendant. "We have never made claims publicly about Robinson's involvement with Clampitt and Godfrey, and we're not leveling accusations now," Koster told reporters. "But there is an ongoing investigation. . . . I want to try this case . . . but my desire to try it takes a backseat to important law-enforcement goals."

Karen Kraft, the public defender who had been appointed to represent Robinson in Missouri, admitted at one point that a plea bargain was under discussion, but she declined to make any comment after the April hearing. Others said, however, that the incentive for Robinson to cut a deal was based upon the fact that Kansas had moved much more slowly than Missouri in reinstating and carrying out the death penalty. According to the latest figures from the Death Penalty Information Center, Missouri had executed sixty people since reinstating capital punishment in 1975. Kansas hadn't executed anyone since 1965 and only reinstated the death penalty in 1994. Robinson couldn't be blamed for thinking he just might cop a plea and beat the death penalty in Missouri and take his chances that his sentence would be overturned on appeal in Kansas.

Several people doubted that Koster could get Robinson to reveal any useful information for a plea bargain. Robinson's former attorneys had approached Morrison and Welch just before the Kansas trial to talk about a similar type of arrangement and they had politely refused in part because they didn't trust a word he said. Some of those in law enforcement also held the belief that Robinson had long ago disposed of the women's bodies in a Kansas City location now covered by concrete. Even if he admitted that was where the women could be found, they'd face a troubling dilemma. "It would be just like the arrogant son of a bitch to send us on a wild-goose chase, spending all kinds of money digging up this [site] for nothing," said one source. "I can just see him sitting back and laughing his ass off."

Some of the missing women's relatives had decided, in any case, they didn't want to learn how their loved ones had died. Karen Moore, Lisa Stasi's aunt, was one of them. "Just speaking for me, I don't know that I want to know," she said moments after the judge had sentenced him to death. "I think there is a little bit of peace in not knowing."

Paula Godfrey's father, Bill, wasn't holding his breath for a confession and appeared confident that the death sentence in Kansas would stand. "He's already facing the death penalty," he reportedly said. "There isn't much more they can do to him, which is a shame."

At the same time, the relatives and friends of Bonner and the Faiths were pushing hard for a trial in Missouri. It wasn't enough that Johnson County jurors had contemplated evidence about their loved ones before they convicted Robinson and sentenced him to death for the murders of the three women in Kansas. They wanted convictions, too. "To remember Sheila

. . . to avenge Debbie," Michelle Fox, Sheila Faith's sister reportedly said. Beverly Bonner's former husband agreed. "It's a matter of principle," explained Dr. William Bonner.

While Koster acknowledged feeling pressure from his constituents, who weren't eager to pay for a second trial, he argued that the only significant extra cost would occur if Cass County had to sequester a jury during a trial, which he predicted would last about 2.5 weeks. Unlike the Kansas trial, where the court-appointed defense attorneys had just billed nearly $500,000 to represent Robinson, the salaries of public defenders in Missouri were fixed, as were those of the prosecutors and the detectives; lab tests, moreover, had already been paid for. "Both the Faith and Bonner families have expressed an absolutely clear desire that we not let up on the prosecution," Koster said recently. "You can't just take a case like this and put it on a shelf and say we are too tired to deal with this, we're too cost conscious to deal with this."

Even if he were to be convicted of capital murder and sentenced to death in Missouri, Robinson was expected to return to El Dorado to resume his solitary existence as his case wound its way through the appeals process. "It will be interesting to see what happens," Morrison said. "We're all kind of learning about this as we go. Kansas has the advantage right now in that our trial is finished and the transcripts are being prepared and we will have a jump on the appeals process of several months, maybe even a year. Yet Missouri has a very well-settled case law for the death penalty. They have it more down to a science, if you will. They run their appeals quicker."

If Robinson were to be sitting in El Dorado, with his Kansas appeal grinding through the system and Missouri obtained its death warrant first, Morrison said it would probably be a matter for the governors' offices of the two states to hash out. "We would work something out," he said. "We might well give Robinson to Missouri to be executed. We're interested in this case in Kansas to develop some good case law. But who actually executes him is of no particular consequence to me."

Under either scenario, Robinson will be an old man, probably close to seventy, by the time he exhausts his appeals. Assuming that Kansas finishes first, Robinson would be moved from El Dorado to the Lansing Correctional Facility, outside of Kansas City, the week of his death. There, on the fourth floor of a century-old stone building, he would spend his last few days in a one-of-a-kind cell less than a dozen paces from the small starkly white room where he would die.

On the appointed morning, Robinson would be allowed a last meal prepared by the prison or $15 worth of food from a Lansing restaurant. If he so chose, he would have an approved spiritual adviser visit him before the execution and be with him in the death chamber. Shortly beforehand, the warden would read the court order of execution, which would be carried out at 11:00 A.M. A six-person team would escort Robinson from his cell down a short hall to the death chamber.

Once inside, the tie-down team would fasten leather restraints around his wrists and ankles. Two medically trained corrections officers would insert intravenous catheters—one of them a backup—to each arm. As many as thirteen witnesses would be escorted into one of three rooms. Three of those witnesses would be of his own choosing and they would sit behind smoked windows, where he could see them and they him. The other witnesses, including victims' relatives, government officials and reporters, would be in two other rooms hidden behind mirrored windows.

Then, the warden would pull back a curtain from the three windows and call the secretary of corrections, who would in turn verify with the Kansas attorney general and governor that there was no legal reason to stop the proceedings. Upon the warden's order, the IV team would push a button to administer the lethal cocktail of drugs, which would travel from an adjoining room through a hole in the wall into his arms. Sodium Pentothal would put Robinson to sleep, followed by pancreozymin bromide to stop his breathing. Finally potassium chloride would stop his heart.

Though not a relative, Debbie Faith's best friend, Suzanne Lawrence, was not shy about saying she would want to witness Robinson's execution, however long it may take for that day to come. "He took two very loving, caring, fun people from this world," said Lawrence, now a young woman living in Orange County, California. "I want to see his face as he realizes he's about to die and go to hell so I know he paid for his crimes."

Others were simply hoping for closure. After waiting nearly two decades, Lisa Stasi's family was finally able to hold a memorial service in Alabama for the missing woman. She now had a headstone next to her brother's grave, which brought her loved ones some small measure of comfort. Still, Stasi's aunt wasn't sure they really would ever recover. "I've had several people ask me about closure," said Karen Moore. "I have really thought about that a lot and I am not quite sure what closure is with Lisa still gone. I just don't know the answer to that question."

Suzette Trouten's mother could identify with Moore. Though her daughter's ashes had been recently returned to her (until the completion of the trial, she had been interred in Lenexa, Kansas, in an unmarked crypt next to Izabela Lewicka), Carolyn Trouten still found the reality of what had happened difficult to comprehend. "I have a picture of Suzy on my dresser," she said. "Every morning I get up and say hello to her. I know she is dead, but I keep wishing that there were some mistake. It's still so hard to believe that she's not ever coming home."

The words seemed to sink in as Carolyn Trouten repeated them softly: "My baby," she murmured, "is never coming home."

Vickie Neufeld could appreciate the fact that she was one of the lucky ones. She had survived her encounter with Robinson and weathered the trauma and public exposure of testifying, but her path had not been easy. When a friend was diagnosed with cancer in 2001, she sent an e-mail to a government Web site seeking to learn more about the subject. A friendly statistician named Doug answered her query and on Valentine's Day, 2003, in a small chapel in Tennessee, they were married. Sadly, however, her story book romance did not have a Cinderella ending. Within a few months the relationship had soured and, as of this writing, Vickie was headed for divorce.

"It's sad because I feel lost," Vickie wrote in a recent e-mail. "I feel like Dorothy and want to hold my little dog in a basket close to my heart, click my silver heels, close my eyes and repeat, 'There's no place like home.' The problem is, when I close my eyes, I cannot envision home. I'm unsettled—not grounded. Lol! And Kansas is definitely NOT home."

She said she could not over-emphasize the connection she felt with Robinson's victims. "They felt like sisters to me— even though I had not met any of them and [they] were of different alternative lifestyles and different from myself," she said. "But I felt this bond like nothing I've ever experienced before. I knew it could have been me that had fallen silent."

Despite her experiences, Vickie still believed the Internet was a wonderful creation. "It puts us in touch with the world," she said. "We have to be wise, however, and alert to signals and red flags that might caution us of potential danger. Robinson was nothing more than a serial killer who made his way online to find more victims. In my opinion, it was never about sex, of any style. It was about pretending to be someone the women desired him to be, then from there finding his way to the path that gave him a great sense of power and satisfaction, finding the way to brutally kill women who trusted him. It was his life's work and he had become very good at it. One can't blame the Internet or meeting online for his actions."

For the time being, however, Vickie had no plans and no desire to date anyone—online or otherwise. "I've got to find some more inner strength to make it on my own," she said. "For once in my life, I am reaching out to others, not [only] online, but in real life. My love is greatest for my children and always has been. Then, of course, Mary Kate has given unconditional love through it all!"

She said her next move would be to relocate to an undisclosed location and study for the licensure exam. If the opportunity arose, she would like to work on a "large scale" as a victim's advocate. "When I say 'large scale,' I mean dealing with victims of the worst crimes," she explained. "I've most of the background and experience needed, though I lack some of the legal knowledge. But one is never too old to learn."

By autumn of 2003, Paul Morrison had just finished up a two-week murder trial—which seemed like child's play in comparison to what he'd gone through with Robinson. "At the end of it, I reminded myself that this time last year, we hadn't even gotten through jury selection yet," he said. "Kind of puts it all in perspective."

As for the detectives who investigated Robinson, life for the most part had gone on as usual—although with the knowledge that they'd probably never work on another case as large and sensational in their lives. The Kansas Association of Chiefs of Police recognized several of them—Rick Roth, Jake Boyer, Dave Brown, Greg Wilson and Mike Jacobson—with special awards for police service. Roth, Boyer, Brown and Wilson also received valor awards from the Metropolitan Police Chiefs and Sheriff's Association. The honors were well deserved.

Life had been anything but usual for Sara Welch, who had her hands full planning a May 2004 wedding. With the trial behind them, Rick Roth had decided the time was right to pop the question to the never-married assistant district attorney. To the sergeant's delight, she accepted. "I was such a confirmed single person that one of the secretaries told me she is convinced my engagement is one of the seven signs the world is coming to an end," Welch said, jokingly. "[Rick] won me over through sheer persistence. He slowly but surely changed my very negative image of marriage as a loss of freedom and individuality to a mutually satisfying partnership."

Describing him as one of the finest people she had ever met, Welch went on to add that Roth had always been very active in his church—taught Sunday school, painted the church and mowed the church lawn. "I doubt if any of his detectives would imagine their hard-nosed, rough-edged sergeant used to spend his Sunday morning teaching third graders. [He's also a] great Dad. Doting Grandpa. Generous to a fault. I am so lucky to have him."

Welch was happy to report that wedding plans were nearly complete. "We have a church, reception site, caterer and DJ," she said. "Bridesmaid dresses are bought. Now I need to get my dress. What is Roth's contribution to the planning and coordination of this event you ask? Zero. Oh well, I should thank my lucky stars he is not involved. His idea of a reception menu is beanie weenies, BBQ potato chips and beer. But I bet he will look pretty dapper in his tux, which is all that matters."

Author's note: On October 16, 2003, as this book was going to press, John Robinson walked into a Cass County courtroom and pleaded guilty to murdering not only Beverly Bonner, Sheila and Debbie Faith, but also Paula Godfrey and Catherine Clampitt. One of his attorneys said his motivations were to avoid a possible death sentence in Missouri and save his family the embarrassment of another trial. When embarking last winter on plea negotiations, DA Chris Koster explained that he hoped to convince Robinson to lead authorities to the bodies of Godfrey, Clampitt and Stasi. But after the October hearing, he told reporters he had become convinced that the women's remains had been "disposed of in a way that were not recoverable."

Johnson County DA Paul Morrison said he was glad of the closure for the families involved. But he called the plea agreement in Missouri "classic John Robinson" and stated that the defendant, whose word could not be trusted, had once again taken advantage of the system. The district attorney added that Robinson would soon be returned to the El Dorado Correctional Facility outside Wichita to await the appeals court ruling on his Kansas death sentence.

Criminal Profile
by Maurice Godwin, Ph.D.

My involvement with the Robinson case began when Dan Clark, a private investigator, contacted me and expressed an interest in my research on serial killers. Clark referred me to attorney Ron Evans of the Kansas Death Penalty Defense Unit, who subsequently hired me as a forensic consultant. As such, I was asked to develop a psychological assessment of Robinson's crimes, which I understood would be used to try to convince him to plead guilty and lead investigators to the bodies of three of his victims, Paula Godfrey, Lisa Stasi and Catherine Clampitt. I signed on in hopes of helping to bring closure to the families of these women. The thinking went that if Robinson cooperated, Evans and his unit might be able to negotiate a sentence of life in prison instead of the death penalty. However, Robinson never accepted this defense strategy and instead replaced his death penalty lawyers with attorney Bob Thomas. At that point, I ceased to work on the case.

Traditionally, a criminal profile is provided in unsolved cases rather than in a situation where the offender has already been detected, arrested and charged. Therefore, this profile should not be construed as a typical offender profile but rather as a post-secondary analysis of how Robinson stacks up against other serial killers and the relationship between his mental state and criminal behavior.

In a few respects, Robinson is considered a typical serial killer (if there is such a thing). To begin with, his victims were primarily white, which supports the data that most serial crimes are primarily intra-racial. His victims, with the exception of 15-year-old Debbie Faith, were between the ages of eighteen and fifty, also in keeping with the average age of serial murder victims. In a study I did of 107 American serial killers, I found that only 3 percent of offenders murdered younger teens.

Robinson, moreover, is similar to other serial killers in terms of the number of his victims. He has been convicted of killing three women—Lisa Stasi, Izabela Lewicka and Suzette Trouten—and on October 16, 2003, he agreed to plead guilty to the murders of five other women he had been suspected of killing—Paula Godfrey, Catherine Clampitt, Beverly Bonner and Sheila and Debbie Faith—in order to avoid a possible death sentence in Missouri. That puts his total number of victims at eight. Likewise, serial killers in the United States have an average of eight known victims.

However, a different picture emerges when Robinson's age is compared to that of other serial murderers. He was fifty-six when he was arrested and subsequently charged with murder in June 2000. In my study, I found that the average age of serial killers at the time of their arrest was thirty. Only 18 percent, in fact, were over the age of forty-two. Clearly, Robinson was older than the typical serial killer when he was arrested. The question is whether he was older than the typical serial killer when he started to murder women.

In my opinion, Robinson's first victim probably wasn't Paula Godfrey. In 1984, when she went missing, he would have been forty years of age, which is old to start a career as a serial murderer. There's a good chance that Robinson murdered women we don't know about dating back as far as the 1970s. There is also a sizeable gap in time between the alleged murders of Bonner and the Faiths in 1994 and Lewicka in 1999. Considering that three of his victims (Godfrey, Clampitt and Stasi) have not been found, it would not surprise me to learn that he had managed to hide the remains of other women.

It is in Robinson's relationships with these women that he really begins to depart from the serial killer norm. Granted, he is just like the roughly half of all serial killers who employed a ruse to lure their victims. But he is different from the vast majority who murdered strangers. Rather than killing his victims immediately or holding them captive for a short period of time, moreover, Robinson first befriended and, in some cases, became sexually involved with them for as long as two years. In this regard, his relationships are more akin to spousal or domestic homicides than serial murder.

What is arguably most unique about Robinson is the way he went about luring his victims and the signature behaviors he exhibited during his interactions with them. In the early years, Robinson utilized local newspapers to place and answer employment and personal ads. He held himself out as a wealthy businessman with international connections who promised rewarding jobs and frequent travel. His modus operandi (MO) changed, however, with the advent of the Internet. Now Robinson could simply log on to Web sites dedicated to BDSM (one of his favorites was alt.com) and browse through countless ads posted by submissive females looking for dominant male partners. He quickly adapted to the new technology and became the first documented serial killer to lure at least some of his victims through cyberspace.

Robinson had several other unusual MO and signature behaviors, several of which support the notion that he carefully planned his murders and took steps to avoid detection. He required his victims to sign and address cards and letters to their families shortly before their deaths and arranged to have other women send the correspondence from different locations in the United States, Mexico and Europe. He bludgeoned his victims and disposed of them in barrels, held onto their personal effects or gave them as gifts to other women and subsequently contacted victims' family members in an attempt to convince them that their loved ones were okay and unavailable simply because they were traveling the world.

What were the motives behind his extreme measures? Robinson was the ultimate con man. He lived his entire adult life creating business scams in order to defraud people out of their hard earned money. Each successful scam undoubtedly gave him a psychological rush—not so much because of the currency he pocketed but because he had outsmarted someone. Soon, however, he found he needed to pull off more and bigger cons to experience the same euphoria. He may have started out by stealing postage stamps but he soon graduated to conning and murdering women.

Robinson clearly profited financially from at least four of the victims. This was certainly true of Bonner and the Faiths. Killing Lisa Stasi and arranging the fraudulent adoption of her daughter to his unsuspecting brother not only made him money but also made him feel important. While his motives for the murders of Lewicka and Trouten are less obvious, the evidence suggests that these women had become a burden. His wife was asking questions about Lewicka and a second girl-friend, Barbara Sandre, was moving into town. In Trouten's case, he had promised to take her to California and Hawaii. but how was he going to do that and keep up the charade at home? We know even less about Robinson's motives when it comes to his involvement with Godfrey and Clampitt. It is not unusual, however, for a killer to exhibit similar behavior in his murders but have different underlying motives for that behavior.

One of the questions that was raised in this case was whether Robinson is a sexual sadist. Richard von Kraft-Ebing coined the term after the Marquis de Sade, whose writings describe a pairing of sexual acts with domination, degradation, and violence. A majority of sexual sadists never engage in sexually sadistic acts, much less a crime. Among those who choose to act on their fantasies, there are many who limit their actions to lawful behaviors with consenting or paid partners.

The Diagnostic and Statistical Manual of Mental Disorders (DSM-IV) definition for sexual sadism is often used to classify the sexual sadist. The DSM-IV was created by the American Psychiatric Association to assist in the identification of all kinds of mental disorders. Psychiatrists, clinical psychologists and other mental health professionals use it to match observed behaviors to particular clinical categories. Each category has a set of criteria that assist the clinician in making a classification of the offender. For example, the DSM-IV states that, to classify someone as a sexual sadist, there must be "recurrent, intense sexually arousing fantasies, sexual urges or behaviors involving acts (real, not simulated) in which the psychological or physical suffering of the victim (including humiliation) is sexually exciting to the person." These fantasies, urges or behaviors must have a duration of at least 6 months; they must also cause significant distress or functional impairment in the person's life.

In my opinion, the DSM-IV description of a sexual sadist matches Robinson's sexual behavior but not his murders. He fulfilled his alternative sexual fantasies with largely willing partners but then decided that they had become a burden and were easily dispensable. Instead of murdering in order to achieve sadistic sexual gratification, I think he viewed the women merely as objects and learned to depersonalize them, which allowed him to psychologically disassociate during his crimes. However, that doesn't mean he wasn't aware of what he was doing and wasn't legally responsible for his actions.

Robinson epitomizes the narcissist whose attitude toward women is marked by feelings of superiority, disdain and scorn. He has lived his life in the form of a 'story,' with himself at center stage, exhibiting the following behaviors:

- Since I am so superior, I am entitled to special treatment and privileges.
- I don't have to be bound by the rules that apply to other people.
- If others don't respect my status, they should be punished.
- Other people should satisfy my needs.

- Other people should recognize how special I am.
- No one's needs should interfere with my own.

Historically, serial killers have experienced intense family conflicts during childhood that fuel their distrust towards the world quite early in life and cause them to turn inward and become self-absorbed. Information about Robinson's childhood is sketchy at best and it is unlikely that a full account will ever come to light, especially since his parents are no longer living. His son reportedly told police that Robinson claimed to have been physically and emotionally abused by his mother. However, Robinson himself has given conflicting accounts to prison psychiatrists over the years, hinting in one that his childhood was ideal while in another that his mother had been a strict disciplinarian who lacked intimacy.

In September 2002, on the eve of the trial, Robinson's lawyers hired Dr. Dorothy Lewis to conduct a new psychological evaluation. She interviewed Robinson twice, spoke with some members of his family and reviewed incomplete documentation currently available on his mental and medical history. She reported that he had a history of severe physical and emotional abuse throughout childhood, resulting in episodic dissociative states. She also discovered that as many as four generations of family members may have suffered from psychiatric illness and that Robinson may have a bipolar mood disorder, although she said substantial additional testing was needed to reach a final conclusion. All further details of her investigation, however, were filed under court seal at the request of the defendant.

Interviews with other serial killers, however, have revealed a hatred of women for wrongs they believe have been done to them in the past. It is possible that Robinson experienced traumatic rejection from his mother or former girlfriends or women he fantasized about. Whether these wrongs were fact or fiction is not the issue; what matters is that Robinson's feelings of hate, anger and rage were undeniably real. In cases in which the offender and his victims were involved in semi-relationships, the amount of anger and rage the offender exhibited was dependent upon the meaning the victim had held for him. The fact that Robinson inflicted blunt trauma to the facial area of his victims suggests that he harbored a significant amount of rage.

It is my belief that Robinson held a 'just world' view of the women he encountered; that is, he felt that each of them deserved what they got. In reality, though, he was turning his loathing and hatred of himself and redirecting it onto these women. What's mystifying, however, is that Robinson conned and became sexually involved with many women whom he did not kill. It could be that the survivors were more inquisitive and displayed a greater level of self-confidence, which signaled to Robinson that they would resist his aggression. Or it could be that just the opposite was true: that he spared the more timid women and killed the self-confident women he both despised and desperately coveted. We simply don't know enough about his victims and survivors to say for certain.

While Robinson appeared impersonal and dismissive of others in terms of his everyday behavior, he actually displayed a high degree of personal attachment in the way in which he dealt with his victims after his crimes. Keeping their personal effects and concealing their bodies in barrels on his property may have been Robinson's way of maintaining control over his objects, possibly to denigrate them even in death. The fact that the farm and the storage locker was a substantial drive from his permanent residence is not important. Serial killers often travel hundreds of miles to crime scenes or victims' graves so they can relive their crimes.

Aggression in serial killers and other criminals has been conceptualized as either instrumental (in pursuit of gain) or affective (an expression of outrage or emotion). Robinson's aggressive actions were mixed, meaning that he displayed both instrumental (cognitive) and affective behaviors. Much of the violence with an instrumental focus was grounded in Robinson's desire for financial gain and to satisfy his psychological need for power and control. His attitude toward and treatment of his victims manifested itself in the form of seeing the women as merely objects, a 'prop' to use and abuse as he saw fit. He viewed these women as nothing more than a 'means to an end.' In the end, though, Robinson was a master of nothing but the plight of his life—death.

ABOUT THE AUTHORS

Sue Wiltz spent more than a decade as a New York correspondent for *Newsweek* and *People Weekly,* where she profiled top-tier celebrities and reported hundreds of features and breaking news stories. Now a freelance journalist, she covered Robinson's capital murder trial for CourtTV.com. Wiltz resides in Indianapolis, Indiana, with her husband, Paul, and their cat and two dogs.

A former North Carolina police officer, Maurice Godwin earned his Ph.D. in investigative psychology from the University of Liverpool in England. Godwin is the author of two books and numerous journal articles on psychological and geographical profiling. He has worked as a consultant on unsolved crimes to investigators and others—including John Robinson's first defense team—and appeared on national TV networks such as Fox, MSNBC and CNN. He lives with his wife, Helen, and their weimaraner, Molly, in Fayetteville, North Carolina.